# Fresh Words
# and Deeds

*History says, Don't hope*
*On this side of the grave,*
*But then, once in a lifetime*
*The longed-for tidal wave*
*Of justice can rise up*
*And hope and history rhyme.*

*Seamus Heaney*

# Fresh Words and Deeds

## The McCaughey Papers

❖

Edited by
**Principal Peter Matheson &**
**Rev Professor Christiaan Mostert**

Introduction by
**Rev Professor (Emeritus) Harry Wardlaw**

**David Lovell Publishing**
**Melbourne Australia**

First published in 2004 by
David Lovell Publishing
PO Box 822  Ringwood
Victoria 3134   Australia
Tel +61 3 9879 1433  Fax +61 3 9879 1348

Cover photo: Noel Butcher, 1988
Design by David Lovell Publishing
Typeset in 10.5/13.5 Garamond
Printed & bound in Australia by Openbook Publishers

National Library of Australia
card number and ISBN 1 86355 106 9

# Contents

## Major Papers

## Shorter Papers

# Sermons

# Commemorations

# Foreword

For a volume of theological papers and reflections that is already superbly furnished with the coeditors' Preface and a colleague's Introduction, to add a Foreword hazards attempting a work of supererogation. Yet no Master of Ormond College could fail to welcome a publication that both keeps Davis McCaughey's distinctive voice alive for his contemporaries and preserves his influence for posterity. So it is a privilege to welcome the publication of this selection of papers, sermons and commemorations that together sample the theological work of the College's fifth Master.

*Fresh Words and Deeds* will usefully and importantly complement *Tradition and Dissent* (Melbourne University Press, 1997), the earlier gathering of essays, addresses and memorials that is focused particularly upon Davis McCaughey's offices in university and public life. Taking both books from the library shelf will show the reader how much the work, like its author's life, is all-of-a-piece. These engagements with the Church and the world, and especially with the university and the professions, are as acute in judgement as they are consistent in approach. To draw upon a comparison he cites more than once, there will throughout be found a balance between respect for the "how" of life—a Benthamite practicality in the utilitarian sense of valuing capacity for getting things done—and an insistence upon the "why" of life—a Coleridgean questioning of purpose, and a moral evaluation of any project, institution or social practice.

These papers will bring us the characteristic fruits of Davis McCaughey's intellect. First, we can depend upon his scholarship. These lectures and sermons preserve the scholarly insight that a rigorous tradition of research and interpretation contributes. Second, we shall find our sense of history enriched. Witness the value of preserving his reflections on the formation of the Uniting Church in Australia, as well as his commemorations of his contemporaries. Third, we shall look to these words for inspiration. Even—especially, perhaps—in the darkest times, his statements communicate a resolute combination of vision and of faith.

Davis McCaughey's ninetieth year sees a new course being charted for the particular institutions of University College and Theological Hall in which much of the thought, writing and work that is reflected in this volume occurred. Indeed, by decision of the College Council in the week this Foreword is written, the Theological Hall and the Joint Theological Library—the twin foundations for theological scholarship here—will be provided with new buildings within the grounds of the College to equip them enduringly for their purposes. It is, I know, the hope of Council, Senatus and Synod alike that in this new setting a renewed relationship between the College and the Hall will develop and grow.

Those charged with responsibility to make this happen are unlikely to do better than to begin with the insights collected in this volume. Its title, borrowing a phrase from the eleventh paragraph of the *Basis of Union* (a phrase Professor Wardlaw associates directly with Dr McCaughey), alone may guide us. For that foundational statement links "fresh words and deeds" to the "inheritance of literary, historical and scientific enquiry" and of "faithful and scholarly" interpretation of Scripture that are the hallmarks of an "informed faith". Such convictions animated the foundation of this College and its association with the Theological Hall; they made Davis McCaughey's leadership in both of such indelible significance; they should suffice to sustain a fruitful future.

All of us who will derive pleasure and challenge from this book are indebted to the editors and their associates for bringing this volume to us.

Most of all, we are indebted to the author, who by example continues to instruct and to inspire us in life and in learning, in faith and in friendship.

Professor Hugh Collins
Master of Ormond College
24.vi.2004

# Preface

The purpose of this little volume is to do honour to a great man. Davis McCaughey has become something of a legend in his own life time, as scholar, teacher, preacher, as Master of Ormond College, leader in church and state. It is fitting that this pre-eminence should be recognised on his ninetieth birthday.

The title of this little volume *Fresh Words and Deeds* is taken from the *Basis of Union*. Talking of the need for scholarly interpreters of the Gospel, it envisages the Church being ready 'when occasions demands to confess the Lord in fresh words and deeds'. The life and thought of Davis McCaughey incarnate that prayer.

Dr McCaughey has a special place in theological education in Australia, in particular in Victoria, first in the Presbyterian Church and subsequently in the Uniting Church. He came to Australia in 1953 to take up the position of Professor of New Testament Studies in the Theological Hall. When he was invited to become Master of Ormond College he at first combined this new responsibility with his work as a theological teacher. When the Mastership of the College became his full-time work he continued to give lectures in the Hall on a part-time basis. He also responded to requests for occasional lectures and short lectures series on various biblical subjects and in various places.

As Davis McCaughey's ninetieth birthday was approaching, two members of the faculty of the Theological Hall, the Principal and Professor of Systematic Theology respectively, set themselves the challenge of gathering a selection of his theological writings. The latter has known Davis since his years in Ormond in the mid-sixties, and is privileged to acknowledge a great debt to his former teacher's influence and unceasing encouragement. Both of us are aware of his stature and the magnitude of his contribution to theological thought and education for half a century. The idea of publishing a book with a collection of McCaughey papers has been actively encouraged by colleagues in the Theological Hall and strongly supported by the present Master of Ormond College.

Davis McCaughey has enriched the life and work of the Theological Hall for decades. It was he who first made this institution internationally known. He was instrumental in sending many of its promising young theologians overseas to further their studies in great places of learning. This volume, apart from enabling the Theological Hall to honour Davis, makes available—to an older generation which knew him well and a younger generation which perhaps knows only his name—a selection of papers on theological and ecclesiastical themes. We already possess a fine volume of his papers and addresses on political and cultural matters. But his writings and papers on exegetical and theological matters, which are at least as close to his heart, are not available to the wider church. We welcome the occasion of his ninetieth birthday as giving us an excuse to remedy this sad state of affairs.

This volume, then, has a very personal focus. As the slightest perusal of its contents will reveal, however, it also stands very much on its own feet. Again and again these papers signal fresh new scholarly initiatives or evidence of pastoral and prophetic insight of the purest water. There is something unmistakeable about a McCaughey paper or sermon. It has a certain unyielding rigour. The reader is never in doubt about the seriousness of the exercise. Equally characteristic, however, is the lightness of touch, the effortless transition into poetry or literature. The lucid, winsome style is itself a clue to the quality of the arguments, and their bearing on the here and now. *Ars est artem celare*; true art never displays itself. One is carried along, never effortlessly, but far more easily than the profundity of the argument would lead one to suspect. We are educated and yet we are entertained, and we are deeply touched emotionally: Quintilian's ancient recipe for true rhetoric!

Those who have had the benefit of being students of Davis McCaughey or who have heard some of the papers and sermons printed in this volume will have no difficulty in hearing the voice, the lyricism of the Irish accent, and the elegance of the McCaughey style. That, we hope, will be part of the pleasure of reading these papers. A lecture by him—but equally a sermon—was always a rich experience; invariably one knew oneself in the presence of a man of powerful intellect, wide reading and insight. On theological subjects, historical or systematic, there were invariably new things to learn about the substance of the faith, the faith of the church catholic; there was never so much as a whiff of sectarian interest. The form in which the ideas were expressed added to their attractiveness, but again and again it was the power of the ideas themselves and the force of the arguments that made the deep and lasting impression.

Some of the papers in this volume explicitly address ecumenical issues, though all of them breathe an ecumenical spirit. This ecumenical outlook extended further to a deep interest in the relationship between Christians and Jews, which continues to be an important theological task for the church. Professor Harry Wardlaw refers in his introduction to Davis McCaughey's association and involvement (and later his patronage) of the Council for Christians and Jews in Victoria. Both the ecumenical outlook and the building of bridges between Christians and people of other faiths have been among his pre-eminent concerns. We tend to take the ecumenical world for granted, even to the point of regarding the theological work which it still requires and the appropriation of its significant achievements as unnecessary. In fact, the progress that has been made in the last half century owes a very large debt to Davis' pioneering work, not only in this country but also internationally.

As a scholar, he inevitably formed friendships across ecclesiastical boundaries. In his work in the World Council of Churches, in particular the Faith and Order Commission, he was in the vanguard of ecumenical leadership in the world, from which the church in Australia undoubtedly derived great benefit. As a churchman he had wide influence, and some of his speeches in the Assembly of the Presbyterian Church of Victoria are remembered decades after they were made. The same could be said for his studies and addresses to the Australian Council of Churches. In whatever forum, his ecumenical work must count among his most significant. In no area could this be more true than in his seminal contribution to the work of the Joint Commission on Church Union. The *Basis of Union*, on which the Uniting Church in Australia was formed in June 1977, is of course the work of more than one individual, but no one played a greater role in its conception, its shape and style, and in bringing to expression its profound theological and ecumenical vision than Davis McCaughey. It is particularly pleasing to be able to include in this volume his own reflections on the most important decisions made in the formulation of this remarkable document, as well as addresses to the first two Assemblies of the Uniting Church in Australia.

This book can only offer a taste of the riches in the McCaughey papers, but we believe it does do that and will whet the appetite of the reader for more. The writings on Scripture, for example, will surprise many of a younger generation by their very early anticipation of a groundswell of change in biblical scholarship, an impatience with a rather clinical approach which had become somewhat mired in historical and philological issues. Davis makes it crystal clear that he respects, and indeed takes for granted, the importance of critical scholarship, but he wants to move on to an awareness of the text as a living whole. The selection of papers in this book will, it is hoped, show this sensitivity to the literary quality of Scripture.

And then there are his sermons. First and foremost—not least because he led such a full life—Davis McCaughey's genius was in person to person, oral communication. Yet, as the sermons in this book testify, he never began with the audience but, as the Germans say, with '*die Sache*', with the business in hand, which, in a sermon, is God: Father, Son and Holy Spirit. From the first word the listener is taken into the heights and depths of faith. The mastery of the communicator ensures, however, an easy passage. The urgency of the message is conveyed not by a staid solemnity, but by apposite quote and earthy touch. We hope the small selection of sermons offered here convey something of this.

Finally, we come to his memorial addresses. One can see from his skill with this genre why he was in such frequent demand. Perhaps we see reflected here something of his life-long debt to Gregor Smith's profound Christian humanism. Let readers judge for themselves why these orations, to use an old-fashioned word, were so unerringly successful. Surely part of the secret is his own enjoyment of people and of life?

It was, of course, more than his skill with words that made people turn to him when someone in public life, in church or education, died. Countless theological students and College residents will testify that Davis took a personal interest in them, their intellectual formation, their development as young men and women. Not without a critical view, he was appreciative of what people in positions comparable to his own sought to achieve and express. Often in awe of his formidable mind, they were nonetheless drawn to him, and were encouraged by him. This interest in people never abated.

We are very grateful to Mark Crees for his diligence in proof-reading, and gladly acknowledge our immense debt to Heather Cameron, for her skills and patience in preparing the papers for publication.

The work of putting together this collection has been a most happy collaborative project for us both. The credit for this largely belongs to the inherent interest and importance of the material; to this day a conversation with his about some of the matters taken up in these essays and papers is an instructive experience. It is a singular honour to be associated with his ninetieth birthday and to offer this tangible expression of our gratitude for fifty years of stimulating theological teaching and leadership.

Peter Matheson
Chris Mostert
24.vi.2004

# J Davis McCaughey

## Harry Wardlaw

T o write an introductory essay about someone whose charac-
ter is as rich and varied as Davis McCaughey's is a tall order. Even before I met
him I had heard of him as one of the most respected leaders of the Student
Christian Movement of Great Britain and Ireland and through fifty years of my
life he has been a greatly valued teacher, colleague and friend. In Australia, which
became his home, he was respected within the church as a church leader and
theological teacher, and in the wider community as a man who made a great
contribution to university education and as Governor of the State of Victoria.

Davis' scholarly career began when he entered Pembroke College, Cambridge, to read for his first degree in English literature. As a field of study Literature was his first love and it is a love he has taken with him through the whole of
his life. This was a fitting preparation for the work he was to do later as a teacher
of New Testament studies and for his ministry as a preacher. He was one of the
most sought after and widely appreciated preachers first in his own Presbyterian
Church and then, when that church went into union, in the Uniting Church in
Australia. This grounding in literary studies enabled him to open the minds of
his students and of many a congregation to the marvellous imaginative richness
of the biblical texts. After Davis had taken his Cambridge degree, he later turned
to the formal study of theology but the deep interest he had developed in secular
literature never left him.

It was at Cambridge that he first became involved with the Student Christian Movement, which at that time was an important agent of the growing ecumenical movement within the Christian Church. Indeed the national SCMs
and the World Student Christian Federation were probably the most important
agencies preparing the way for the formation of a world council of churches in
the pre-war days of the 1930s. The Council as we now know it was actually
established soon after the war ended. The great hope of that time was that we
might see within our lifetime the coming of an ecclesial unity embracing all

Christians. In reality this vision was probably limited to the non-Roman Catholic churches of the West. The Roman Catholic Church at that time still held the view that it already embodied in itself the unity of the church and it simply remained for other Christian bodies to recognise the fact and return to their true and proper home. The Eastern churches represented a different kind of challenge, though it was probably only through a few Russian émigrés like Nicholas Berdyaev that their voices were heard at all in WSCF circles. While the question of churches coming together commonly presented itself, to Protestants at any rate, as an issue confronting national church denominations, the wider implications of our use of the word 'ecumenical' were never overlooked. In this connection the WSCF was very important. Furthermore, the fact that the Federation had its central offices in Geneva, along with the League of Nations and several other worldwide agencies, served to remind us that the ecumenical vision born in the first half of the twentieth century was not confined to the Christian churches. As far as Davis McCaughey was concerned, the hope of moving towards a genuine re-unifying of the church across the world has remained with him throughout his life.

In addition to these Christian pre-occupations, the European world of Davis McCaughey's student days was going through a period of bewildering upheaval. The great European war of 1914-1918 shattered hopes of continuing progress that had been entertained by some nineteenth century western idealists. Then in the early 1930s, when Davis was an undergraduate student, the whole Western world found itself reeling under the impact of the most disastrous economic depression the capitalist world had ever known. In the centre of Europe the German National Socialists of Hitler's Nazi Party were locked in a struggle with the international socialists of the Comintern, as it was represented in the German Communist Party. While Davis was an eighteen-year-old undergraduate in Cambridge, this struggle reached a decisive and fateful outcome on 30 January 1933, when the leaders of the German *Reichstag* invited Hitler to take on the office of Chancellor.

The full implications of this development were not recognized immediately even in Germany, let alone in England, but with bewildering rapidity Hitler made it clear where his dreams of a great German empire were leading him. The impact of these events on the life of the British SCM has been vividly documented by Davis himself in his survey of the period in his important book *Christian Obedience in the University*. In that book we also have a good introduction to the formation of his own Christian, ministry as it began in the SCM.

In August 1936 Davis joined a group of fourteen members of the British

SCM, crossing the Atlantic to attend a reading party together with leaders of the corresponding student movements in Canada and the USA. Here the American theologian, John Bennett, unfolded to them the theological thought of Reinhold Niebuhr, whose writing made a deep impression on Davis and became a significant guide to his own theological development.

Having finished his undergraduate studies at Cambridge, Davis did not immediately go on to formal theological study. Instead he became Irish Secretary in the SCM, a position he occupied from 1937-1939. It was after that that he turned to theological studies, first at the Presbyterian Theological College in his native Belfast and then at New College in the University of Edinburgh. In Edinburgh the ground was laid for Davis' New Testament studies, which he pursued under the guidance of Professor William Manson.

Prominent in New Testament studies at that time was the voice of C H Dodd. His little book *The Apostolic Preaching and its Development* had been recently published. Dodd argued that all of the New Testament writings were primarily proclaiming a message rather than merely recounting things that had happened or telling us how we should live. The best guide to the content of this proclamation is found in the actual sermons recorded in Luke's Acts of the Apostles, together with certain preaching sections of the apostolic letters of St Paul. Davis saw what an important light this throws on our understanding of the New Testament. Indeed, I remember him using this book some years later as a starting point for the first course he taught in Ormond College in 1953. Dodd, along with Niebuhr, was perhaps the theologian who influenced Davis most through his student days.

After ordination and a period of ministry in the Presbyterian Church in Ireland, Davis returned to the SCM in 1946, to serve first as Associate Study Secretary and from 1948 as Study Secretary and Editor of *The Student Movement*. It was at this time that the friendship with Ronald Gregor Smith, who was then Editor of the SCM Press, had its beginnings. Like Davis, Gregor Smith had been a student of literature. He studied in Edinburgh, where Herbert Grierson was his teacher, and after graduation he too went on to read theology at New College, though at that time the two did not meet. Along with his study of English literature, Gregor Smith also developed an interest in German language and literature, which led to him playing a part in the post-war re-construction of German universities in the British zone of occupation. This was important in giving Gregor Smith the opportunity of developing his dialogue with the great German theologians of the 1930s, '40s and '50s. The continental connection also stimulated his interest in the Danish writer, Søren Kierkegaard.

These things were important for the work he did as Editor of the SCM Press. It was at this time that a deep friendship between Davis McCaughey and Ronald Gregor Smith developed and the influence of Gregor Smith can be seen in some of Davis' subsequent writings. [See his Lecture 'The Formation of the Basis of Union'.]

Late in 1952 Davis received a call to come to Melbourne to take up the chair of New Testament Studies in Ormond College. He took up this position at the beginning of 1953 and generations of theological students can bear witness to his success as a teacher. I have already said something about how training in literary appreciation fitted him for the task of helping his students discover the imaginative power of the New Testament. He did not neglect detailed issues of textual analysis, dates, authorship, manuscript variation and so on, but his central concentration was on the unity and strucure of the text seen as a whole. I particularly remember his lectures on the Gospel according to St Mark. In those lectures he showed us how effectively the evangelist ordered all his material in the world through the death and resurrection of Jesus Christ. Everything in the book leads on to the cross and then beyond the cross to that small band of women standing by an empty tomb, where they received the message that Jesus was not there in the grave but was going ahead of them into Galilee. Davis knew better than to be diverted into useless conjectures as to what actually happened or how it happened. His task was to show us how powerfully Mark shaped his writing to convey the inner truth of the events to the sympathetic reader. He drew our attention to the way Mark shows how what *really* happened in these events was both hidden and revealed: hidden in the empty tomb, yet revealed as the mystery of the kingly rule of God coming into the world.

Davis may question this account of what he was saying in those lectures but it is certainly how I remember them. In any case I am sure he would accept my central point about the importance of bringing the Christian Gospel to bear on the imagination of those to whom it is proclaimed. He knew well the importance of the imagination in Christian preaching. Indeed, I think that Davis helped many of us see the extent to which the truth of Christianity can be validated in the realm of the imagination. It is essential that we retrain our respect for the centrality of imagination in human life and in our receiving of the rich tradition of faith which we have inherited from centuries of Christian history. When it comes to discovering the truth there is, in the sphere of the imagination, a great difference between those things that are authentic and those things that are bogus, false or empty.

It is not only in his study of the Biblical texts but also in his preaching that

Davis shows how these canonical writings can be illuminated by looking to other great works of literature. Many people have dismissed the suggestion that the Bible might best be studied as a work or a collection of works of literature, on the ground that such an approach will lose the real power of the Gospel which the Scriptures are proclaiming. However, the claim is not that the Bible is *nothing more* than a collection of literary works but it that it is *not less than* a collection of literary works. What we have here are works of literature that are surely also more than just works of literature. To recognise that we are dealing with literary texts when we approach the Scriptures is certainly important. Davis McCaughey saw this very clearly and this contributed to his success as a first-rate teacher of New Testament studies. Yet Davis' interests were never narrowly confined to New Testament Studies. The whole field of theology and of Christian discipleship in his own time occupied his attention constantly.

In the wider field of theological studies through the 1920s and 1930s Reformed Churches in Europe had been moving in new directions under the influence of the Swiss theologian, Karl Barth. This led to intense discussions into which thinkers like McCaughey and Gregor Smith were inevitably drawn. Davis McCaughey entered into all these theological developments with the kind of critical and imaginative enthusiasm that was to mark his work in the following years. Along with the voice of Barth, there were his German contemporaries, Gogarten, Bultmann and Tillich, (who moved from Germany to the USA in 1933) and in America Reinhold Niebuhr and his brother, H Richard Niebuhr. In the post-war years the writings of Dietrich Bonhoeffer captured the imagination of a whole generation of Christians. Davis' excitement when a selection of Bonhoeffer's letters and papers from prison was published in an English translation in 1953 indicated the direction of his theological thinking at that time. He told his students that this book was so important that they should all buy it, even if they had to sell their beds to pay for it!

Soon after he began teaching at the Theological Hall in Ormond College he arranged for Gregor Smith to visit Australia, to give a series of lectures (the Love Lectures), which opened up the importance of Bonhoeffer's thought and also the thought of existential theologians like Rudolf Bultmann and Friedrich Gogarten. This was a very important contribution for us here in Australia at that time.

In addition to these theological conversations and his conversation within the churches, his contacts in Ormond College and in the University were constantly drawing him into dialogue with a wide circle of scholars of various kinds, philosophers, scientists and social commentators. He had had a good deal of opportunity for such associations before he came to Australia, both in the SCM and the WSCF, and he was very ready to open up such paths of dialogue and to keep them open. In view of this, it was not surprising that a new call was put to Davis from the Council of Ormond College which wanted him to take on the responsibilities of Master of the College. Ormond is a University College for students of all faculties of Melbourne University as well as for students of the Theological Hall.

Davis was reluctant to give up his teaching work in the Theological Hall and the Theological Faculty did not want to lose him. At first it was thought that if a new lecturer were appointed in New Testament studies, then he might be able to serve as both Master of the College and Professor of Biblical Studies in the Theological Hall, and that plan was adopted. After some years operating that way, however, it became clear that the demands of these two jobs together were more than one man could do justice to. While continuing to lecture on an occasional basis in the Theological Hall, his major work was in the College.

The work Davis did in strengthening and enriching the life of the College is a story that cannot be told within the limits of this essay. From the point of view of Christian ministry, he continued to act as a pastor to students in the College. When he saw the major turning away from the churches that was one characteristic of the cultural revolution that took place through the 1960s and '70s, he established a chapel within the College itself, where evening services were held every week. This was a change from the expectation that students would attend the local parish church generally known as the College Church, in the hope that the local parish and the student community might be united with each other.

The best indication of Davis' view of the Christian presence in the university is found in his 1958 book *Christian Obedience in the University*. Quoting Bonhoeffer's proposal that we should speak of God not on the borders of life but at its centre, Davis writes 'The attempt by men and women in the Universities to see their work in the light of faith is an attempt to do just that. What they ask for and what they offer is not a new scholasticism but a new attitude' [140].

Davis' primary associations were in the University of Melbourne. But he also showed interest in seeing how the Christian presence might be accommodated in the newly emerging Monash University and at La Trobe, Melbourne's third university, where he was a member of the council which planned the form of the university. This council first explored the possibility of organizing the whole university on a collegiate basis, so that every undergraduate student would be associated with one or another of a group of university colleges. This was a bold and interesting idea; three residential colleges were in fact established, although the idea was never implemented in its entirety.

Since Dr McCaughey's work in the church is at the centre of my attention, I must say something about his contribution to ecumenical relations. Before he came to Australia he was already well-known in ecumenical circles through his contributions to the SCM and the WSCF. I think it was on his way out to Australia that he first met Father Gabriel Hebert of the Anglican Society of the Sacred Mission; together they discussed their mutual concern for ecumenical relationships between churches in the land to which they were travelling. Between them they started planning for the observance of a week of prayer for Christian Unity, which came to be observed by churches in Australia between Ascension Day and Pentecost. Such a week was already being observed in the Northern Hemisphere but the date fixed for that did not suit the rhythm of the southern year. There was wide support for this in the churches and it has become an established observance in the calendar of many Australian churches. When he had settled in Australia Davis quickly established a reputation as one of the wisest contributors to discussions of inter-denominational relations. At the same time he continued his involvement in the World Council of Churches for some years serving as a member of its Faith and Order Commission.

At the time of his coming to Australia the Presbyterian Church, the Methodist Church and the Union of Congregational Churches were reflecting seriously on the possibility of those three denominations at least uniting with each other. With the example of the newly established Church of South India exciting our imagination, the possibility of bringing the Anglican Church in Australia into this conversation was explored but this proved too much to hope for. A joint commission of the three denominations, the Congregational Union, the Methodist and Presbyterian Churches was formed and began its work in 1957. Davis was a member of that Joint Commission. The present volume includes a very valuable reflection about the work of that Commission and in particular about the way in which it understood its responsibility both in regard to the heritage of faith received from previous centuries and the hope for the future promised in the Gospel. One important development in the course of that Commission's work which Davis does not discuss in that article is the very creative proposal made in the second report of the Commission that the newly forming denomination might adopt an episcopal form of church order. This would have been a new departure for all three of the participating denominations. Associated with this proposal was a suggestion that a Concordat be entered into with the Church of South India. At that time the South Indian Church was still seen by many as a kind of prophetic sign of things hoped for in the ecumenical movement. The Concordat was to be sealed by representatives of the Church of South India participating in the inaugurating act in which the new pastoral bishops-in-presbytery would be commissioned. I do not know how far Davis himself was committed to that, but in the event it proved to be too daring a proposal to gain acceptance from any of the three participating churches. Whether such a development would have linked the Uniting Church in Australia into what might have become a new denominational 'family' in the world church I do not know. Be that as it may, the opportunity was missed.

No doubt the hope was that such a new denominational family might prove to be a vanguard in a general move towards one unified church throughout the world, with the further prospect of a Concordat with the Roman Catholic and Orthodox churches, all being gathered into one united communion of the Holy Spirit.

However, the document which was finally accepted as a basis for the three denominations going forward together was a splendid re-affirmation of our faith, in language which while unmistakably twentieth century, insisted on the importance of the church continuing to seek guidance in the earlier confessions of faith which belonged to its history. It is a document which speaks at every point of how God is acting in the church and what God is saying to the church, rather than setting out a succession of particular beliefs about the divine nature or the divine being. Instead of offering us a catalogue of dogmatic articles of faith, this Basis speaks of the actual dynamics of faith as it is lived out in church and world. In this regard at least, I find a vitality in the final form of the Basis which I did not see to the same degree in the previous report. I also believe I can see the hand of Davis McCaughey in the style of the writing.

Thus while I believe we lost something important in giving up the proposal for pastoral bishops in accord with the Church of South India, I think there are other ways in which we gained a more dynamic basis for our church life. The style of the Basis as we have it addresses the modern imagination more directly than the earlier text would have done. This may well be the first requirement for any attempt we make to give an account of the faith, the hope or the love that is ours in the church.

One element in the *Basis of Union* which I know gave particular satisfaction to Davis was the paragraph numbered 11 which 'acknowledges the work of faithful and scholarly interpreters of Scripture' and commits the Uniting Church to enter into the inheritance of literary, historical and scientific enquiry which has characterized recent centuries. Lukas Vischer, who was at that time the secretary of the World Council of Churches' Faith and Order Commission, re-marked to Davis that this was the only union proposal he knew of that con-tained such a clause.

When the Union of the three denominations was finally consummated Davis was elected first President of the new Uniting Church Assembly, serving a term as President through the final years of his time as Master of Ormond Col-lege. When he retired the Mastership of the College, Davis continued to con-tribute to the life of the University of Melbourne and for a time acted as Deputy Chancellor.

A further call to serve the community came to Davis when the Premier asked him to accept nomination as Governor of the State of Victoria. After some hesitation, he accepted the challenge and took up this quite demanding role. He set himself two standards from the outset. First, he would not give any speeches that other people had written and, second, he would not make any speeches that did not have something to say. These might seem obvious princi-ples for any governor to adopt, but when you think of the endless succession of occasions on which a governor is asked to speak, he was surely setting himself very demanding standards.

Being a secular appointment and above politics, it must sometimes have been somewhat difficult for Davis to say what he really thought without re-straint. I remember listening to him speaking at the dawn service on Anzac Day. The service was inevitably couched in Christian imagery and language, yet it was a civic event with a congregation that included people of other faiths and of no faith at all. So it was not exactly a Christian occasion. Davis began his address by saying, "A wise Jew once said" and he then gave us a text from the prophet Amos. It was, I thought, a splendid example of how a Governor could retain his own integrity while still retaining the kind of neutrality that the office demanded.

One of the things Dr McCaughey did as Governor which showed the creative character of his mind was to invite to lunch at Government House people in the community that he thought should be talking to each other, but who in the ordinary course of events were unlikely to meet together. Then, having given them a first class meal, he set them talking. Perhaps any responsi-ble Governor should do no less, but I think it was something for which his life experience had prepared him peculiarly well. In any case, it was surely a valuable way of exercising that ministry of reconciliation which was his Christian calling and which he demonstrated in other areas, such as his patronage of the Council of Christians and Jews in Victoria. Davis was already a participant in this Coun-cil and the inter-faith conversations it promoted, and it was entirely consistent with the Governor's office that he should now extend his name as Governor to the Council.

The Governor's office did not altogether prevent Davis from exercising his ministry as a preacher, though clearly it restricted him from accepting preaching engagements outside occasional appearances in the pulpit of his own church. The question as to whether one who holds, or has held, office in a religious denomination should ever be appointed Governor under the kind of constitution we have in Australia has become something of an issue in recent years. But it can hardly be thought that we should seek people without any strong convictions when choosing our governors. There are doubtless complicated issues involved here but it seems to me that Davis showed in splendid measure how a person with a strong faith commitment may nonetheless display the kind of restraint and proper neutrality that the office requires.

At the end of his term as Governor Davis really did retire, to continue writing and giving occasional addresses, as well as preaching in the pulpits of the Uniting Church. He also went as the occasional preacher to a celebration of the hundred and fiftieth anniversary of New College in the University of Edinburgh, where he had had an important part of his theological education.

I have been attempting to sum up the life of Davis McCaughey and more particularly to say something of the theological thought that created and sustained him, and as I think of the breadth of his interest and his capacity to throw light on so many different aspects of human existence, I am reminded of that great American theologian Reinhold Niebuhr who was so important in Davis' early development. Davis spoke of how in the middle of the 1930s it was Niebuhr '... who excited men [sic], gave direction to feet inclined by panic to run down many political by-ways, and gave to their thought about their fellowmen [sic] a realism which did not cut the nerve of political action ...' I think that realism and that sense of balance have remained with Davis through the whole of his life, holding him back from extravagant flights of revolutionary enthusiasm and leading him on to creative and imaginative ventures of reformation. I appreciate very much this opportunity to salute him and to give thanks to our God for all that we have gained from this great man.

# Major Papers

✤

# Theology and Imagination

## An address given at the conferring of the degree of Doctor of Divinity *honoris causa* on Professor Eduard Schweizer of Zurich by the Melbourne College of Divinity
### 3 October 1975

A long time ago A. N. Whitehead wrote:

The justification for a university is that it preserves the connection between knowledge and zest for life, by uniting the young and the old in the imaginative consideration of learning. The university imparts information but it imparts it imaginatively. At least this is the function which it should perform for society. A university which fails in this respect has no reason for existence. This atmosphere of excitement, arising from imaginative consideration, transforms knowledge. A fact is no longer a bare fact: it is invested with all its possibilities. It is no longer a burden on the memory: It is energising as the poet of our dreams, and as the architect of our purposes.[1]

What is true of the University as a whole is true also of theological studies pursued with academic intent, and recognised as being on the same level of seriousness as other University disciplines. Those who have sat at Eduard Schweizer's feet have certainly had communicated to them knowledge connected with zest for life. They have been made to think in 'an atmosphere of excitement, arising from imaginative consideration [which] transforms knowledge.'

Regrettably it has not always been so. Let me quote Whitehead a little further:

The tragedy of the world is that those who are imaginative have but slight experience, and those who are experienced have feeble imaginations. Fools act on imagination without knowledge; pedants act on knowledge without

---

[1] A. N. Whitehead, *Aims of Education* (London: Benn, 1929) 139-140. In R. H. Titmuss in 'The University and Welfare Objectives', *Commitment to Welfare* (London: Allen & Unwin, 1973).

imagination. The task of a university is to weld together imagination and experience.

It is the task of theological teachers and students also; but perhaps no field outside the study of law has, over the centuries, attracted so many pedants. You remember Mr Casaubon in George Eliot's *Middlemarch,* whose 'Christian hope in immortality seemed to lean on the immortality of the still unwritten Key to all Mythologies', to which description the author adds:

> For my part I am very sorry for him. It is an uneasy lot at best, to be what we call highly taught and yet not to enjoy: to be present at this great spectacle of life and never to be liberated from a small hungry shivering self—never to be fully possessed by the glory which we behold, never to have our consciousness rapturously transformed into the vividness of a thought, the ardour of a passion, the energy of an action, but always to be scholarly and uninspired, ambitious and timid, scrupulous and dim-sighted.

Now, how are we to be saved from the Scylla of pedantry, and the Charybdis of folly? How does imagination operate in the study of theology? I want to make three suggestions, without however suggesting that this is an adequate introduction to the topic, much less an exhaustive treatment of it. In all three cases we might bear in mind that in English thought we have, since Coleridge, been taught to make a distinction between Imagination and Fancy.[2]

Coleridge, you remember, speaks of the primary imagination as the 'living power and prime agent of all human perception, and as a repetition in the finite mind of the eternal act of creation in the infinite I AM.' The secondary imagination, he says 'dissolves, diffuses, dissipates, in order to re-create ... It is essentially vital, even as all objects (as objects) are essentially fixed and dead.' Imagination then is that power which enables us to see the datum—be it biblical text, historical instance, doctrinal formulation—in all its vitality. Fancy on the other hand, in Coleridge's words, 'is indeed no other than a mode of memory emancipated from the order of time and space.' 'Imagination brings what is there creatively to life, Fancy is not regulated or regulative but is a free associative power' which has its own place in human perception, no doubt. I am not, however, at the moment asking for a more fanciful approach to theology, but a more imaginative.

The first way in which this may be done is by a fresh look at our pedagogical methods and presuppositions. Whatever may be true of teaching at other levels, the primary, the secondary or the technical, study of any subject at the tertiary level (in a manner worthy of a university) must always be undertaken in a way that questions itself. There is no place in the study of theology for un-

---

[2] *Biographia Literaria,* Everyman's Library, 1930 (and in many other editions), chap. XIII.

thinking repetition. The theological teacher must constantly be asking: is my course of lectures strictly necessary? Is this individual lecture in this course strictly necessary? What does it contribute to the study of the whole? Universities may say that they welcome new knowledge, that they are always open and willing to pursue new subjects of study (provided of course the government will pay for it, and no one will have to sacrifice any existing activity to make it possible); but they are notoriously bad at cutting out and burning the dead wood. Indeed some are quite good at carving patterns out of the dead wood, playing their own intricate games with pieces of dead wood in the name of pure scholarship. That way lies pedantry. I want to be so bold as to ask whether the study of theology can be exempt from this criticism.

Like many of you I conceive it to be my duty, at least from time to time, to keep myself acquainted with what has been published in current periodicals. Indeed a number of those in biblical disciplines come into my study. More, many more, increasingly many more are to be found in this and other libraries: theological publication, including the proliferation of writing for periodicals, has been a growth industry (although like many other industries which expanded rapidly in recent decades it is now facing some considerable problems). We must, however, often ask the question: to what end? Again and again I am tempted to deface the periodical which I am reading by almost carving at the conclusion the words: So what? Was this article strictly necessary for any other purpose than to promote the name of the young author? Or to show how clever some individual was at moving the counters of a game which he was taught when he studied for his PhD?

My purpose is not to abuse or scold, but to illustrate: if we were called upon to justify the writing of that article or the giving of that lecture, to show why it is strictly necessary, then there is some hope that its significance would come alive for readers other than other pedants. And if we are asked, necessary for what?

And justify to whom? The answers are really quite simple, although of course capable of considerable sophistication.

Necessary for what? For the enlargement and deepening of our under-standing of God and man and their inter-relation: for I take it that is the subject matter of theology. If all our theological disciplines are required to point to that, then imagination has come to the rescue of knowledge—'a fact is no longer a bare fact: it is invested with all its possibilities. It is no longer a burden on the memory: it is energising as the poet of our dreams, and as the architect of our purposes'. This presupposes theological teachers who are highly self-critical, and who are secure enough in their spiritual and personal lives to be able to raise and entertain fundamental doubts about the value of much that they are doing. This leads me to the second question: justify to whom? Oddly enough, the answer to this (painful and testing though it may be) is 'to our students'. If we cannot, in this process of teaching, justify to our students the subjects we study and the disciplines which we undergo, then to what end are we pursuing them? In recent years many teachers have had to spend long (and sometimes tedious) hours in discussions with students about curriculum reform; and if in the process we have learnt to be tough-minded in our dealing with one another that is no harm, and the discussion must continue. But I am thinking more of the justification which is built into the way in which we present our material, the fundamental doubt and faith about the necessity of pursuing this topic which should creep into all we say and do. The transcending power of imagination, its re-creative power, begins when teaching and learning are no longer conventional communications but a dangerous voyage between the rocks of folly and pedantry.

A second way in which imagination may reassert itself in the study of theology has particular reference to biblical studies, but also applies more widely: we have to lay hold of a more capacious criticism than is provided by historical method alone, and that will include a freshly discovered literary criticism appropriate to the great documents of the faith, biblical and post-biblical. Perhaps particularly in the Anglo-Saxon world the study of history has become a self-justifying activity. Most of us have at least a smattering of knowledge of the history of at least one of the arts, but we are singularly weak in critical appreciation. Unless someone else told us we would not know why one picture is better than another; and even our assessment of films is often still on the level of 'I know what I like'.

In the case of the Old and New Testaments historical investigation has been so successful in breaking up the monolithic fundamentalism of a previous age, and its contribution to our knowledge of the setting of individual books in the life of Israel or the Church so great, that we are rightly grateful for all its achievements. We know more about the books of the Bible than any previous generation, we even think that we know something about a certain number of the biblical authors, and we perceive behind the text those strangely named characters the Yahwist, the Elohist, Deutero-Isaiah and Q! Historical imagination has worked powerfully to reconstruct for us literally almost a hundred different circumstances in which God had a controversy with his people Israel or with their successors in the churches (which we now refer to in the plural) of New Testament times. The work is genuinely imaginative, not fanciful; and it would be churlish to deny that it has engendered excitement, just as it would be philistine to go back on the great achievements of the period of historical enquiry.

Similarly historical studies have introduced a healthy relativity into the study of ancient creeds, dogmas and confessions. We know better what their authors were saying, or trying to say, in the language of their own day. We are less prone to idolatry of a particular period in the Church's history: be it the New Testament, the Patristic, the Middle Ages, the Reformation, the Enlightenment or the Evangelical Revival. We owe so much to the historians that it seems dangerous to say that history, like patriotism, is not enough; but we must say that for at least two reasons.

It is not enough first because to exercise the historical imagination—if left to itself—is self-defeating. Albert Schweitzer saw this over seventy years ago. If we really do our historical homework thoroughly, the past becomes not more familiar, certainly not more congenial but more remote. You will remember Schweitzer's words about the quest for the historical Jesus:

> It set out, believing that when it had found him it would bring him straight into our time as a Teacher and Saviour. It loosed the bands by which he had been riveted for centuries to the stony rocks of ecclesiastical doctrine, and rejoiced to see life and movement coming into the figure once more, and the historical Jesus advancing, it seemed, to meet it. But he does not stay; he passes by our time and returns to his own. What surprised and dismayed the theology of the last forty years was that, despite all forced and arbitrary interpretations, it could not keep him in our time, but had to let him go. He returned to his own time, not owing to the application of any historical ingenuity, but by the same inevitable necessity by which the liberated pendulum returns to its original position.[3]

Since Albert Schweitzer wrote these words we have had *Formgeschichte* (the history of the forms of biblical speech), *Überlieferungsgeschichte* (the history of the traditions behind the text), and *Redaktionsgeschichte* (the history of the editorial process): all plotting out a process, essentially, necessarily remote from our present preoccupations and purposes. Indeed Käsemann has remarked that it is the job of the historian to uncover the alien character of the past.[4] That is salutary, but it is not enough.

It is not enough for a second reason, namely that it always tends to take us

---

[3] Albert Schweitzer, *The Quest of the Historical Jesus* (London: E T, A & C Black, 1948), 397.

[4] 'On the subject of Primitive Christian Apocalyptic', English Translation in *New Testament Questions of Today* (London: SCM Press, 1969), 111, n 2.

behind the text. It does not move from the text forward, but through the text backwards to a more remote process and history. It is time to apply to the text a more authentic literary criticism. Much is happening in the realm of so-called secular literary criticism which we neglect to our peril. It is worth remembering that the Christian Church found the Scripture of the Old and New Testament compelling to the imagination for centuries before there was any historical knowledge of their place and occasion of origin; and it may be worth asking 'how?'. A distinguished American critic has written an important essay entitled "The Intentional Fallacy".[5] What is significant for the critic is not what the poet or novelist intended but the poem, the writing which he has left us. What has to be interpreted is not his intention, but what he wrote.

What such a literary criticism would mean is beyond the scope of the present address, just as it is beyond my competence to delineate. But hints are to be found in the work of James Barr and others, that we may be at the beginning of a new and exciting approach to the age-old task of elucidating the text in its distinctiveness; and in doing so we shall be wise to learn from the lively exponents of contemporary literary criticism, some of whom—certainly in France and in North America—have begun to look at some biblical texts while we have been burrowing in antecedents, preoccupied with some questionably relevant studies in the history of words, fascinated by the *Umwelt,* the surrounding world. We need a new generation of biblical scholars whose literary imagination is as developed as the historical imagination of their predecessors.

This leads to a third observation on the place of imagination in theology: it may help if we were to go about our study with a new awareness of the problem of our Christian identity. Christianity, for better or for worse, has been a great literary event; and we who study theology have access to it chiefly through its literature. Moreover, to acquire a faith a man must learn a language, to pray he must use words (or at least the Church in which he prays must do so), to pass

---

[5] W.K. Wimsatt, *The Verbal Icon* (University of Kentucky Press 1954 and London: Methuen & Co 1970). One might perhaps put alongside this some sentences from Helmut Franz's essay "Das Wesen des Textes" Z thK LIX (1962), 190, quoted by J.M. Robinson in "Hermeneutic since Barth" in *The New Hermeneutics* (New York: Harper & Row, 1964) 46: "The basic thing about a text is not what the author intended to express in words by following up a given point of view. Rather, basic is what wills fundamentally to show itself and have its say prior to or apart from any subjective intent. The question to the text would then not be the question as to the [author's] perspective, but rather: 'What shines forth in this text? What shows itself in this text?'"

Or again perhaps T S Eliot:
> It seems, as one becomes older,
> That the past has another pattern, and ceases to be a mere sequence —
> Or even development.

on his faith he must be articulate. Christian writing (including that in the Old Testament) is the literary deposit of a series of language-events which occurred first in Israel and has been continued in the history of the Church. This is our literature. It is in these writings that we find our cultural identity; or, do we? That is the problem, the great question with which we must now go to our study.

Professor Graham Hough in an essay on "Criticism as a humanist discipline"[6] has remarked succinctly: 'The literature of the past is what it always was; the business of criticism is to insert it into the living fabric of the present.' We can apply that: Christian writing is what it always was (like secular writing it is always growing in volume); the business of theology is to insert it into the living fabric of the present. This is an immense imaginative exercise, from which the Christian Church has never been free. The question, who are we now in relation to this great body of literature?, is always with those who would be theologians. To date, however, the question has often been approached with altogether too narrow a preoccupation, sometimes that of denominational self-justification — as though, laughably, the biblical writers, the fathers of the Church and all their successors were really at heart Englishmen preparing the way for *ecclesia anglicana*, or men whose only possible residuary legatees was tridentine Rome, or either Barthian or liberal protestantism. Even that most impressive 20th century attempt to insert the literature of the past into the living fabric of the present undertaken by the existentialists, we now see to have been conducted within too narrow confines.

Our problem of identity is at least two-fold. The first may be called the doubt about ourselves: can we really insert into the living fabric of our lives anything more than a small, and arbitrarily chosen, selection from the great Christian literary tradition? The problem, we know, is not simply one of size, or of time or linguistic competence to master it. The problem is one of sympathy. And yet we would not be theologians unless at least some fragments of that literature, in another of Coleridge's phrases *finds* us' 'and finds us at greater depths of our being.'

Our internal problem, however, turns out to be also an external problem: how is it that between us and so many of our contemporaries there is such a rift on this matter? We are not only children of the Christian tradition, we are also deeply embedded in contemporary culture, and many Christians (especially perhaps in parts of Africa and Asia) find themselves deeply sympathetic to that

---

[6] In *Contemporary Criticism*, Stratford-upon-Avon Studies 12, edited by Malcolm Bradbury and David Palmer, Edward Arnold, London 1970, p. 50.

culture. We too would not wish to be separated from our contemporaries, espe-cially our younger contemporaries, to whom our Christian language and litera-ture are unintelligible.

How Christian theology is to come to terms with this problem, I do not know. I only know that it will require a gigantic imaginative effort. Let me conclude, however, with an instance which may or may not be either illuminat-ing or comforting. There are lots of early Christian writings which are con-cerned with this question. I pick on one, familiar to us all. It is a passage from Mark's gospel.

You remember how the fourth chapter opens with the story of the seed and how it is destroyed by a series of antagonistic elements: the birds, the sun, the thorns, each in turn preventing it from germinating or growing to the point at which it bears fruit; and yet there is a harvest of miraculous proportions. The story is told by Mark in such a way as to pick up the theme of conflict and antagonism of the preceding incidents and to prepare the way for his fuller exposition of how the message concerning Jesus fares in the world. Then imme-diately he precipitates the problem of identity. The twelve ask Jesus about the parables, this strangely simple mode of speech so unlike other religious talk; and they receive the answer: 'to you the mystery of the kingdom; for those outside everything in parables.' For the disciples the knowledge, the assurance, of God's final reign (his eschatological kingdom, if you like) over everything; for other men, everything (*ta panta*), the whole world lies around them in these parables. And the parables are not esoteric stories; they are about ordinary things, at which men may look and see nothing, which men may hear and understand nothing. Between the disciples and the others there is a terrible rift, and yet they are looking at the same world and it is described to them in the same simple para-bles—simple enough to be misunderstood; weak enough to be destroyed by the birds, the sun, the thorns. The disciples are men to whom understanding is *given*. That is to say, some part of this strange and often unimpressive narrative *finds* them. So their task is to put a lamp on a stand; for what is secret will come to light.

The task of theology is just that. Not to advertise its nostrums with neon signs, nor to think that it can steer a search light and penetrate the darkness of the world, but modestly to hold up a lamp — so that perchance those who look out into the darkness with us may gradually, as our eyes become accustomed to the half-light in which we live, see there the conflicts and the crucifixion of a man who is and is to be the Lord of us all. In tracing his way we lose ourselves, and so are found.

# The Formation of
# The Basis of Union

## A Lecture given before the Synod of Victoria
## October 1994[1]

In responding to your kind invitation to me to give this lecture, I find myself faced by two difficulties. First, there is a historical enquiry which might properly be undertaken about the consultative procedures adopted by the three churches—the Congregational Churches of Australia, the Methodist Church of Australia and the Presbyterian Church of Australia—as they sought a basis of union in the period from 1957 until they entered the Uniting Church in Australia in 1977. Against that day when we enter into discussions tending towards union with another Church, it may be of importance to have a critical analysis of the procedures adopted on the previous occasion. That cannot be done without reference to the formidable collection of archival material now lodged in the Mitchell Library in Sydney.

As is probably well known by members of this Historical Society, that remarkable man, Robert Macarthur—formerly a minister of the Presbyterian Church, now a minister of the Uniting Church—persuaded most of us who were involved in that process to lodge our papers in that Library. Anyone wishing to make a thorough investigation of the union negotiations will from now onwards need to spend some time in those archives. I would suppose that my case is similar to that of others: I no longer possess any papers belonging to that period, only an index to my papers held in the Mitchell Library. All that I can do is to speak from memory. I would greatly have enjoyed spending some days working in Sydney. It would, for instance, be fascinating to learn how other members of the Joint Commission saw our task, and to note perhaps how our minds changed or our spirits developed as the consultation proceeded.

It could be a useful study of how a group of people learn to think together, with influences from without and from within the group; especially interesting

[1] Previously published in the Proceedings of the Uniting Church Historical Society, Synod of Victoria Vol. 1, No. 1, Dec. 1994. Reproduced by permission.

when the people involved, the personnel, changed as much as they did in the process. Henry Wells once remarked that he thought that he and I were the only people who had been present at the first meeting of the Joint Commission, had been members throughout and were present at the Inaugural Assembly.

Be all that as it may that enquiry must await another occasion, and almost certainly another enquirer.

A second approach also runs into a difficulty. It would be possible to give a straightforward account of the different literary stages through which the material in print passed as we follow the work of the Joint Commission on Church Union on its way towards the production of the Basis of Union. But this has already been done—and, as is necessary, at greater length—by Andrew Dutney in his admirable and generous book *Manifesto for Renewal,*[2] and by Michael Owen in his magisterial General Introduction to the historic documents of the Uniting Church in Australia[3]. I am not sure how widely those books have been used. They deserve to be studied carefully, if the process is to be understood. To try to cover the same ground more briefly in a lecture would be to attempt to summarise a summary: a procedure which would be somewhat insulting to a literate audience, inducing a high degree of boredom.

So I turn to a third approach, one which I was required to adopt for the first time nearly thirty years ago, and ask: what were some of the theologically significant decisions made in forming the Basis of Union? I select three which may be seen to have had controlling significance, and must continue to do so.

## The First Decision

In forming the Basis of Union we were putting into the hands of the uniting churches, and of the Uniting Church, an instrument whereby they might call their members into a deeper commitment to the faith and worship of the Christian Church in its fulness. We came together *and we stay together* to bear witness to the Church's faith in its fulness.

Negatively, this meant that we rejected what in sophisticated terms was called 'comparative ecclesiology', or in more colloquial language 'ecclesiastical carpentry'. This had far-reaching influence on our method. It was not our custom in the Joint Commission to ask for comparative statements of the views of the denominations entering union, on critical items of doctrine. We were not there to reshape the lives of our several churches so that they might the more

---

[2] Andrew Dutney, *Manifesto for Renewal* (Melbourne: Uniting Church Press, 1986).
[3] Michael Owen, *Witness of Faith* (Melbourne: Uniting Church Press, 1984).

readily fit together, like the legs and seat of a well-made chair, on which we might sit with comfort.

We were there to try together to understand the Gospel afresh. We were there to invite our churches together to enter into a fuller appreciation of what it meant to belong to the One Holy Catholic and Apostolic Church: that Church which in a memorable phrase of Bishop Oliver Tomkins is 'none of us yet all of us'—'none of us' meaning 'no one of us alone' or 'no one of us yet', but in God's sight all of us because called to bear witness to him, to show forth his glory.

If the process was not a matter of carpentry, fitting together the separated parts of the church, neither was it to be understood as an anthology: choosing the best pieces out of each of our traditions and, as in a hymnbook or other anthology of sacred writing, saying 'When you put all these pieces together you have the faith and life of the church in its fulness'. No! the perfection of the church's life and of our understanding of its faith, lies in the future. In the imagery of the book of Revelation, it is in a vision of the end that the marriage supper of the Lamb takes place and the Bride is presented as made ready for her husband. This is part of what theologians might call the eschatological dimension of the church's faith and life: that to which we are called, to which we are to go, passing this way as pilgrims. Here we have no continuing city; we seek one to come. Together we were to set our faces in that direction.

The significance of this faith and hope which holds us is set forth in the *Basis of Union* not only in its forward look, its 'not yet', but also in its stress upon the road along which we (all of us, the whole church) have come to this hour. There is a faith delivered to the saints, just as there is a hope of our calling. So the *Basis of Union* takes us back along the way by which the Church has come to this hour. Through the witness of contemporaries, by hearing the evangelical preaching of John Wesley, with minds informed and intelligence sharpened by the Confessions and Catechisms of our Reformation forebears, in the use of the Apostles' and Nicene Creeds—'framed in the language of their day and used by Christians in many days'—we are led through sacrament and scripture to the One who is the Way, the Truth and the Life.

The *Basis of Union* shows us what it might mean to enter more fully into 'the faith and unity of the Holy Catholic and Apostolic Church built upon the one Lord Jesus Christ' (para. 3).

In all this there is no freedom from error, no promise of the security of always being right. The *Basis* ends with a prayer for correction. To be a member of the Uniting Church (or any other church) is to be put at a place where we stand before God, and therefore are made the more liable to know our defects:

The hour-glass whispers to the lion's paw,
The clocktower tells the gardens day and night
How many errors time has patience for,
How wrong they are in being always right.[4]

The Scots Confession is one of the reformers' documents to which our attention is drawn. In its preface it acknowledges this possibility of error in words that Ronald Gregor Smith describes as 'disarmingly revealing':

> Protesting that, if any man will note in this our confession any article or sentence repugnant to God's holy Word, that it would please him of his gentleness, and Christian charity's sake, to admonish us of the same in writing; and we of our honour and fidelity, do promise unto him satisfaction from the mouth of God (that is from his Scriptures), or else reformation of that which he shall prove to be amiss[5].

It is striking that John Knox (or whoever wrote those words) invites admonition in writing, and promises to answer in words drawn from scripture. Christian discourse (like any other human conversation) depends upon us speaking the same language. Indeed conversation between God and members of the human race, this man, that woman, depends upon there being a common language—a fact which God himself recognised, indeed established, in the incarnation, the Word made flesh.

The *Basis of Union* unashamedly invites us to learn a certain language, the language or languages in which faith has been passed on from generation to generation. It says remarkably little about religious experience but in a score of ways reminds us that 'faith comes from what is heard, and what is heard comes by the preaching of Christ' (Romans 10:17). The two substantial reports of the Joint Commission—*The Faith of the Church*[6] and *The Church: Its Nature, Function and Ordering*[7]—allude constantly to the articulate, the literate tradition of the Church. However much the framers of the *Basis of Union*, and the Church for which they framed it, may fall short of their own best aspirations, again and again they invoke or echo a tradition greater than the contemporary community of which they are a part. I am not nowadays a great reader of reports to Synods or Assemblies, but those I do read sometimes appear a little thin in their references to the great tradition of Christian thought and writing. In the first chapter of the Warfield Lectures, which he was preparing at the time of his death, Ronald Gregor Smith asserts:

---

[4] W H Auden, 'Our Bias', *Collected Shorter Poems, 1927-57*, (London: Faber, 1966).
[5] Owen, *Witness of Faith*, 1964.
[6] Originally published by the Joint Board of Christian Education. (Melbourne:1959, republished 1978).
[7] Melbourne: The Aldersgate Press, 1963.

Certainly, without the willingness to think through the received documents of our tradition, I could not venture to stand before you now, or to account myself a reasonable heir not merely of the documents of the Reformed tradition, but also of the whole material of the Christian tradition. For the readiness to understand our past is the prime prerequisite for facing the future in a responsible way[9].

He concludes that memorable chapter on 'Faith and Doctrine' with the following words:

> Faith without doctrine is a wildly swaying weathercock driven around by every gust of the arbitrary imaginative or speculative power of man. Doctrine without faith is a sullen and joyless taskmaster, the slave-driver with the whip. There is no immutable doctrine; but the reality of the doctrinal tradition keeps faith from fantasy. The two must go together; but the greater of the two is faith.

Granted the truth of the last phrase, the question still must be pressed: is Christianity in Australia (in the Uniting Church) more under threat from an undue preoccupation with the formulations of the past or from fantasy, trends, fashions?

It is not only the language of the past but the books in which 'the reality of the doctrinal tradition' (as Gregor Smith puts it) are preserved which are precious (I was going to say, sacred). At the present time theology, like other humane studies, is in many countries going through a period of reassessment. Among the matters for discussion are those relating to our literary traditions: the possibility of a canon of preferred literature is being called in question. So too I detect among us an unwillingness to think again the thoughts expressed in the great traditional writings of the Christian Church. Let us not be swept away by loss of nerve on this point. It may be encouraging to observe that among those—Christians and others—who have experienced the most searing attacks on their religious and cultural traditions (I refer to those who lived and sometimes died at the hands of Stalinist regimes in Russia and Eastern Europe), the existence of a literary tradition has been highly valued.

Let me give you one example, from Czeslaw Milosz, a Polish poet, in a poem entitled 'And yet the Books':

> And yet the books will be there on the shelves, separate beings,
> That appeared once, still wet
> As shining chestnuts under a tree in autumn,
> And, touched, coddled, began to live

---

[8] *Ronald Gregor Smith, The Doctrine of God,* (London: Collins, 1970), 25-26.

In spite of fires on the horizon, castles blown up,
Tribes on the march, planets in motion.
'We are,' they said, even as their pages
Were being torn out, or a buzzing flame
Licked away their letters. So much more durable
Than we are, whose frail warmth
Cools down with memory, disperses, perishes.
I imagine the earth when I am no more:
Nothing happens, no loss, it's still a strange pageant,
Women's dresses, dewy lilacs, a song in the valley.
Yet the books will be there on the shelves, well born,
Derived from people, but also from radiance, heights[9].

# The Second Decision

We turn now to a second critical decision which flows from the first: a decision
about how you conduct negotiations tending towards union. Granted that the
*Basis of Union* put before the uniting churches a possibility of standing together
and afresh before the faith by which the Christian Church lives, how do the separated churches move into union, and why should they? Would it not be sufficient
to issue agreed statements and remain separate institutions or organisations?

Let us take the second of those questions first. The perception that there is
a faith and life of the Church leads inescapably into a deeper awareness that God
in Christ has called into being one fellowship of the Holy Spirit to do his bid-
ding. This is clear from Scripture, it is affirmed in the creeds, and it was so
understood at the Reformation, which was to restore and renew the face of the
Catholic Church. But how do churches separated by historical forces of one
kind or another come together?

It became increasingly clear that abandonment of the comparative method
involved abandonment of comparative ecclesiastical (and implied moral) judgements. If we are serious about asking 'What is God's will, for the true and full
life of the Church?', we must surely regard it as at least inappropriate to be
giving each other marks for the extent to which we have responded to that will
with the inevitable tendency to give oneself, or one's own denomination, rather
higher marks than we give to the other parties. A better way must be found; and
as we proceeded we became aware that that way is the road along which God
always leads his children into a fuller and richer relationship with himself. It is
the way of justifying grace as that is set forth in the Epistle to the Romans; and

---

[9] Czeslaw Milosz, *Collected Poems, 1931-1987* (London: Penguin Books, 1988).

we were required to apply that to our life as churches, just as we would be required again and again to apply it to the life of the Uniting Church.

Looked at this way there are four great moments in the way from disunion to union, and in the constant way of renewal along which a reformed Church is led, *ecclesia reformata et semper reformanda*: a reformed Church, always to be reformed. Let me elaborate.[10]

1. The first of these is the moment of acknowledgement of the given character of the Church's faith. There is a Word of God come among us in Jesus Christ, to whom decisive witness is borne in Scripture, confessed in creed, in whose life the believer participates through Baptism and the Holy Communion. This is not of the making or invention of any of our churches. This is the given basis of the Church's life. This acknowledgement leads, however, to another moment.

2. This is the recognition that none of us has borne witness to that faith in its fulness. This awareness springs not from a comparison one with another but from a realistic assessment of church life as we know it when it is measured against the given provisions of the church's life. What we in effect said to our churches was that unless they come together as penitents they would be better not to come together at all.

3. The third moment is that in which the divided churches recognise that, in spite of their defects and failures, God has blessed them. He has acknowledged the words spoken so that his Word has been heard; he has drawn people to himself by means of the sacraments administered in divided churches; he has blessed with the gift of his Spirit their separated communities. Divided churches can therefore do no less than acknowledge what God has acknowledged, each recognising with gratitude the presence of God in its own past and in that of the other. We come together only because the miracle of forgiving grace has been worked in each of us. Here is the counterpart of the Pauline 'while we were yet sinners Christ died for us' (Romans 5: 8).

4. The fourth moment is also Pauline. It arises when the strong negative is given to the question: 'Are we to continue to sin that grace may abound'? (Romans 6: 1). Since God has blessed the churches in their divided

---

[10] This fourfold response was elaborated in the first Report of the Joint Commission, *The Faith of the Church*, 29-31. The formulation used here is largely that adopted when I addressed the Faith and Order Commission of the World Council of Churches in 1964, printed in *The Ecumenical Review*, January 1965, and later reprinted by the Joint Board of Christian Education.

state, what is the point of reunion? And the answer must be that we have been delivered from the past in order to seek a new life in Christ. A basis of union is not to be thought of primarily as a negotiated agreement between members of human institutions but as a call to the churches to come together and seek amendment of life.

This approach by way of the rhythm of the Gospel eliminates the possibility of churches approaching the question primarily in terms of the 'contribution' of one or more denominations to the fulness of the coming great church. Instead, it assumes that the reality of the church's faith and life is *given*, that we hide it from one another and from the world, that nevertheless the goodness of God is greater than human sinfulness, and that we are called to try to remove from our lives those things which contradict the gracious and reconciled relationship in which we stand.

## The Third Decision

The third critical decision to which I would draw attention was to offer this Basis of Union as the basis in faith, the standing ground, for the Uniting Church. We certainly never intended that it should only be of significance at the time of union. There was no intention that the Assembly of the Church would be in control of the *Basis,* but rather that the commitment explicitly made by the Uniting Church in the *Basis* should control the life of the Assembly, as of every other part of the Church's life[11]. To hold office within this Church it was necessary for ministers and others to 'adhere to the *Basis of Union*'; and the *Basis* describes its understanding of that phrase as 'willingness to live and work within the faith and unity of the One Holy Catholic and Apostolic Church as that way is described in this *Basis*'.

Since this has become of critical importance for the life of the Uniting Church, let us see if we can obtain light on what such 'adherence' might mean by reference to two other critical destinations, one made between philosophers and the other of John Stuart Mill in his essay on Coleridge[12] drew attention to

---

[11] The point is well made by Michael Owen in a sentence in the General Introduction to *Witness of Faith*: 'There is such a thing as the substance of the faith, but, rather than seek to spell it out in one more set of formulations, the Uniting Church has pledged itself to continue to seek and to receive that substance under the guidance of certain historic texts' (20).

[12] Reproduced in part in *The Oxford Book of Essays*, edited by John Gross, Oxford: University Press, 1991. The essays in full can be found, with difficulty, in Mill's *Dissertations and Discussions*. Happily F. R. Leavis edited them with an Introduction, *Mill on Bentham and Coleridge* (London: Chatto and Windus, 1950).

an important difference between Bentham and Coleridge. Coleridge has been, he writes,

> almost as truly as Bentham, 'the great questioner of things established'; for a questioner needs not necessarily be an enemy. By Bentham, beyond all others, men have been led to ask themselves, in regard to any ancient or received opinion, Is it true? and by Coleridge, What is the meaning of it? The one took his stand outside the received opinion, and surveyed it as an entire stranger to it: the other looked at it from within, and endeavoured to see it with the eyes of a believer in it; to discover by what apparent facts it was at first suggested, and by what appearances it has ever since been rendered continually credible—has seemed, to a succession of persons, to be a faithful interpretation of their experience. Bentham judged a proposition true or false as it accorded or not with the result of his own inquiries; and did not search very curiously into what might be meant by the proposition, when it obviously did not mean what he thought true. With Coleridge, on the contrary, the very fact that any doctrine had been believed by thoughtful men, and received by whole nations or generations of mankind, was part of the problem to be solved, was one of the phenomena to be accounted for.

'The Uniting Church', we are told in the *Basis of Union*, 'lives and works within the faith and unity of the One Holy Catholic and Apostolic Church' (para 2). Adherence to the Basis is 'willingness to live and work within (that) faith and unity' (para 14). There is no doubt a place for a Benthamite scrutiny of the truth of propositions which are found in credal or confessional affirmation, and the question 'Is it true?' may, on the lips of an outsider, purge from us a too facile acceptance of every formulation of the faith. But adherence to the *Basis* is more Coleridgean than Benthamite, reminding us that 'a questioner need not necessarily be an enemy'. He can be from inside, asking 'What did it and what does it mean?'

The Uniting Church through its *Basis* lays a great burden upon its ministers. Their particular calling is not only defined in paragraph 14. They are called to enter a tradition of 'faithful and scholarly interpreters of Scripture' and to reflect deeply upon God's living Word, exposing themselves to a wide range of contemporary thought. They in particular are committed to an understanding of the evangelical and confessional writings mentioned in paragraph 10, asking always the question of Coleridge looking at the creeds, at Scripture itself, 'with the eyes of a believer … to discover by what apparent facts it was at first suggested, and by what appearances it has ever since been rendered continually credible'. To adhere to the *Basis of Union* comes mighty close to living in the Communion of Saints.

My second illustration, or illumination if it be such, comes from the sphere of politics and history[13]. Edmund Burke, as is well known, was the most articulate opponent of George Grenville over the taxation of the American colonies in the late 18th century. When Grenville died Burke paid a generous tribute, neither uncritical nor unkindly, to him in the House of Commons. After recognising Grenville's 'well-earned rank in Parliament', his 'thorough knowledge of its constitution, and a perfect practice in all its business', he speaks of Grenville's limitations, defects to be 'sought in the particular habits of his life'.

> He was bred in a profession. He was bred to the Law, which is, in my opinion, one of the first and noblest of the human sciences; a science which does more to quicken and invigorate the understanding, than all the other kinds of learning put together; but it is not apt, except in persons very happily born, to open and to liberalise the mind exactly in the same proportion. Passing from that study he did not go very largely into the world; but plunged into business; I mean into the business of office; and the limited and fixed methods and forms established there. Much knowledge is to be had undoubtedly in that line and there is no knowledge which is not valuable. But it may be truly said that men too much conversant in office are rarely minds of remarkable enlargement. Their habits of office are apt to give them a turn to think the substance of business not to be much more important than the forms in which it is conducted.
>
> These forms are adapted to ordinary occasions; and therefore persons who are nurtured in office do admirably well, as long as things go on in their common order; but when the high roads are broken up, and the waters out, when a new and troubled scene is opened, and the file affords no precedent, then it is that a greater knowledge of mankind, and a far more extensive comprehension of things, is requisite than ever office gave, or than office can ever give.

I have quoted this at such length partly because at this stage in a lecture you deserve to hear a really great piece of English prose. I draw your attention to Burke's description of a certain habit of mind, because the church on earth always also suffers (like other institutions) from inescapably being in the hands of men and women who have the habits of office. This does not only apply to a few, to holders of office, to members of Legal Reference Committees (although to them especially); it applies to us all as we adopt the *personae*, play the role of being members of Councils of Elders, Presbyteries, Synods, Assembly. We become 'men and women conversant in office', 'rarely [with] minds of remarkable

---

[13] For what follows see Conor Cruise O'Brien, *The Great Melody: a thematic biography of Edmund Burke* (London: Sinclair-Stevenson, 1994), 108-110.

enlargement ... apt to think the substance of business not to be more important than the forms in which it is conducted'.

Such people, and that includes all of us when we hold office, when we are members of governing bodies, will always tend to prefer to have a Constitution and Regulations to rely on than a Basis of Union to reflect upon. For most of the time, for much of our business affairs, that is all right: 'as long as things go on in their common order'. But what if for the Church 'the high roads are broken up, and the waters out, a new and troubled scene is opened, and the file affords no precedent'? Then we must learn what it means to adhere to the Basis of Union, for it points us to that greater knowledge of the ways of God with his people scattered over many centuries and lands, and it may for us in such critical hours offer a more extensive comprehension of things than ever office gave, or than office can ever give.

Looking at it now as one spared the problems of office, I cannot help wondering whether too much time and energy are sometimes spent on trying to work out what the church should be doing to commend itself more effectively to the world.

On the twenty-second day of June 1977 the three churches entering union laid upon the table the resolutions passed in their respective governing bodies which took them into union. Farquhar Gunn, a man who held office without loss of enlargement of spirit, who was in the chair, asked us all to stand and sing 'Praise God from whom all blessings flow'. He then invited Dr Harold Wood to lead us in prayer and we commemorated, or Dr Wood drew into our memories in God's presence, the many gifts which God had bestowed upon men and women in various times and places, by which gifts we too would live. I have rarely heard such a prayer. I have rarely so been taught to pray. I am glad to learn that that prayer has been recorded. It should be taken into our private prayers, when we go into our room and shut the door and pray to our Father who is in secret, with the assurance that 'your Father who sees in secret will reward you' (Matthew 6: 4).

The *Basis* itself ends with a prayer, and with that this lecture should finish.

> The Uniting Church prays that, through the gift
> of the Spirit, God will constantly correct that which is
> erroneous in its life, will bring it into deeper unity
> with other Churches, and will use its worship,
> witness and service to God's eternal glory
> through Jesus Christ the Lord. Amen

# Living in Two Worlds

## The Cardinal Knox Lecture at the Catholic
## Theological College, Melbourne
## 13 August 1993*

You do me great honour in inviting me to give this lecture, associated as it is with the name of Cardinal James Knox.

With many of you I have not only respectful but also affectionate memories of Cardinal Knox. I had the privilege of being a member of the bi-lateral conversations between members of the Catholic and Presbyterian Churches before the Presbyterian Church entered union with the Congregational and Methodist Churches to form the Uniting Church in Australia. These took place under the joint chairmanship of Archbishop, later Cardinal Knox and The Very Reverend Norman Faichney. We met alternately at Raheen and at Ormond College, and our meetings always included lunch at which my wife was customarily present when we met at Ormond College. From this there grew warm friendships so that Cardinal Knox, although rather eschewing farewell occasions, agreed that all the members should lunch together with him before he left for Rome. He insisted that we should subsequently visit him in Rome which my wife and I did on two occasions, enjoying the hospitality of that kind shy man.

I also remember with gratitude his insistence that the Eucharistic Congress of 1973 should have an ecumenical dimension. To that end, a small committee met in my study at Ormond and were kept informed about plans as they developed, and we were encouraged to make our contribution. Some of you may remember that two of the visiting theologians on that occasion were notable Protestants: Jürgen Moltmann and Lukas Vischer. I often think that the form of address 'Your Grace' was singularly apt in the case of James Knox. He was a gracious man both in the secular and the theological sense of that word. It is a pleasure to recall him to memory tonight.

* Previously published in a slightly modified form in *Pacifica*, Vol 7, 1994, the Journal of the Melbourne College of Divinity. Reproduced by permission of The Pacifica Theological Studies Association, PO Box 271, Brunswick East, Victoria 3057, Australia.

About seven years ago a distinguished American literary critic, Michael Seidel, published a book entitled *Exile and the Narrative Imagination*.[1] 'An exile', he writes in his first sentence, 'is someone who inhabits one place and remembers or projects the reality of another'. In the substance of the book Professor Seidel discusses Daniel Defoe's *Robinson Crusoe*—'Crusoe's Island Exile'; Joseph Conrad's *Lord Jim* and *Heart of Darkness*; James Joyce's *A Portrait of the Artist* and *Ulysses*; the 'expatriated adventurer', as he calls Lawrence Sterne's *A Sentimental Journey* in which the author 'propels his Parson Yorick to France after the opening sentences and never returns him'; 'the lone exile' Henry James' *The Ambassadors* and *The American Scene*; and then finally the exile from Russia, Vladimir Nabokov in *Ada* and *Pale Fire*.

Even a cursory reading of this study—and it deserves much more—brings home to the reader two things. First, how often an experience which has been of decisive importance for a period of history, in our case the modern world, is disclosed in the work of artists, poets and other imaginative writers. Secondly, in observing how different authors have used the occasion of exile, or have described it and reacted to it, we learn how our own imaginations have been shaped by these events and their interpretation. Often writers do this for us ahead of time, so to speak. Defoe and Sterne, Henry James, Joyce, treat of issues that have become more acute, and of experiences which have become more widespread in the twentieth century. They join Odysseus and Ovid and Dante in casting light upon a condition which has been that of many, willingly or unwillingly, in the twentieth century. 'The exile is someone who inhabits one place and remembers or projects the reality of another'.

One thinks of one's own *trivial* experience. When I became a citizen of Australia I was asked the inevitable journalist's question: 'how do you feel?'. Without too much reflection I replied: 'I still feel Irish, but Australia is home'. That, of course, is the relatively happy experience of many, still to feel Italian, Greek, Vietnamese, but to have found in Australia a home. More *momentous* is the experience of literally millions across the face of the earth, who have been uprooted from their home and through perils by land and on water have found themselves separated from family and friends, knowing nothing of their fate, in a country of which they know little, are scarcely welcome and will never again be 'at home'. Every human and natural disaster spills out its hundreds of thousands of refugees to inhabit a strange place and at least to remember if not project the reality of another.

---

[1] Michael Seidel, *Exile and the Narrative Imagination* (New Haven and London: Yale University Press 1986).

We might pause and reflect on that 'remember' and 'project'; for it is memory and hope that keep people human through both the ordinary and terrible experiences of life.

Allow me to remind you of two of the great figures of the twentieth century who were committed to the task of keeping memory alive. It has been a characteristic of totalitarian regimes, Stalinist or fascist, to try to suppress the past, to spread disinformation. Few governments love the truth.

Anna Akhmatova[2] was born in 1889, and was already established as a poet before World War I. When the Russian Revolution took place, she refused to go into exile, that is to say into physical exile:

> No, not beneath a foreign sky,
> Not sheltered by a foreign wing —
> I was where my people were,
> Where, alas, they had to be.

She remained in Stalinist Russia, and in particular identified herself with the women who waited, with diminishing hope, for their imprisoned husbands and sons. Her vocation, however, was not only to be a Russian who remained in Russia, but also a Russian woman who suffered with other women.

> Magdalene wailed and lamented,
> The beloved disciple stood as though in stone,
> But no one dared to cast a glance
> To where the Mother, silent, stood alone.

Akhmatova then 'turns from the depiction of the woman alone in sorrow who becomes universal by becoming one with Mary the Mother of Christ, to describe again the many Marys to whom she dedicated [a group of her] poems' (Haight).

> I pray not only for myself
> But for all those who stood with me
> In savage cold and July heat
> There, beneath that blind red wall.

For it is her vocation to be not only a Russian woman but also to be a poet, to pray and describe the terrible events through which she and others had lived. In

---

[2] The translations used are taken from Amanda Haight's study *Anna Akhmatova, a Poetic Pilgrimage* (New York and London: Oxford University Press, 1976). Since that date there has been published a number of selections and translations. *The Complete Poems of Anna Akhmatova*, translated by Judith Hemschemeyer, edited with an Introduction by Roberta Reeder, were published in two Volumes by the Zephyr Press, Somerville, Massachusetts, in 1990.

brief not to allow to be forgotten. More positively, to remember; and to articulate that memory.

The often quoted 'Instead of a Preface' to her series of poems *Requiem* may perhaps be cited again:

> In the terrible years of the Yezhov terror I spent seventeen months waiting in the line outside the prison in Leningrad. One day somebody in the crowd identified me. Standing behind me was a woman, with lips blue from the cold, who had, of course, never heard me called by name before. Now she started out of the torpor common to us all and asked me in a whisper (everyone whispered there):
> 'Can you describe this?'
> And I said: 'I can.'
> Then something like a smile passed fleetingly over what had once been her face (Leningrad, 1 April 1957).

Humanity at least fleetingly restored, hope not allowed completely to die, by the word. D M Thomas, the English (or perhaps I should say Welsh) poet writing about her funeral in 1966:

> The crowds who swarmed to Akhmatova's funeral, in Leningrad, filling the church and overflowing into the streets, were expressing her country's gratitude. She had kept the 'great Russian word', and the Word [capital W], alive for them. She had outlasted her accusers: had so exasperated them that, as she put it, they had all died before her of heart attacks.[3]

She had never left the land.

> I am not one of those who left the land to the mercy of its enemies.

In that sense she was not an exile, but remaining where she was, suffering at most internal exile, through years when evil and terror reigned she remembered and projects a reality which will not be smothered or destroyed.

It would be possible, and indeed profitable, to occupy the whole of the time set aside for this lecture, by reflecting further on Akhmatova and reading to each other her poems. But I want to put beside her another writer with a similar commitment. Elie Wiesel's story is, I take it, well known. The basic document for understanding him is the account in *Night*[4] of his childhood in a small town in Transylvania, a devout and studious boy in a devout Jewish family; of how his friend the Beadle at the synagogue disappeared because one day 'they', the im-

---

[3] From the Introduction to *You Will Hear Thunder, Akhmatova: Poems,* translated by D. M. Thomas (London: Secker and Warburg, 1985).

[4] Elie Wiesel, *Night* translated from the French by Stella Rodway (London: Penguin Books, 1961).

personal 'they', expelled all the foreign Jews; how they learnt in the spring of 1944 of 'Jews in Budapest living in an atmosphere of fear and terror'; of how the Germans came and set up two ghettos in the town, Sighet, and the Jews recreated their lives there. He and his family are moved from one ghetto, the larger, to another; and ruthlessly, group after group are herded into cattle-trucks and the transportation of the Jews of Sighet begins. The terrible conditions of life in the cattle trucks is succeeded by the greater horror of Birkenau and Auschwitz, the furnaces and the burning of children. He and his father are separated from his mother and sister, and they never see each other again.

He was engraved with a number on his left arm. 'I became A-7713. After that I had no other name'. It would be wrong to summarise further, for as Robert McAfee Brown has commented, 'Of all Wiesel's work, *Night* is the one that most cries out not to be touched, interpreted, synthesised. It must be encountered at first hand'.[5]

Suffice it to say that as the Russian front grew closer, Auschwitz looked like being over-run. Those who had survived are compelled to move, weak and sick though they are, to Gleiwitz and then to Buchenwald. Wiesel's father dies on the way. Three days after the liberation of Buchenwald Wiesel became very sick and was transferred to a hospital. One day he was able to get up and look at himself in the mirror, a thing he had not done since he left the ghetto.

> From the depths of the mirror, a corpse gazed back at me.
> The look in his eyes, as they stared into mine, has never left me.

So ends this spare and unsparing tale: only 125 pages of a Penguin sized book, but an Inferno, a descent into Hell. We can say that, for Hell is not only a place of physical torment—this Hell is that—but of separation, from the entry to Auschwitz with the order 'Men to the left! Women to the right' until when his father is dying the head of the block at Buchenwald advises him: 'Here there are no fathers, no brothers, no friends. Everyone lives and dies for himself alone'. A place of separation also from God. It would be insensitive to try to trace that reality as it impinged upon the spirit of a sensitive boy; but some phrases are unforgettable. At an early stage: 'I did not deny God's existence, but I doubt his absolute justice'; later, 'Where is God now?' and 'What are You, my God?'

At the Jewish New Year: 'This day I had ceased to plead. I was no longer capable of lamentation'. And at Yom Kippur, the Day of Atonement: 'I no longer accepted God's silence ... In the depths of my heart, I felt a great void'. 'It's the end', said the Rabbi from Poland, 'God is no longer with us'.

---

[5] Robert McAfee Brown, *Elie Wiesel, Messenger to all Humanity* (Indiana: University of Notre Dame Press, 1989).

Wiesel waited ten years to write his account. As is well known, he subsequently wrote a series of novels which are, as it were, commentaries on that basic text. This is, however, not the appropriate time to follow him on those journeys of exploration. We must leave him, as we left Akhmatova, to speak for himself. But, and here the resemblance to Akhmatova is striking, he too was compelled to write.

The first essay in a collection of reminiscences entitled significantly *From the Kingdom of Memory*[6] is entitled 'Why I write'. He answers in a number of ways, but underlying them all

> The fear of forgetting: the main obsession of all
> those who have passed through the universe of the damned.
> The enemy relied on people's disbelief and forgetfulness.

Or again, 'I owe the dead my memory'.

Again and again, in his essays and addresses, in fiction and in hortatory prose, speaking to the Reichstag or receiving the Nobel Prize, Wiesel returns to his theme, Remember. For out of that memory which the perpetrators of the crime, and the onlookers, are so anxious to forget, comes some hope. Remembering the children who were herded to their death in Auschwitz, 'For my generation', says Wiesel, 'hope cannot be without sadness'. Remembering too our children and our grandchildren he adds, 'Let the sadness contain hope too'.

In one of his essays Wiesel quotes from that strange but influential Jewish writing the *Book of Splendour* 'When Israel is in exile, so is the word'. In one sense both Akhmatova and Wiesel both refused to go into exile. Akhmatova would not be driven from Russia, would not be silenced by the terror of Stalin, would not be separated from her fellow Russian women.

Wiesel will not be separated from his people, from their memories or their hope, however troublesome, indeed agonising the reappraisal of those memories and hopes given what has happened. The traditional language of Jewish prayers no longer satisfies him. 'The word has deserted the meaning it was intended to convey. The displacement, the shift is irrevocable.' Yet he must testify. He must write. He must speak the word. There is no escape. Like the Jeremiah whom Wiesel so much admires, there is in his heart as it were a burning fire shut up in his bones, and he is weary with holding it in, and he cannot.

I am aware that I have taken you by a strange route into my chosen theme for tonight, living in two worlds. When I first proposed this topic I thought of going back to two books, both influential in my younger days: A D Lindsay's

---

[6]  Elie Wiesel, *From the Kingdom of Memory*, Reminiscences (New York: Summit Books, 1990).

*The Two Moralities: Our Duty to God and Society* where the ethics of grace is put into tension with the ethic of 'my station and its duties'.[7] That does need further exploration, as does a re-examination of Reinhold Niebuhr's *Moral Man and Immoral Society*[8] where the contrast between personal and social ethics becomes almost absolute. I also reflected that the kinds of situations to which I was required to give attention as Governor for over six years, affirming the value of what many good people are doing in society, occasionally warning myself and others about the aberrations which beset us in the modern world, required a different vocabulary from that which I was accustomed to use from pulpit or in theological discourse. I ought to have learnt something about living in or at least speaking of two worlds. Maybe at a rather elementary level that too calls for a little more critical investigation. But somehow all this did not seem immediately illuminating for the world of the exile, the world disclosed to us in the writings of Anna Akhmatova and Elie Wiesel, speaking of both memory and hope.

I take it for granted that as Christians we know ourselves to belong to two worlds, that now we 'see in a mirror dimly, but then face to face', that now we 'know in part', but then shall we 'understand fully, even as we have been fully understood', that here we survive by faith, by hope and by love, and that the greatest of these is love. I assume too that the instructed Christian knows that he or she stands in a great succession going back to Abraham who obeyed when 'he was called to go out to a place which he was to receive as an inheritance; and he went out not knowing where he was to go ... He sojourned in the land of promise as in a foreign land'. He was an exile. 'He looked forward to the city which has foundations, whose builder and maker is God'.

And I remind myself and you that that great writing, the letter to the Hebrews, from which that description comes, says of Christians also that 'here we have no lasting city, but we seek a city which is to come'.[9]

Yet, most notably, this, what theologians would call eschatological perspective, is held together with two other notes: one is the sufficiency of Christ's death as a sacrifice for sin, the awareness that Christ died outside the gate, the supreme exile, and that we may be called to 'go forth to him outside the camp, bearing abuse for him'; the other is the persistent demand for basic virtues:

> Let brotherly love continue.
> Do not neglect to show hospitality to strangers.

---

[7] A. D. Lindsay, *The Two Moralities: Our Duty to God and Society* (London: Eyre & Spottiswode, 1940).

[8] Reinhold Niebuhr, *Moral Man and Immoral Society: A Study in Ethics and Politics* (New York: Scribners, 1932)

[9] Hebrews 13.14

Remember those who are in prison, as though in prison with them;
and those who are ill-treated since you also are in the body.
Let marriage be held in honour, and the marriage bed be undefiled.
Keep your life free from the love of money, and be content with what
you have.
Do not be led away by diverse and strange teachings.[10]

Humbly we receive all this, placed in this world with unremitting obligations to
it, but belonging to a new world which God inaugurated with the call of Abraham
and remade in the death of Jesus who became the pioneer and perfector of our
faith, the one who came to us so that ultimately we may go to him.

Granted all that, what do we say to each other at the end of the twentieth
century about living in two worlds? What in particular if we bear in mind the
disclosure of new dimensions of evil and suffering within the century which is
drawing to its close? What do we say to a world of emigrants and immigrants, of
exiles, of refugees, of those separated from family and friends, and where God
himself is silent? How do we keep the faith, and perhaps just manage, almost
despite ourselves, to convey it to others?

These are questions far too difficult for me to answer. At the risk of being
trivial and banal, let me try however to feel my way forward. I am aware of the
danger of falling back into clichés. There are theological clichés, there are spiritual clichés, as well as literary clichés. A cliché, I take it, is a phrase or a mode of
thought into which we retreat to save us the trouble and perhaps discomfort of
facing reality. With all the hazards with which the attempt is surrounded, let us
try to discern a few signposts on our way.

1. First, as we draw towards the end of the twentieth century do not let us
   put its lessons behind us. From Akhmatova and Wiesel and others we
   have learnt to see and remember the terror that was Stalin and the horror
   that was the holocaust. Evil was given a new face; and the terrible thing
   is that it was a human face. Men and women did these things. Men and
   women acquiesced in these monstrous crimes. Men, women and children suffered almost, although not quite indescribably. We owe it to the
   dead, and we owe it to generations yet unborn to remember these things.
   Moreover, in different shapes and forms these crimes are repeat-
   able. We live in a monstrous world where people excuse themselves
   (probably you and I do) with talk of compassion-fatigue. Of course
   there is a danger, always a danger, of thinking of our small irritations
   and corruptions as more important than they are. I remember Donald

---

[10] Hebrews 13.1-5,9

McKinnon once describing those who within a democracy were inclined to compare its corruptions to the calculated cruelties of totalitarian states as 'the melodrama of the comfortable'. Nevertheless, far short of ethnic cleansing there are always people who want to get rid of each other, who want to silence each other, who want to pretend that what happened wasn't as bad as it was, that the great evil of some of our entrepreneurs was not greed or the lust for power or the love of office but a mistake in not being able to pay their debts and a miscalculation in being found out. There are those who want to falsify the evidence and spread misinformation in war and in peace. Since evil is perhaps not altogether calculable, it is difficult to know whether it is now more manifest in the world than in previous centuries; but what is certain is that in the twentieth century the human race learnt how to do evil, inflict suffering on fellowmen and women and children, with a degree of sophistication never previously available.

The twentieth century has left us with great benefit. That we cannot deny: we know how to control pain, and to eliminate some diseases previously regarded as fatal. We have learnt something about racial and gender prejudice which we did not know, or did not choose to recognize before. But that is not the whole story. The cry 'Remember' must be heard across the whole scene, and it is a sombre call.

2. Secondly, the memory of the twentieth century to which our attention is drawn renders extraordinarily difficult the selection of an adequate vocabulary in which to speak about—or for that matter to—God. We are no longer dealing with the polite intellectual agnosticism of a Matthew Arnold who can claim that

> ... rigorous teachers seized my youth,
> And purged its faith, and trimmed its fire,
> Showed me the high, white star of Truth,
> There bade me gaze, and there aspire.[11]

Nor can it be met by the power of Protestant preaching, nor by the syllogisms of well-rehearsed Catholic thought. Certainly those who hold the Christian faith and those who in a sense are its custodians, not simply as bishops and doctors of the Church but as priests and ministers of the Gospel who Sunday by Sunday and week by week must hold

---

[11] Matthew Arnold 1822-88, 'Stanzas from the Grande Chartreuse' (1855), *Poetical Works of Matthew Arnold* (London: Collins, 1929).

to that faith more deeply than ever before. They must have a range of reference in the history of Christian thought and worship and practice on which they can draw at most unexpected moments. They will not have nostrums, pet schemes for alleviating the world's sorrows, easy answers to the agonizing questions forced upon men and women in the twentieth century. They will live in the household of faith, with whatever difficulty, and they will constantly nourish their minds and spirits, seeking a deeper understanding of what the Christian faith has been, is and might become for the sons and daughters of God. But then they will go out, not with 'easy speeches' which Chesterton rightly perceived only 'comfort cruel men'.[12] They will go out with a certain sensitivity, almost tentativeness.

Michael Seidel in the book *Exile and the Narrative Imagination,* to which I referred at the beginning of this lecture quotes from *Either/Or,* a parable of Kierkegaard:

> If I imagined two kingdoms adjoining one another, with one of which I was fairly well acquainted, and altogether unfamiliar with the other, and I was not allowed to enter the unknown realm, however much I desired to do so, I should still be able to form some conception of its nature. I would go to the limits of the kingdom with which I was acquainted and follow its boundaries, and as I did so, I should in this way describe the boundaries of this unknown country, and thus without ever setting foot in it, obtain a general conception of it. And if this was a task which engrossed my energies, and if I was indefatigable in my desire to be accurate, it would doubtless sometimes happen that, as I stood sadly at my country's boundary and looked longingly into the unknown country, which was so near to me and yet so far away, some little revelation might be vouchsafed to me.[13]

The 'end of the familiar' as Professor Seidel puts it, may mark 'the beginning of the unknown'. Even John Bunyan, that great man of faith, when he got Christian and Hopeful to the Celestial City and saw them through the gate, heard indeed the angelic host sing 'Holy, Holy, Holy is the Lord'. And after that they shut up the gates: 'which when I had seen, I wished myself among them'.[14] But Bunyan has to go back to the City of Destruction and find Christian's wife and children who had

[12] G. K. Chesterton, 'O God of Earth and Altar', *The Collected Poems of G. K. Chesterton* (London: Methuen, 1939)

[13] S. Kierkegaard *Either/Or,* 2 Volumes (New York: Doubleday Anchor Books, 1959).

[14] John Bunyan, *The Pilgrim's Progress*

been unwilling to go with him on pilgrimage.

In the beautiful English words of the Anglican Liturgy 'it is meet right and our bounden duty' that we should praise God and with the angels sing the Sanctus; but when we go from that the gate is shut, and for some it has never been opened. They have never had a glimpse across the boundary into that other kingdom, and when they have they have found it impossible to believe that God is just and good. The cry of Weisel rings in their ears: 'What are you, my God?' Like Job at best they only know 'the outskirts of his ways; how small a whisper do they hear of him!'.[15] Yet out there are women, and I suppose some men, who—readily lost in the crowd—would come up behind Jesus and who keep on muttering to themselves 'If I only touch his garment, I shall be made well'.[16]

3. This leads to the third and last observation with which I shall weary you.

We have already noted that the New Testament writing which most fully develops the thought of the Christian life as a journey, a pilgrimage of faith, no road for the weary or faint hearted, is also that which speaks at least as clearly as any other of the decisive character of Christ's death. We cannot talk about living in two worlds without taking with radical seriousness an event which happened within one of those worlds, crucified under Pontius Pilate. That event, that redeeming event not only opens for us a way into another world, but because it is a redeeming event within history, it would alter the way in which we live within history. Given what we have learnt about how man lives with man, how man lives with woman, how men and women and children suffer together, and the cruelty which afflicts us all, is there anything specific which we can say about what that redemption means, about how we should be living on our way from the cross of Christ to the final consummation, the summing up of all things in him?

I want to suggest two directions to which we should turn our thoughts, and leave to others to work out their significance. The first is with reference to forgiveness. Professor John McIntyre in his recently published book *The Shape of Soteriology*[17] urges us to review again the different theories of the atonement and

---

[15] Job 26.14
[16] Mark 5.28
[17] John McIntyre, *The Shape of Soteriology, Studies in the Doctrine of the Death of Christ* (Edinburgh: T & T Clark, 1992), 129.

ask ourselves how the different models 'lay out the paths which men and women are to follow to find their way to forgiveness'. It is in his view 'supremely important' that the descriptions of the death of Christ, 'at different times, in different cultures and societies' should be 'offered from the very start, as the basis for forgiveness'.

I leave that task with you, but I also leave a question: 'What short of forgiveness is going to break the nexus of cause and effect in the conflicts to which human life is prone?' If the message of Jesus and the message about Jesus and his death have at their centre the proclamation of the forgiveness of God and the obligations upon men and women to show forgiveness, is this not central to the human condition as we enter the twentyfirst century? The twentieth century has been, is marked, deeply wounded by conflict, between races, between men and women, between traditional enemies and new enemies defined in ideological terms.

> O cease! must hate and death return?
> Cease, must men kill and die?
> Cease, drain not to its dregs the urn
> Of bitter prophecy.
> The World is weary of the past,
> Oh, might it die or rest at last!

So Shelley at the beginning of the nineteenth century; but the cry is unheeded.[18] Cease! The cry unheeded perhaps because ineffective. Ineffective because it knows not forgiveness. That alone can overcome hatred, it is stronger than death. What does that mean? This is a task for younger theologians, and for every Christian. The future of the human race depends upon it.

By way of transition to my very last point, let me quote John McIntyre's final words:

> What we have not so far taken account of, in all our deliberations, is the role which we as brothers and sisters play in the mediation of forgiveness to those about us. Two points: first, by refusing to forgive, we may actually be preventing the forgiveness of God reaching others, and so bringing the purposes of God to frustration. Secondly, if we do not forgive those who have offended us, we shall not ourselves know forgiveness (Mt. 18. 23-35). No account of the shape of soteriology, however otherwise impeccable, can afford to ignore the final finishing touch thus given to it by human agency.

---

[18] P. B. Shelley, 'Hellas' lines 1096-1101, *The Complete Works of Shelley*, edited by T Hutchinson (London: Oxford University Press 1921).

My final point is this: men and women are called by God, are redeemed by Christ into responsible relationships. As far as I know, God did not say at the beginning 'Let us create market forces to look after the wellbeing of my creatures'. He said 'Let us make man (i.e. human beings) in our image' with responsibilities in and for the created world. So God created in his own image, male and female created he them. Similarly I am not aware that the new man and woman in Christ has been redeemed to a state of passivity, to await the succeeding of recession with recovery, the turning of the wheel of the trade cycle. He and she have been redeemed to love neighbour as self, and that means making sacrifices and taking responsibilities.

A besetting sin of the developed world, both eastern communist which has collapsed and western capitalist which fails the human, is determinism. With this comes depersonalisation. Wiesel becomes a number in the concentration camp, no longer has a name. The unemployed man and woman, the younger person leaving school or university without a job becomes a statistic. It is a modern sophisticated way of slotting people away and in effect ignoring them. There are even people who pretend that the homeless and the unemployed don't exist, just as there are those who pretend that the holocaust did not happen. Such blasphemies are not available, should not be options for the Christian. In the Christian understanding of life in two worlds there has always been a place for judgment. Indeed the notion of judgment ties together the two worlds. It describes how the two worlds meet.

> For we must all appear before the judgment seat of Christ, so that each one may receive good or evil, according to what he has done in the body.[19]

Is Paul still stuck in the language of apocalyptic? Is this just old fashioned mythology? Before we dismiss it as such, it would be good to remember the parable in Matthew 25, with its disturbing: as you did it … as you did it not to one of the least of these, you did it … did it not to me.

# Virtue in the World

## The Norman and Mary Miller Lecture
## delivered before the Synod of Queensland
## Uniting Church in Australia, 8 May 1995
(Previously published in Trinity Occasional Papers, Vol No 1995)

Early in his important book, with the forbidding title, *The Analogical Imagination*, with the sub-title 'Christian Theology and the Culture of Pluralism' David Tracy asserts,

> ... we must recognise that Christian faith, as trust in and loyalty to God and to Jesus Christ, demands a fundamental trust in and loyalty to the world in all its ambiguity ... Christian faith demands that every theologian affirm the world and thereby pay heed to the legitimate demands for justice in society and for intellectual integrity in the academy ... the universalist thrust of Christian self-understanding demands a real affirmation of the world, and thereby a real coming to terms with the publics of society and academy.[1]

There is no shortage of voices speaking for a new engagement between religions and the societies in which they are placed. Lesslie Newbigin in a series of books, lectures and articles has called more and more insistently for the gospel to be given its public face *vis-à-vis* the cultures in which the Church finds itself. Pope John Paul II wishes that the teaching of which he is the custodian should be applied to the whole of society. In encyclicals and other instructions he not only tells the faithful how they should behave, but he asks that that teaching—for instance about abortion, euthanasia and a number of related issues—should be incorporated into the laws of countries where forces can be marshalled to make this effective.[2] He and some of his closest followers speak of the 'second evangelisation of Europe'. A 'public legal status' for Christianity is seen as fundamental to the re-Christianising of Europe. 'The state must recognise that a basic frame-

---

[1] David Tracy, *The Analogical Imagination: Christian Theology and the Culture of Pluralism* (London: SCM Press, 1981), 49-50.
[2] On what follows see Gilles Kepel, *The Revenge of God: the Resurgence of Islam, Christianity and Judaism in the Modern World*, English Translation (Cambridge: Polity Press, 1994).

work of values with a Christian foundation is the precondition of its existence' says Cardinal Joseph Ratzinger. 'It', he adds, 'must learn that there is a continued existence of truth which is not subject to consensus but which precedes it and makes it possible'.

Across the Atlantic the Moral Majority, Liberty University and considerable forces in many of the churches seek to save America by the application of biblical precepts to public life. 'Americans' wrote the spokesperson for one association known as Operation Rescue, 'have a grave responsibility to vote in those leaders who will rule America justly, under divine guidance'. There can be little doubt about who is to provide the divine guidance: Christians of a fundamentalist persuasion.

Gilles Kepel, in a book published in France three years ago and now available in English translation, has traced the parallels and differences between these phenomena in Christianity, Protestant and Roman Catholic, and recent developments in Islam and Judaism: political and theological conservatives of an extreme kind in each case imposing or seeking to impose their convictions upon societies as a whole.

No doubt there are appropriate as well as inappropriate ways for religious bodies to make known in public the teachings of their authoritative books about human life in society. No doubt there are acceptable as well as unacceptable ways for churches and other religious groups to influence the formulation of laws by which the whole community must abide. It is not, however, of that which I would speak (except perhaps indirectly) tonight. I want to ask you, with me, to start at the other end and ask what it might mean, with David Tracy, to 'trust in' and be 'loyal to the world in all its ambiguity', to 'pay heed to the legitimate' demands for justice in society and for intellectual integrity in the academy'. So we shall ask in the first place, not what as Christians we may bring to the world, but what we shall find there. It is well for those of us who are ministers, and in some sense theologians, to remember that that world is the one in which most members of the Church live most of their waking hours. There they make their living, there they live with their families, there they meet their neighbours, at work and in leisure. Those neighbours will sometimes share their convictions about what is the right thing to do, in bringing up children, in the politics of the neighbourhood or the workplace, about what is best for the country and its citizens, and sometimes they will disagree.

Some matters they will think to be important and some unimportant, but they have to live and work together. Perhaps more often than we think, they will wonder what is the right thing to do, and wonder how you determine that.

This leads to a further preliminary observation. There can have been few periods in recent history when there has been so much talk about ethics as in our own time. Bio-ethics or medical ethics flourish as never before. Institutes are given to their study, some very good ones in Brisbane. Business ethics is now a topic on its own, as it were. There are good reasons for the prominence given to discussion of ethics in these two cases. The human race has in the twentieth century given itself a fright with developments in medical practice and science and in the use and abuse of financial markets, and in the treatment meted out by some employers to employees, by employees to each other, not least by men to women. So there is a lot happening that raises ethical questions, and when a really big question arises there are not too many equipped to deal with it—or so it is thought.

At a more reflective level the word 'value' or 'values', and even the word 'virtue' has come back into our vocabulary. There are some people brave enough to suggest that that impersonal force, the market, in which we are supposed to believe with superstitious awe as controlling our destiny, may be manipulated or controlled by human beings actually making judgments on behalf of other human beings. Maybe the market is not value-free. Maybe somebody actually decides what shall be fed into the computer! Insofar as that decision is good or bad it is a moral decision. 'Morality is a dimension of human behaviour, the dimension whereby behaviour is described as good or bad', says Enda McDonagh, a distinguished Roman Catholic moral theologian, with disarming simplicity.

So human behaviour as moral behaviour is on the agenda. It is amongst the given factors to be discussed. The essay of McDonagh from which I have just quoted is entitled 'Morality and Christian Theology'. Of this McDonagh says,

> The order of words in the title 'Morality and Christian Theology' is therefore important. One begins with morality as a human phenomenon and subsequently seeks to understand or illuminate it theologically. The human phenomenon has to be given its full value before any attempt is made to interpret it in Christian fashion. And the human phenomenon is wider than the phenomenon of Christianity or the Jewish-Christian tradition. In fact, … morality is a universal human phenomenon and has to be treated as such. It is this universal which provides the source material for reflection by the Christian theologian as well as by other theologians or philosophers. To confine the theologian in his reflection on morality to the gospels or the Bible would be to restrict his basis of reflection improperly from the beginning.[3]

---

[3] Enda McDonagh, *Gift and Call* (Dublin: Gill and Macmillan, 1975), 3.

Perhaps I may add one piece of theological justification to this approach. Some Christian discussion of the world of politics and intellectual enquiry which starts from the Bible or the Christian tradition and moves outwards involves too restrictive a view of God's relation to the world he has made and sustains. It does not need to be argued, I hope, that God's will is that all his creatures, his created order of human beings, should live in order and in peace. His watchful care is over all his creatures, and is not restricted to those who know his name; and there are many more who do not know or explicitly acknowledge him than do so. Such men and women are frequently organised into institutions and communities for good as well as for evil purposes, and as with the life of the Church, the ambiguities of life are intertwined in all our living together. Thus we come to understand David Tracy's injunctions to 'recognise that Christian faith, as trust in and loyalty to God and to Jesus Christ, demands a fundamental trust in and loyalty to the world in all its ambiguity'. After all, God is not sitting here in the Church waiting to be taken out there into the world. He is the One who goes before us in all our doings. He is the Creator-Redeemer who makes his way known to men and women where they are, often in language strange to the churchman and churchwoman.

How do we (again in Tracy's words) 'pay heed to the legitimate demands for justice in society and for intellectual integrity in the academy'?

To explore this question further I turn in the central part of this lecture to thoughts suggested by Alasdair MacIntyre particularly in his extremely important, if not easily read, book *After Virtue*.[4] MacIntyre must not be held responsible for my use or abuse of his thought. Those who would engage in controversy with him must do so directly not through the distorting mirror of my references to his writings. I must admit to using some of his suggestions for my own purposes.

---

[4] Alasdair MacIntyre, *After Virtue, A Study in Moral Theory*, 2nd Edition (Indiana: University of Notre Dame Press, 1984). Themes introduced in *After Virtue* have been taken up and developed by MacIntyre in *Whose Justice? Which Rationality?* (Notre Dame Press, 1988), and in his Gifford Lectures, *Three Rival Versions of Moral Enquiry* (Notre Dame Press, 1990). They have given rise to a widespread discussion within and outside the academy. Particularly helpful for Australians is the treatment to be found in Ian S. Markham *Plurality and Christian Ethics* (Cambridge University Press, 1994). For comment on the wide range of topics raised, see *After MacIntyre: Critical Perspectives on the work of Alasdair MacIntyre* edited by John Horton and Susan Mendus (Indiana: Notre Dame Press, 1994).

In the central chapters of this book (10-13) MacIntyre examines what was regarded as virtuous in a number of societies: heroic societies, for instance Homer; Aristotle's view as expressed in *The Nichomachean Ethics*, what Aristotle believed 'to be the rational voice of the best citizens of the best city-state', that is Athens. From Aristotle, MacIntyre moves to the medieval period in which the Aristotelian tradition is taken up and developed. The chief development is 'from a humanly realisable earthly' end or purpose in life 'to an otherworldly destination requiring divine assistance' (Markham p. 131)

This all sounds like good academic lectures; and it is that but it is more. MacIntyre has by this recital, and by the addition of the New Testament, Benjamin Franklin and Jane Austen, provided himself and his readers with a wide range of examples of what men and women have regarded as virtuous, on which he can call in the subsequent discussion. First he observes that 'differences and incompatibilities between different accounts at least suggest that there is no single, central, core conception of the virtues which might make a claim for universal allegiance'—although he goes on to remark that each was exclusive in its claims:

> For Odysseus the Cyclopes stand condemned because they lack an agriculture ... For Aristotle the barbarians stand condemned because they lack the polis (city) and are therefore incapable of politics. For New Testament Christians there is no salvation outside the apostolic church [I am not sure that he is right about that]. And we know that Benjamin Franklin found the virtues more at home in Philadelphia than in Paris and that for Jane Austen the touchstone of the virtues is a certain kind of marriage and indeed a certain kind of naval officer (that is a certain kind of English naval officer)[5]

The main point remains: they are different and frequently incompatible, each list of virtues being conditioned by the society in which they were observed. This is important for us in a multicultural society: not every cultural group in Australia holds as precious, at least to the same degree, the same virtues. Some are different and may be incompatible.

It is scarcely necessary to illustrate: what is regarded as virtuous among some Aborigines may be in sharp contrast to what is regarded so among later settlers of Anglo-Saxon or Celtic or Mediterranean origin; who is regarded as a virtuous woman in a Moslem community may provide us with a different view of womanhood from that provided by the Western European tradition. We could multiply examples; and they would only render more urgent MacIntyre's second observation, or question: are we or are we not able to disentangle from these

---

[5] MacIntyre, *After Virtue*, 186.

rival and various claims a unitary core? In answering that question in the affirmative, MacIntyre delineates three stages in the logical development of the concept (of virtue) which have to be identified.

I want to use these three suggestions of MacIntyre as pointing us to the way in which a public morality may be recognised, and/or developed.

1. The first thing to be recognised is that the practice of any serious human endeavour has certain virtues—what MacIntyre calls 'goods' (good things, moral attributes)—internal to itself. For our purpose let us concentrate our minds on two human 'practices' to help us understand what we are talking about: science and painting or one of the visual arts. In the pursuit of each of these the practitioner—the scientist or the artist—to be successful must subject himself to certain disciplines, must acknowledge certain activities as good, as it were, in themselves: what MacIntyre calls 'internal' goods, or values or virtues. The scientist or the artist may achieve fame, wealth, standing in the community, influence in his discipline, and these are relatively harmless or quite good things, but they are external.

What makes the work of the scientist virtuous is that adherence to the search for the true answer to the question asked, that refusal to tamper with the evidence in order to provide a popular or politically acceptable answer, and the acceptance of a number of other constraints, all in order to extend knowledge and thereby enlarge the human beings awareness of their environment. Science is wisdom before it is power.

Similarly it is not the size of the sum paid for a work of art that makes a picture good. The picture has value insofar as it moves beyond the banal and the commonplace and depicts nature or the human scene, the human body, the human perception of colour, design and other factors in a new and enlarging way. A distinguished art historian once said that he could no longer look at the Australian landscape in the same way as was his custom once he had seen how Fred Williams had depicted it. Some of us have had the same experience when we have looked at the art of Aborigines. The human imagination had been enlarged.

'Practices have a history' says MacIntyre. 'The standards are not themselves immune from criticism, but nonetheless we cannot be initiated into a practice without accepting the authority of the best standards realised so far'. Or again, 'to enter into a practice is to accept the authority of those standards and the inadequacy of my own performance as judged by them'.

Much of what we have said about the practice of science or the visual arts could also be said, with appropriate modification about the practice of medicine or the law, about the craft of furniture making the practice of farming or a whole series of human occupations. To cheat in the pursuit of the science, the execution of a work of art, the performance of a manual skill is to prostitute it for some lesser gain. To perform to the best of one's ability within the inherited tradition, and to make one's own small contribution with integrity, this is virtue; and it is being pursued every day all around us.

Those of us who recognise it in our fellow human beings and their activities are not conferring value upon it, as we might put a price-tag on an article for sale in a bazaar, we are doing simply that, recognising or acknowledging virtue in the world around us, showing trust in and loyalty to those worldly activities in all their ambiguity.

Much has been said and much could be said about how in the twentieth century honourable practices have been contaminated by being brought under the dominance of powerful and power-seeking groups. Truth-telling, a virtue on which journalism as a practice depends, has been violated by the substitution of propaganda for accurate reporting. Good government is difficult to discern and to judge because it is brought to our attention through the distorting techniques of advertising. We could all multiply examples: where virtue is required for the fulfilment of a practice you can be certain that the possibility obtains of vice being present. The distortion of truth is not simply erroneous—to err is human—it is vicious. To err is to make a mistake. To distort is to say Evil be thou my Good. Newspapers often apologise for errors. They rarely acknowledge distortions. To restore 'virtue' to our vocabulary brings with it its opposite, 'vice'.

Enough, however, has perhaps been said to bring before us the first stage in the rehabilitation of virtue as a public or civic good: not simply as a by-product of religion but as present in a whole series of human activities, in all their ambiguity. The practice of these activities is destroyed if we do not observe the rules, whether written or conventional. Therein resides virtue.

2. In the second stage of recovery or discovery of virtue, MacIntyre draws our attention to what he calls 'the narrative order of a single human life'. What does he mean by that?

As I understand it (and that qualification needs to be put before much that I have said in this lecture, especially when representing the views of other people), we are asked to look afresh at two contrasting concepts, one very ancient, one modern. The first takes us back to the beginning of Aristotle's *Nichomachean Ethics*: every human pursuit has its corresponding end (*telos*), the end of the practice of medicine is health, of shipbuilding is a vessel, of domestic economy is wealth. It will be noted that our English word 'end' (like its Greek equivalent) carries two shades of meaning. An end can signify the last moment in a sequence of events; or it can refer to the purpose of life as in the opening question and answer of *The Shorter Catechism* of the Westminster Assembly, 'Man's chief end is to glorify God, and to enjoy him for ever.' Every life has its full significance as related to its end in both senses.

The second more modern way of speaking about a human life is in terms of the roles a man or woman has to play. We even speak of role models. But Shakespeare did it more memorably in the oft-quoted speech of Jacques:

> All the world's a stage,
> And all the men and women merely players:
> They have their exits and their entrances;
> And one man in his time plays many parts,
> His acts being seven ages.

The trouble with such a description is that it makes our lives consist of a series of unrelated, or barely related episodes. Sartre among twentieth century writers so presents us with characters who lose all integrity because they are not related by bonds of responsibility to the society of which they are a part, nor is one part of their lives related by cause and effect to any other part. They are disintegrated characters, both in the historical or temporal continuity of their lives and in their moral fibre: their integrity is diminished. Death is simply the last episode.

It is of interest to observe how we revolt from that, even in this relatively secular age. When someone dies we customarily wish to mark that event by a recollection of their lives to some degree in its entirety. We have ceremonies in which their achievements are recited: their telos, purpose in life is recalled now that the *telos*, the *finis*, the finish has been reached. Frequently still this is done in the setting of a Church's worship, so that this little piece of history in the narrative of the life of this man or this woman may, by prayer and Scripture reading, be taken up into a larger story, an end and a beginning marked by Eternity. It is, in

MacIntyre's phrase, in the narrative order of a single life that virtue is perceived, even if the fragmentary or partial character of the virtue is not frequently referred to on such an occasion.

One virtue which we seek in looking at the lives of our fellows is consistency.

> For a virtue [says MacIntyre] is not a disposition that makes for success only in some one particular type of situation. What are spoken of as the virtues of a good committee man or of a good administrator or of a gambler or a pool hustler are professional skills professionally deployed in those situations where they can be effective, not virtues. Someone who genuinely possesses a virtue can be expected to manifest it in very different types of situation, many of them situations where the practice of a virtue cannot be expected to be effective in the way we expect a professional skill to be.[6]

It is the search for consistency which makes the reading of biography or novels such a profitable exercise in our enquiry after virtue. When Conor Cruise O'Brien entitles his biography of Edmund Burke *The Great Melody*[7] (a phrase taken from Yeats) he would show that contrary to some other interpreters he sees Burke's reaction to American independence, to Catholic emancipation in Ireland, in the impeachment of Warren Hastings, and his attitude to the French Revolution as consistent one with another; and all that despite those moments, faithfully recorded, in which Burke failed to maintain the great melody. 'To pay heed', in this particular instance, 'to the legitimate demands for justice in society' does not involve whitewashing its agents. Ambiguity remains characteristic of human affairs, but ambiguity does not exist unless virtue and its corresponding vice are in the field.

Biography and indeed autobiography (as we think of Facey's *A Fortunate Life* or Sally Morgan's *My Place*) often give us a glimpse into lives made virtuous, or in struggle to achieve virtue, by pursuing an end, a telos, in both senses of that word. Because of the capacity for self-deception, and sometimes because of diffidence it is particularly difficult for autobiography to be faithful in presenting the ambiguity of life, but sometimes its aspirations come through. It is in fiction, in the hands of important novelists that form and content can come together to disclose the operations of virtue and vice in the narrative order of a single life.

---

[6] *After Virtue* p. 205.
[7] Sinclair Stevenson, London, 1993.

Alasdair MacIntyre has a telling reference to two of Jane Austen's novels *Mansfield Park* and *Persuasion* in which constancy is set forth as a virtue, or rather as a basis of all virtues. We may recall that Dr Johnson said that courage was the basic virtue for without it all the others fail; but in *Persuasion* Anne Elliot, the central woman character, argues that constancy is a virtue which women are more apt to practice than are men. And without constancy all the other virtues to some degree lose their point. Courage and constancy, the masculine and the feminine expressions of a virtue fundamental to classical eighteenth century England. In *Mansfield Park* Fanny Price disobeys her guardian and refuses to marry Henry Crawford. This says McIntyre 'can only be because of what constancy requires. In so refusing she places the danger of losing her soul before the reward of gaining what for her would be a whole world'. That that is not an exaggerated claim is brought home to us when we remember Jane Austen's devastating exposés of the way in which unmarried women were treated in her society, and when we note that Fanny Price is unusual among Jane Austen's central characters by being devoid of charm. Some readers have found her unattractive. 'She pursues virtue for the sake of a certain kind of happiness and not for its utility'. In other words we come across in this fictional character one who perceived in Kierkegaard's words that 'purity of heart is to will one thing'.

3. I have spoken of how virtue is disclosed in the serious practice of a discipline, be that in science, the arts or in a craft. And we have looked at how it may be perceived in the life of an individual oriented towards his or her end. A third stage has to be accomplished if we are to achieve virtue in our public life, and that MacIntyre discusses under the concept of tradition.

The existence of a tradition is already implied in what we have said. To become a scientist or an artist or a craftsman implies that these activities have been pursued before any individual took them up. The virtues necessary for good scientific work are inherited. Every work of art is in some measure in conversation with other artists who preceded us, just as it is in some measure a challenge to those who will succeed us. No contemporary craftsman invented the wheel, however much he may wish to improve the use to which it is put.

I want to concentrate, however, on one manifestation of virtuous living, namely that which is embodied in the professions and crafts to which men and women belong. Too often perhaps associations of men and women who are bound together because they belong to the same profession or trade are regarded with suspicion: such associations—it is assumed—only exist to protect the financial and other material interests of their members. Why this should be viewed with suspicion by people in other occupations I am not sure, unless it is an instance of always assuming that other people are less honourable than we are. But to defend the interests of members of your trade or profession is not necessarily a dishonourable thing. If nurses had not spoken out on behalf of nurses, or teachers on behalf of teachers, members of these professions would probably still be treated as shoddily as was once the case.

As Reinhold Niebuhr frequently reminded us, 'society is moved by the cry of its victims'. If professional and trade associations have at times appeared only to be concerned with the material interests of their own members, then that is part of the ambiguity of life. They have in practice also been concerned with passing on the skills and knowledge which characterise those activities, and in doing so have shown themselves to be the custodians of some virtues.

Let me, however, narrow the discussion to what has sometimes been called the learned professions. There is a whole series of these, and their number is increasing with the diversification of learning and of occupations requiring a base in systematic thought and constant intellectual enquiry. We readily think of the practice of medicine, of the law, and of clergy in the churches as learned professions. What do we mean by that? What are the marks, the characteristics of such professions? There are, I suppose, three or four.

First, practitioners in these professions are equipped with a body of knowledge which is not readily available to other members of the community. That body of knowledge is an ongoing, developing, self-correcting process. Doctors are dependent upon the ever-changing science of medicine, lawyers upon the developing and ever-increasing complexity of the law. Not all doctors are themselves medical scientists and not all lawyers have the responsibility of interpreting and re-interpreting the law. But the good practitioner will keep himself or herself abreast with those aspects which are relevant to their field of practice.

The second characteristic of a profession is that a member uses that body of knowledge into which he has been introduced for the benefit of his or her client. The true professional always puts the interest of the client before his own interests.

A third characteristic flows from this, although its observance has sometimes been shaky: a member of a learned profession customarily does not use knowledge or authority or standing for self-aggrandisement or to gather great wealth. Honour may be conferred upon him or her: it is not the *telos*, the aim, the end of the professional's activity. Members of a profession will be rewarded by payment of salaries or fees on a scale adequate to relieve them from financial anxiety, adequate to enable them to keep up-to-date in the knowledge which is the basis of their calling, and to lead a tolerably civilised life, but not such as to enable them to amass wealth.

A fourth mark of a professional is that he or she belongs to a profession, a company of peers whose discipline is accepted, whose guidance is valued, and whom the individual practitioner regards as custodians of the virtues without which the profession will cease either to be learned or honourable. It may be that the professional association has a large say in who is qualified for entry into the profession and who should no longer be recognised. Most important, however, is the support and guidance available from peers.

> Every individual [wrote Paul Tillich], even the most creative, needs
> given structures that embody the experience and wisdom of the past,
> that liberates him from the necessity of having to make innumerable
> decisions on his own, and that shows him a meaningful way to act in
> most situations.

Good ethical decisions are most frequently made by those who do not stand alone, who know that there are others who have faced these questions before and who have the capacity to support us - a capacity born out of experience. Few of us are called to be lonely individuals going to a martyr's death. If so called the way will be clear. It will not be of our making.

I have been arguing that virtues have to be recognised as operating internally in certain practices if those arts, sciences and practical skills are to fulfil their roles in society. I have suggested that there are certain virtues which enable us to give an account of a single human life as relatively consistent, and that virtues are inherent in the organisation of our lives in groups of people fulfilling the same calling, clearly observable in the organisation of a profession. On the larger scale it is one of the boons of our existence in this country at the end of the twentieth century that we have inherited a tradition whereby the basic purpose of the law is to set people free to order their lives in professions and other ways to serve the common good. Social democracy, for all its ambiguities, depends for its working on responsibilities being exercised and decisions made by countless people at different levels, in different locations and occupations. Many of these decisions are moral decisions which they make for themselves and for their neighbours.

Treatment of men and women as responsible human beings is under threat today in a variety of ways. I mention one: we might call it the managerial revolution. Those who would improve the performance of many institutions, especially in health, education or welfare, frequently suggest that this could be done by better management. So there has grown up a race of managers of whom it is believed that they have the skill to manage any institution - be it a hospital, a school, a factory or a university. What is forgotten is that each of these and lots of other occupations has its own *telos*, purpose, and managers cannot define that for them. At best, good management is a means to an end, it is not an end in itself. Health is an end, learning is an end, discovery is an end, good craftsmanship is an end, compassion is an end, the upholding of the law is an end, but efficiency and profit-making are not ends in themselves; they are instrumental virtues, enabling other good things to happen.

Moral decisions are made in the effective practice of certain human activities pursuing their proper ends, and of course they must do so efficiently; but it is the end that must always be kept in view. Virtuous actions depend upon the consistent attitudes of individual practitioners, and upon a tradition of moral dealings perhaps of a conventional kind, preserved in institutions, such as universities and hospitals, or in professional associations. So virtue is sought and found in all its ambiguity in the world. Where in all this does the Church come in? How does the Church fulfil its historic responsibility for the well-being of the society in which it is placed?

Let me be almost telegraphic in my brevity; but something must be said about this, especially to this audience. In each case, I want to try to make clear what I mean by 'Church'.

First, there are two continuing and in a way over-riding responsibilities which belong to the Church organised institutionally to enable representative Christians to act together. One of those abiding responsibilities is to speak for and defend the interests of the weak, the poor, the disabled, and for those whom society however organised tends to put at a disadvantage. That responsibility does not need to be argued for. But another continuing responsibility also merits attention. The Church has a firm responsibility to keep alive the long history of reflection on moral questions, from Abraham and the Law and Prophets to our own time. This—what we might summarise as moral theology—must run parallel with our respect for the task of the academy (the University) to keep alive the long history of moral philosophy: in the European tradition from Socrates until today; in other traditions from other ancient origins. On the fly leaf of a recently published book there appears a quotation from Goethe:

> He who cannot draw on three thousand years
> is living from hand to mouth.

We Australians are great improvisers. The nature of the life we have imposed on each other, and which nature has imposed upon us over the last 200 years has made improvisation a necessity. Part of the vocation of the Church is to stop us living from hand to mouth.

Secondly, we may look at the Church as expressing its life through the majority of its members whom we customarily call the laity. Perhaps Luther's most significant contribution to Christian social thought was to bring the notion of call (*Beruf*) out of the cloister into the market place: every man and woman has received and continues to receive a vocation, a call from God to serve him in that place in which it pleases God to place her or him. Calvin's emphasis on the sovereignty of God covering every aspect of human life reinforced the view that there is no place where a man or woman may go but that there he or she may be required to be obedient and show forth God's glory by the work of their hands and their brains, in the way they treat other people, giving and receiving responsibilities, in the way they handle goods and money: in families, localities, in the nation and now in international life.

The Christian man or woman will fulfil his or her calling in the kind of world which I have tried to describe, in which many different activities make up the whole, but each of which has its own virtues without which it will fail to fulfil properly the purpose for which it exists. The Christian lay person involved will frequently, indeed normally, find support for the fulfilment of his or her vocation among fellow members of a profession, trade, neighbourhood—more readily than in the fellowship of the Church.

It is not really possible for groups in congregations or presbyteries or synods to appreciate sufficiently sensitively, looking at them from the outside as it were and spasmodically, issues as they arise for accountants, medical practitioners or other professionals, or for that matter the problems that have to be faced by young mothers. The last mentioned may be fortunate and sometimes find other young mothers in the Church, but it must not be forgotten that the Church is not a clinic. There are clinics not controlled by the Church and there are places where young mothers must and can support each other, which happen in a random way here and there in most societies.

To determine how members of the Church with diverse occupations are to support one another is a matter of some difficulty; but perhaps two things may be said. The first is that as in so many matters we must remind ourselves that the Church's primary function, its *telos*—its end in heaven and its purpose on earth—is worship. We must learn afresh how the diversity of our callings, our secular callings, are taken up in worship: in the prayers of intercession, and in that great act of intercession which is the Eucharist, the whole of human life held in the presence of God from whom our lives receive their full significance, our virtues find their origin and their fulfilment, our vices their forgiveness, and our ambiguous existence its acceptance in the divine love.

The second thing is this: we live in a period when the professions are held in low esteem, and trade associations are regarded as no more than self-serving. The fellowship of the Church could be, perhaps sometimes is, a place where we learn mutual respect because we see in the commitment to the world of work of our brother and sister in Christ an acknowledgment of the demand, the presence, the succour of God in the secular world, delivering us from isolation, from disease, disorder, lawlessness, and enabling his human children to respond to his wisdom and holiness by making something beautiful of their lives upon earth.

And—thirdly—what of the clergy, the ministers of the gospel? I use the word clergy purposefully, for they are or should be 'clerks' that is men and women of learning, custodians of the gospel for the benefit of the people, learned in the ways of the people of God. Perhaps it is time to recover the sense of the ministry of the Church as a profession, with some of the same marks as other professions, set apart for a distinctive task. So we might understand other professions better, so they might understand us. The doctor has his surgery, his home visits and his continual and continuing refreshment by learning and learning afresh what belongs to best practice. We in the Ministry have three focal points to our lives: the pulpit and table, the people for whom we must care in sickness and in health, in their lives, in their homes and constituted by their work and the society in which they live, and (I fear sometimes neglected as a poor third focal point) our studies.

Much could be said about each of these, but let me leave you with a comment upon the third, the study. There traditionally the minister prays for the people, there he or she refreshes mind and spirit by constant reflection on what the Church of God has been from the call of Abraham to today, there ministers quicken their imagination by a serious engagement with the human scene in many of its facets and still today these are not simply locked in computers but expressed in writing. It is still true today that the reading of books, including so called secular books, enlarges the mind, quickens the spirit and renders the imagination more open to the world of men and women and children whom God made for his glory.

'And yet the books' (wrote the Polish poet Czeslaw Milosz having lived through many of the turmoils of the twentieth century).

> And yet the books will be there on the shelves, separate beings,
> That appeared once, still wet
> As shining chestnuts under a tree in autumn,
> And, touched, coddled, began to live
> In spite of fires on the horizon, castles blown up,
> Tribes on the march, planets in motion.
> "We are," they said, even as their pages
> Were being torn out, or a buzzing flame
> Licked away their letters. So much more durable
> Than we are, whose frail warmth
> Cools down with memory, disperses, perishes.
> I imagine the earth when I am no more:
> Nothing happens, no loss, it's still a strange pageant,
> Women's dresses, dewy lilacs, a song in the valley.
> Yet the books will be there on the shelves, well born,
> Derived from people, but also from radiance, heights[8].

That is true supremely, but not only, of the book of books.

---

[8] Czeslaw Milosz *The Collected Poems (1931-1987)* (London: Penguin Books, 1988).

# Literary Criticism
# and the Gospels

## A rumination (chiefly) on Mark

T his paper was previously published in the *Australian Biblical Review*, Vol. XXIX, October 1981. Many scholars have discussed since that date the theme suggested in my essay. Study of the Gospels as wholes and elucidation of narrative sections, and in particular of parables, continues to add to our understanding, and the literature on this subject is growing apace. Likewise much has to be learnt from developments in literary criticism in the last 15 years. It would, however, be foolish—indeed foolhardy—for me to attempt to summarise the developments of these years. I therefore leave the essay as it first appeared, except for the elimination of one or two infelicities in the writing. On reading again what I wrote fourteen years ago I am struck by the need to take up each Gospel so to speak on its own merits. The original sub-heading of this essay was simply 'A Rumination'. I now see that it should have been 'A Rumination (chiefly) on Mark', and have amended accordingly. Each of the other Gospels requires separate treatment and each is receiving it not least from the Australian scholar Francis Maloney whose literary critical work on the Fourth Gospel repays most careful attention.

## I

Mark (we assume) is the earliest of the four books which we call by the name Gospel, although it is increasingly doubtful whether it is helpful to think of them all as 'gospels': maybe they are books of four different kinds, even though they have a common purpose. A rigorous literary criticism might suggest that they are not all of one *genre*. At any rate let us start by assuming that Mark is *sui generis*: certainly it once was.

We know that we must read it as a whole. Many of us have never forgotten the illumination which came when we first read R H Lightfoot's *The Gospel Message of St Mark*,[1] Harvesting the fruits of his Bampton Lectures (*History and*

---

[1] R H Lightfoot, *The Gospel Message of St Mark*, Oxford: Clarendon Press, 1950.

*Interpretation in the Gospels*),[2] Lightfoot enabled us to see Mark as a theological writing in its own right, as it were. He anticipated much of the work of the Redaction critics. He taught us how to use, in the study of Mark's Gospel, Schleiermacher's hermeneutical circle: to (read the parts in the light of the whole, and the whole in the light of the parts. Many others have developed this theme, have walked this road since then, just as a few had done before. When we are alert critically, as serious students of the New Testament, we no longer read one Gospel in a harmony of the three Synoptics, let alone the four. We try to allow one Gospel to stand out from the pages of the New Testament, and tell us what it has to say.

In some ways this is more difficult in reading Mark than in studying Matthew or Luke. Source criticism alone suggests to us the distinctive notes struck by the two later writers. We know when they depart from Mark, and have a reasonable assurance of where they differ from one another and their common source, and we can recognise their editorial work and the distinctive material which belongs to each. But Mark is not well read when you look at it as though it were simply the rather crude first attempts at something taken over, polished and completed by the other two. It stood by itself, it spoke to believers, it nourished faith in a Church which did not yet know Matthew or Luke; and its distinctive notes are not well characterised as naiveté or crudity, or at least not so because they seem that way as compared with Matthew or Luke. It is not an appropriate procedure to move back to Mark through Matthew and Luke. We should ban Huck's Synopsis from our study of Mark; but set it out as a separate text. Nowadays that would be accepted. But it is well to remember that for centuries Mark was the poor relation, the country cousin among the Gospels, only receiving the attention which could be spared from acquaintance with the richer relatives, Matthew and Luke.

Now, how are we doing this? By criteria which are deeply historical. Let me illustrate what I mean by the historical approach by reference to two important recent commentaries: that by Eduard Schweizer[3] and that by Ernst Haenchen, *Der Weg Jesu*.[4] They are both extremely important and valuable books. To risk some rather wild generalisations, if you ask what it is that makes the Gospel of Mark come alive for each of these authors, you receive an interestingly contrasted answer. For Schweizer Mark comes alive when you see his form of the

---

[2] R H Lightfoot, *History and Interpretation in the Gospels* London: Hodder and Stoughton, 1935.
[3] *The Good News According to Mark* Eng.Tr. (London, SPCK, 1971).
[4] Alfred Töpelman (Berlin, 1968).

Christian message in contrast to, in amplification of the early Christian tradition. You see faith, faith in the risen crucified one, taking shape, being accepted in the historical development of the life of the Church. Those who have read his commentary, and other writings, or listened to Schweizer know the tremendous and challenging emphasis on the call to discipleship, which is at the centre of his exposition. Discipleship is discipleship under the cross, taking up the cross and following the crucified living one, and involves a steadfast obedience to his Word which calls men. Chapters 9 and 10, after the first prediction of the passion at the end of chapter 8, are shaped in Schweizer's exposition by the need to strengthen the Church in her task of discipleship in a number of directions: in controversy with 'enthusiasts', in the life of the Church, in relation to marriage, to treatment of children, in the handling of possessions and so on. By way of contrast, for Haenchen Mark comes alive as you investigate the relation between the proclamation of the Gospel writer and the events and teaching of the pre-Easter Jesus. Note his subtitle 'an exposition of Mark's Gospel and its *synoptic parallels.*'

Both writers are concerned with what all this might mean for the reader today. They do not want to stop at exegesis, they at least hint at the hermeneutical task; and again anyone who knows Schweizer knows that he wants to preach Jesus. The basis of all this is however material expounded as a result of historical enquiry: on the axis in one case, of the early Christian message and its development in Mark, in the other case, of the life and teaching of Jesus and its representation by Mark, faith (it is to be supposed and hoped) comes alive for men of other days. Form-criticism and redaction-history lie behind this. As we see and hear of faith developing in other times and places, it becomes more real for us. Admittedly the medium of this is the words of Mark's Gospel; but what is conveyed is what happened *historically.*

Continuing our rather wild generalisations about recent writing on Mark, note must be taken of the important work of Howard Clark Kee, culminating in his *Community of the New Age.*[5] This is a book so full of matter that it will be some time before most of us have assimilated the results of all its enquiries. The main thrust of Kee's writings are, however, apparent: he would 'employ a social-cultural-historical method in New Testament study, and do so by beginning with one of the most enigmatic books in the New Testament: the Gospel of Mark'. The end which he has in view is a clearer understanding of the community for which Mark wrote his Gospel. In other words, Kee's is an historical enquiry using modern sociological insights about the nature of sectarian and

---

[5] H C Kee, *Community of the New Age* (The Westminster Press: Philadelphia, and London: SCM Press, 1977).

millenarian groups to cast light on one community in early Christianity. To be sure, Kee discusses the literary antecedents of Mark; and his work is full of illuminating perceptions of Mark's style and structure; but all this is in the service of historical enquiry. It cannot, and must not be neglected.

By way of contrast with Kee and distancing himself somewhat not only from Bultmann and Käsemann but also from what he calls 'American exegesis', is Joachim Gnilka whose two-volume Commentary has recently appeared in the series *Evangelisch—Katholischer Kommentar zum Neuen Testament*.[6] Again it is impossible to summarise or assimilate at one reading the riches of this magisterial work; but for our present purposes we may note the way in which Gnilka arrives at an understanding of the text of Mark. He sees the text as containing certain signals, which direct the reader's attention to its message and purpose; he picks up certain themes (discipleship, Israel and God's people, the preaching of the Kingdom of God) as providing the essential clues to Mark's theology. The message of the book, and of the text, are of greater interest to him than an analysis of its historical antecedents or than speculation about the characteristics of the Church which brought his Gospel into being or which this Gospel was written to serve.

It is not part of the purpose of this article to make a survey of recent writing on Mark's Gospel: it would be beyond our competence. Starting with Lightfoot and ending with Gnilka we observe, however, a tendency to look at Mark as a whole as the text stands before us and ask what it (the text) says to, discloses to us. This leads into the second part of this paper.

# II

For centuries before there was historical enquiry, faith was quickened and sustained by words written, tales told, psalms recited, hymns sung. Indeed we might say that, over the whole history of the Church, faith and hope and love have been kindled and kept alight by the reading of certain texts, and by hearing them. The books of the Bible—or passages from them—have taken on the form of address. This has been true when readers and hearers have had the most inaccurate views of authorship, milieu, date of the books being read, and even when they have misunderstood the genre of the particular writing before them. It should only make for clarification when greater accuracy can be gained on questions usually treated under the misleading name of 'Introduction'. But as we know the matter does not end there: Indeed most matters of introduction only

---

[6] Joachim Gnilka *Das Evangelium nach Markus* (Zürich: E K K Benzinger Verlag, 1978).

remove dust from the furniture, which must still be seen as having its appropriate place in the room if we are to live there.

This preoccupation with the author and his historical setting is relatively recent. Certainly we suggest to students that they should ask the question: who is saying what, to whom and in what circumstances? But, if we are honest, we must admit to ourselves that frequently we do not know the answer, or that the answer which we would give is at best tentative. It is 'diachronic' to use a technical term of the structuralist: it assumes that the human person is the creator of significations. It is always looking for the speaker, the writer, the author, the community which created such modes of address. The text itself is only a means to the clarification of our perception of such personal, social, historical events or situations. So we cannot read a text without a commentary which tells us of sources behind the text. In one of his essays, T S Eliot regrets having appended notes to *The Waste Land*.[7]

> It is not because of my bad example to other poets that I am penitent: it is because my notes stimulated the wrong kind of interest among the seekers of sources. It was just, no doubt, that I should pay my tribute to the work of Miss Jessie Weston; but I regret having sent so many enquirers off on a wild goose chase after Tarot cards and the Holy Grail.

On how many goose chases have we started students with our comments?

Few scholars will wish to deny that the hermeneutical circle in which we operate requires us to see the text within its historical and cultural context; but there has been a growing uneasiness at the appearance that that is the end of the matter.

> There are texts [writes R C Tannehill][8] whose primary purpose is to convey information, but this purpose is not characteristic of the Gospel texts, especially not of synoptic sayings. As their form shows, these texts are shaped for a different function. When the scholar uses these texts as sources of information about historical events, persons, or views which lie behind them, he is forcing concerns which are subordinate in the texts into a dominant position … it means that the scholar and the text are working at cross purposes, and the information must be extracted in spite of the stubborn efforts of the text to speak in its own way.

How do we enable the text to speak in its own way?

Before we can answer that question it would be well to take note of the

---

[7] T S Eliot, 'The Frontiers of Criticism', a lecture delivered at the University of Minnesota in 1956, reprinted in *On Poetry and Poets* (London: Faber, 1957).

[8] R C Tannehill, *The Sword of His Mouth* (Philadelphia: The Fortress Press, 1975).

immense reinforcement of our uneasiness which comes from two major sources. The first is a historical study: Hans Frei in *The Eclipse of Biblical Narrative*[9] takes us through a detailed study of eighteenth and nineteenth century hermeneutics to show how modern exegesis grew up in an atmosphere of systematic neglect of the realistic character of biblical narrative. The reasons for this are extremely complex, and are treated in great detail by Frei in a book which is at times as difficult as it is rewarding. With gross over-simplification we may say that the Bible was used in the period under review as a quarry from which to gain rocks with which to support a dogmatic system, or stones to throw at that edifice and hope to crack it. Moreover, the debate about historical reliability which dominated so much of this period was conducted in the midst of a confusion that stories which are history-like are necessarily historical. To quote Frei himself in a summary of his thesis, early in his book:

> A realistic or history-like (though not necessarily historical) element is a feature, as obvious as it is important, of many of the biblical narratives that went into the making of Christian belief. It is a feature that can be highlighted by the appropriate analytical procedure and no other, even if it may be difficult to describe the procedure—in contrast to the element itself. It is fascinating that the realistic character of the crucial biblical stories was actually acknowledged.
>
> Biblical commentators again and again emphasised the simplicity of style, the life-likeness of depiction, the lack of artificiality or heroic elevation in theme in such stories as the first three chapters of Genesis, the story of Abraham's willingness to sacrifice Isaac, or the synoptic Gospels. In other words they believed that representation and depiction and what they represented, had a great deal to do with each other and came very close in these stories ... Some commentators (however) explained the realistic feature by claiming that stories are reliably or unreliably reported history. Others insisted that they are not, or only incidentally, history and that their real meaning is unconnected with historical reporting. In either case, history or else allegory or myth, the *meaning* of the stories was finally something different from the stories or depictions themselves, despite the fact that this is contrary to the characteristic of a realistic story.[10]

The 'appropriate analytical procedure' was not available to biblical exegetes very largely because it was not available in secular literary studies either in England or Germany, and that despite the growth of the novel in English during the nineteenth century.

---

[9] H Frei, *The Eclipse of Biblical Narrative* (New Haven and London: Yale University Press, 1977).

[10] Frei, *Eclipse,* 10-11.

If Frei tells where we went wrong, Paul Ricoeur[11] seems to provide us with a philosophical and theological justification for taking texts seriously as occupying an intermediate ground, 'a moment of grace' between antiquarian history (the original meaning) and contemporary relevance (what it means for us). Ricoeur would suggest an approach which frees us from what Wimsatt calls 'the intentional fallacy' and 'the affective fallacy'. On the one side lies the danger to which much commentary writing is subject which takes as its end a penetration 'behind the text' to what the author originally meant; on the other side lies a danger of only seeing significance in a text when it is meaningful to us. When the author put what he had to say into a written text he released into the world something which has a life in its own right: it was a creative act, and the creature (the written text) now has its own relative autonomy. This stands not only outside the author but also *extra nos*; it speaks of an alien world. There is always a distance between us and what is written; we are addressed by the text. To use different terms, the text itself again becomes the focus rather than the author, as tends to be the case in historical criticism, or than the reader as in existentialist interpretation.

To return to our main question: how then do we enable the text to speak in its own way?

Both in France and America a quick answer to that question would seem to be by the application of structuralist principles to the interpretation of the text. The approach is well summarised by Dan O. Via:

> According to a definitional essay by Jean Pouillon, structure in the structuralist sense is to be distinguished from the internal organisation or arrangement of a text, and it is precisely the making of this distinction which differentiates the reality from the appearance of structuralism. Structure,

---

[11] It is difficult to find one's way in Ricoeur's writings, and particularly difficult for some of us who have scant philosophical equipment to master Ricoeur's extensive writings, which however remain so suggestive as surely to be relevant to our concerns. Probably the best place to begin to try to understand Ricoeur's contributions to our present subject is through the three essays, 'La tâche de l'hermeneutique', 'La Fonction hermeneutique de la distanciation' and 'Hermeneutique philosophique et hermeneutique biblique' in *Exegesis: Problemes de méthode et exercises de lecture,* edited by F Bovon and G Rouiller (Paris: Delachaux et Niestle, 1975). Attention should also be given to the relevant sections of *The Philosophy of Paul Ricoeur, an Anthology.* C E Reagan and David Stewart (Boston: Beacon Press, 1978), and *The Conflict of Interpretations* (Evanston: Northwestern University Press, 1974). There are a very few pages (62-68) on Ricoeur in Patrick Henry, *New Directions in New Testament Study* (Philadelphia: The Westminster Press, 1979, and London: SCM Press, 1980).

properly speaking, is the hidden or underlying configuration that can offer some explanation for the more or less visible or obvious pattern in the text.[12]

We now have a number of examples of what a structuralist interpretation of biblical texts might look like; and the first impression is that this is a world for the young, strong and free. There would appear to be some methodological and philosophical objections (as well as temperamental ones) to placing oneself in that straitjacket; but the discussion ought to be left to those competent to judge. One comment may be permitted in passing. Towards the end of his autobiographical volume *A World on the Wane,* Claude Lévi-Strauss[13] writes: 'Our argument is, in brief, that men have always and everywhere undertaken the same task, and assigned to themselves the same object; all that has differed is the means employed'. Is that true? Have all men and women 'always and everywhere' undertaken the same tasks when they have put pen to paper? Is there a deep structure which underlies all the texts they write by various means, in different genres? We would need to know a lot before we could be sure.

While some must pursue a structuralist analysis, perhaps a more modest start might be suggested for the rest of us in using literary critical analysis to bring to light the simplicities and subtleties of biblical texts, their naiveté and their sophistication.

So the third part of this paper makes some suggestions:

# III

1. The need to distinguish between the older and the newer literary criticism, and to take each seriously without neglecting the other.

Literary criticism which is more than the tedious information contained in the Introductions has a long and honourable history. No scholar worthy of the name is now likely to ignore Gunkel's often quoted remark: 'To study a writer without defining the literary types he uses is to start building a house with the roof'. That definition continues, and becomes more refined, more accurate with the passing of time. One thinks immediately of Bultmann's many contributions, for instance of how his relatively early study of the style of Pauline preaching and the cynic-stoic diatribe has become a part of every later commentator's

---

[12] In *Interpretation,* April 1974, summarising Pouillon's essay: 'Présentation: un Essai de Définition' in *Les Tempes Modernes,* 22 (1966).
[13] C Lévi-Strauss, *A World on the Wane* (London: Hutchinson, 1961).

inheritance in interpreting some critical passages in Paul's writings.[14] One thinks of Käsemann's essay on 'Sentences of Holy Law in the New Testament';[15] or of Amos Wilder's *The Language of the Gospel.*[16] In this connection Hans-Dieter Betz and others serve us well by exploring further the form and character of New Testament writings in the setting of literary conventions prevailing in the Graeco-Roman world.

Study, however, of how the older literary criticism, which is really literary history, calls out for supplement by a newer style Betz's Commentary on Galatians[17] provides a useful case of criticism which more properly could claim that name. Betz suggests, indeed demonstrates that Paul's letter is to be understood as an example of a genre of which we know something from contemporary or near contemporary sources, the apologetic letter. In expounding the epistle, Betz makes use, most illuminatingly, of Greek and Roman studies in rhetoric, of Aristotle, Cicero and Quintilian. His analysis of the letter shows how the argument is carried forward according to certain recognised conventions, if not rules. Galatians was written and read by those who would understand, almost instinctively, the methods employed. This is all extremely illuminating, and is essential groundwork. Yet since the text stands there calling for an interpretation which is more than literary-historical it is legitimate to ask how else do we see it, in addition to our recognition of it as a specimen of Graeco-Roman epistolography? We may perhaps suggest, taking our clue from Frei, that the letter to the Galatians is also a series of interwoven narratives or stories: there is the story of Paul himself, of his relations with the Church in Jerusalem and with Peter in Antioch; there is the much older story of Abraham, and of Hagar and of Isaac; there is the recent story of the Galatians' baptism, and of their life in the Spirit with its two-fold threat from a return to legalism and from licence, giving way to life in the flesh. This calls for the careful reading and patient listening about which the literary critic may perhaps be able to teach us a thing or two.

---

[14] R Bultmann, *Der Stil der paulinischen Predigt und die kynisch-stoische Diatribe*, FRLANT 13, 1910.

[15] A Wilder, *New Testament Questions of Today* (London: SCM Press, 1969).

[16] New York, Harper & Row, 1964. Published also under the title *Early Christian Rhetoric* (London: SCM Press, 1964).

[17] Betz in *Hermeneia—a Critical and Historical Commentary on the Bible* (Philadelphia: Fortress Press, 1979).

2. We must listen afresh to what is being said and written by contemporary literary critics, and test the water to see whether it will irrigate our sometimes rather dry studies.

This will be a formidable undertaking for literary criticism in English studies alone, let alone other European languages, is a full-time occupation of professional colleagues. Yet we cannot afford not to listen. Let us take a few examples, which must be regarded as random.

2.1 Is the reading of a biblical text more like reading a poem or reading a work of prose fiction? An obvious answer to that might be that it depends upon whether the part of the Bible being read is poetry or prose. All right. Rephrase the question: is the reading of a Gospel more like the reading of a poem or of a piece of narrative prose, fiction, history-like, history? Again, at first the answer seems obvious: a Gospel is less like a poem than it is like a piece of prose with a narrative framework. But what is the difference in the way in which these two types of literature are approached? 'The difference between verse and prose is self-evident, but it is a sheer waste of time to look for a definition of the difference between poetry and prose', W H Auden quoted by David Lodge in *Language of Fiction*,[18] the first part of which would repay careful study by any interpreter of the Bible.

It has been our custom to think of narrative prose in terms of characterisation and plot; and since in, say, Mark's Gospel there is very little characterisation and the plot is rather obvious it might be assumed that literary critical analysis has little to contribute to our understanding of that text. But what if the Gospel has more in common with poetic fiction than with anecdote told to convey character or to savour a swift development of plot or incident? For here, to use some phrases of Professor J M Cameron in a passage quoted by Lodge, you have a writing which 'exists only as *this* description,[19] these words in this order. What is said and how it is said are thus not distinguishable in the way they are in other forms of discourse'. Now it is certainly true that the parables of Jesus are poetic fiction, even though we might demur at the Gospels as wholes being described in that way. But Mark's Gospel can no longer be thought of as a description of events which might be described in other

---

[18] David Lodge, *Language of Fiction, essays in criticism and verbal analysis of the English Novel,* (London, Routledge & Kegan Paul, 1966)
[19] David Lodge, *Language of Fiction,* 33-38.

ways. What is said and how it is said are indistinguishable. If we are to listen to this text it will be to *these words in this order*.

2.2 Further illumination may be gained if we recognise that the Gospels, particularly Mark, have much in common with the Short Story. It would at least be comforting to hard pressed students of the Bible to know that they do not always have to go to full-length novels for the kindling of their imagination. Short stories will sometimes do; and they should certainly influence preachers.

Without taking space to develop we may note two critical points in short stories which correspond to two of the *cruces* in the interpretation of Mark. The first concerns beginnings. Fairy tales frequently begin with the conventional opening 'Once upon a time' - 'a convention which meant that people agreed to believe the most fantastic impossibilities provided they occurred long ago and far away enough; and they did so for the sufficient reason that it amused them to do it'.[20] But writers of short stories try to make their tale more plausible through 'a preamble in which the writer tells us how he came into possession of the facts': one might note Luke's technique in this regard (Luke 1: 1-14). When we turn to Mark we find ourselves in the presence of what O'Faolain calls 'one of the most successful inventions of the true modern short-story ... Maupassant more than anyone else showed readers that if they were, as we say colloquially, "quick on the uptake", they could dive into the narrative without any explanations, preambles, elaborate introductions, apologies or other notations as to place, time or occasion.'

So Mark's opening of his Gospel jumps *in medias res*: 'the good news of Jesus Christ the Son of God'. The effect of this is (to quote Professor Donald Juel)[21] that 'from the outset the reader knows what no one in the story ever knows: Jesus is the Messiah, the Son of God. .Everything that occurs is ironic. Jesus' enemies are made unwitting witnesses to the truth. The "messianic secret" is not a secret for the reader, but is for everyone else in the story'. May we not take this further and say that having readers 'in the know' may explain some of the asides in the Gospel; and may cast light on the strange oscillation between indicatives and the imperatives in chapter 13?

---

[20] Sean O'Faolain *The Short Story* (London: Collins, 1948)
[21] David Juel commenting on H. C. Kee 'Aretologies, Hellenistic "Lives" and the sources of Mark' (Berkeley: Centre for Hermeneutical Studies, 1974).

Perhaps more puzzling than the beginning is the closing of Mark's Gospel: why does it end without an ending? The practice of short story writers may throw some light on this also. O'Faolain points out that the short story itself is a convention:

> There is no such thing as a short-story; all life's stories are long, long stories; or perhaps one may say that life is one long (or short) story; either way, to chop up life is to pretend that life is not continuous but spasmodic or intermittent ... With a short story it is one of the anxieties of the writer that the episode shall *seem* more than an episode or disjunction.

Or again, 'a tiny bit of life (has to) speak for the whole of life'. Was this Mark's problem? What for him was the most important and definable episode ever occurring had to be seen to speak for the whole of life. Many of Chekov's short-stories end with a road opening out into an unknown future. 'And they went out and fled from the tomb; for trembling and astonishment had come upon them; and they said nothing to anyone, for they were afraid.'

# On re-reading 1 Peter

## Presidential Address
## to the Fellowship for Biblical Studies
## Melbourne, 1982

The 'mental set' with which this essay approaches 1 Peter is not that of one whose primary object is to find out information about the socio-economic circumstances in which it came into being, but of one who sees a literary text sitting there on the page demanding analysis, interpretation and understanding as a piece of writing. In doing so we may have to use a number of different literary critical techniques before we can be satisfied that we have taken the text with due seriousness. Professor Quinn on the title page of his book quotes some words of R S Crane which students of the New Testament might make their own: 'The final test of any critical language is what its particular scheme of concepts permits or encourages us to say, in practical criticism, about individual works.'[1]

## I

1 Peter appears on the page before us in the form of a letter. The epistle as a literary form in the New Testament has been fairly thoroughly discussed, and its characteristic formulae—opening thanksgivings, benedictions, doxologies and the rest—isolated and analysed. We know something of the influence of Paul on subsequent Christian writing so that the epistolary form is adopted as a Christian mode of communication.[2] Recently some scholars have turned with renewed vigour to the study of the letter in the Graeco-Roman world. To take an outstanding example, Hans-Dieter Betz has shown in his commentary how the letter to the Galatians owes much of its rhetorical force to the conventions of the

---

[1] *The Languages of Criticism and the Structure of Poetry* (Toronto: University of Toronto Press, 1953), 115.

[2] See Helmut Koester, *Introduction to the New Testament* (Philadelphia: 1982), Volume II, 54-56, and bibliographies, 52 & 112.

apologetic letter.[3] It may be that a fuller acquaintance with the conventions within which Paul was writing will explain or even remove what have sometimes been taken as confusions, ascribed varyingly to his emotional state, his rabbinic methods or to the assumption that he has been interrupted in the middle of dictation.

When we turn to 1 Peter we move out of the convention of the personal letter. We have a document which belongs to that stage at which

> the epistles of the N. T. shade into the theological treatise literature, and the few apostolic pseudepigrapha which we possess represent no pure type, but are either theological treatises which make use of certain elements of letter, or literary experiments that have deliberately been made pseudonymous.[4]

The writing before us retains the form of address; but by way of contrast with Paul's undisputed letters it lacks the intensely personal, indeed vibrantly personal, note. To take what is perhaps the most extreme case: Paul's letter to the Galatians gains much force from the interweaving of three 'stories' (to use the terminology of Dietrich Ritschl and others[5]), that of Paul himself, that of Abraham and that of the Galatian Christians. The author is powerfully present addressing his readers through the letter. 1 Peter is not only unconventional as a letter, it is also impersonal in tone. The person of the author disappears after the first verse only to reappear, not named, in the conclusion (5: 12), except for his emergence at 5: 1: 'So I exhort the elders among you, as a fellow elder and a witness of the sufferings of Christ'. Only in these two places do we find the first person singular, and the first person plural is only found in the opening section, 1:3-5. Far from this being the equivalent of the apostolic 'we' found in Paul, for instance in the Corinthian correspondence, its sole use in 1 Peter is in a confessional statement. Otherwise the personal pronoun is in the second person. As a result, although the document continues to be in the form of an address to those in certain circumstances, the style objectifies the situation. There is effected a certain detachment of author from reader.

It must be conceded that this distancing of the author from the reader is characteristic of all texts. In the case of biblical texts, when exegesis moves too

---

[3] *Galatians:* in the series Hermeneia - A Critical and Historical Commentary on the Bible (Philadelphia: Fortress Press, 1979).

[4] W Schneemelcher, 'Apostolic Pseudepigrapha' in E. Hennecke: *New Testament Apocrypha* edited by W Schneemelcher (English Translation edited by R Mc L Wilson, London: Lutterworth Press, 1965).

[5] Dietrich Ritschl and Hugh O. Jones, '*"Story" als Rohmaterial der Theologie"*: *Theologische Existenz Heute,* 192. München 1976).

rapidly into homiletics, this distance is forgotten. It is overlooked that, in Ricoeur's words,

> the writing-reading relation is not a particular case of the speaking-answering relation. It is not a relation of interlocution, not an instance of dialogue. It does not suffice to say that reading is a dialogue with the author through his work, for the relation of the reader to the book is of a completely different nature. Dialogue is an exchange of questions and answers; there is no exchange of this sort between the writer and the reader. Rather, the book divides the act of writing and the act of reading into two sides, between which there is no communication. The reader is absent from the act of writing, the writer is absent from the act of reading. The text thus produces a double eclipse of the reader and the writer. It thereby replaces the relation of dialogue, which directly connects the voice of one to the hearing of the other.[6]

We must leave aside reflections of what this hard fact about the nature of a written text says to those who would expound the Scriptures, and in particular what it says to preachers. The force of Ricoeur's contention is brought home vividly by a careful reflection on 1 Peter; and might be illustrated in a number of ways if we compare the reading of 1 Peter with the reading of what at first sight is a very different writing, T S Eliot's poem, *The Waste Land*.

F R Leavis commented on that poem: 'it would be difficult to imagine a completer transcendence of the individual self, a completer projection of awareness'.[7] Those of us who, having been taken through the search for sources by the commentators and who having observed the heightening of the sense of urgency at 4: 12, are left wondering whether we have here one coherent work, should perhaps re-read 1 Peter with a different question in mind: do we not here have 'a projection of awareness' of what it was, and of what it might be, to be a Christian in an antagonistic world? Here we have something like a meditation, a reflection using traditional materials no doubt, a tapestry on which is woven a picture of what it means to take the humbler part. A further comment by Leavis on *The Waste Land* may help us to adopt an appropriate mental set in reading 1 Peter:

> The unity of *The Waste Land* is no more "metaphysical" than it is narrative or dramatic, and to try to elucidate it metaphysically reveals complete misunderstanding. The unity the poem aims at is that of an inclusive

---

[6] Paul Ricoeur, *'What is a Text?'* in *Hermeneutics and the Human Sciences* (Cambridge University Press: Chatto & Windus, 1981), 146.
[7] F R Leavis, *New Bearings in English Poetry* (London 1938), 93.

consciousness: the organisation it achieves as a work of art is of the kind that has been illustrated, an organisation that may, by analogy, be called musical.[8]

The inclusive consciousness of 1 Peter is presumably of those who cannot feel at home in this world and who therefore are called upon both to hope fully, without reserve (1:13), and to love constantly, with an undivided heart (1:22). This imperative may confront them in a variety of circumstances, as the baptised, as citizens, as household servants, as wives of unbelieving husbands; in the normal vicissitudes of life, and in times of persecution. All is held together by their identification with Jesus, the crucified, risen one. They are committed to live in a new way in relation to 'every fundamental human institution'[9] 'Creature', says Goppelt commenting on 2:13, 'implies not only that man is indebted to God and not to himself, but also he is committed to a historical road. Therefore the submission is to every human creature, that is to say to every man in that destiny which the Creator as Lord of history has given him'.[10]

In this kind of writing then the person and personality of the author matters much less than in a private letter. It makes literary claims. It aims at becoming a public document. What role does the author play? The briefest answer to that is that he plays the role of 'Peter'; but how does he play it? Again, some illumination might be gained from reflection on Eliot's *Waste Land* but this time from Eliot himself. Readers of that poem will remember how—in the third section entitled 'The Fire Sermon'—the comments of Tiresias are inserted into the sordid little seduction scene:

> I Tiresias, though blind, throbbing between two lives,
> Old man with wrinkled female breasts, can see
> At the violet hour, the evening hour that strives
> Homeward, and brings the sailor home from sea,
> (II 218-21)

and again, resuming the intrusion some lines later:

> I Tiresias, old man with wrinkled dugs
> Perceived the scene, and foretold the rest –
> (II 228-9)

And then just before the end of the scene:

---

[8] Leavis, *New* Bearings, 103.
[9] E G Selwyn's translation of *pase anthropine ktisei* at 2:13.
[10] L Goppelt, *Der Erste Petrusbrief* (Göttingen: K-EKNT, 1978), 183.

(And I Tiresias have foresuffered all
Enacted on this same divan or bed;
I who have sat by Thebes below the wall
And walked among the lowest of the dead.)

'Peter' is a presence who sees what is in fact the substance of the writing. He is also one who shares the tasks given to some among his readers: in this he may be distinguished from Tiresias, he is more nearly 'a character' in the drama when he writes: *So I exhort the elders among you as a fellow elder and a witness of the sufferings of Christ as well as a partaker of the glory that is to be revealed* (5: 1). He stands on the Christ-ward side of his readers, constantly referring them to the sufferings of Christ (1:11,19; 2:4ff; 21ff; 3:18ff, 4: 1,13; 5:1).

Before we leave consideration of the relation of the author to reader it may be helpful to consider what Paul Ricoeur describes as "Play" as the mode of being of appropriation.[11] There is not space to represent the subtlety of Ricoeur's argument, only to draw attention to some aspects of it. 'Play', writes Ricoeur, 'is not determined by the consciousness which plays; play has its own way of being. Play is an experience which transforms those who participate in it'. It seems that the subject of aesthetic experience is not the player himself but rather 'what "takes place" in the play'. What happens when we go to a theatre, where a play is performed (using one sense of the word 'play') is that the lights go out and another world is disclosed to us, indeed we may to some extent be said to enter into another world. 'Everyday reality is abolished and yet everyone becomes himself.' In play there occurs what Gadamer calls a "metamorphosis" *(Verwandlung)* '... Art only abolishes non-metamorphosed reality. Whence the true *mimesis:* a metamorphosis according to the truth. In this sense, we shall speak of recognition rather than cognition. In a theatrical representation, we recognise characters and roles. Therein lies the paradox: the most imaginary creation elicits recognition.'

Because of decades of preoccupation with the historical context of biblical writings Christian exegetes have been slow to see that their reading of Scripture is very like entering into a play, taking part in a game or being present at a theatrical production. The author takes upon himself a role, that of 'Peter' in I Peter; or Paul takes upon himself the role of apostle in writing to the Galatians or the Corinthians. He too is 'metamorphosed'. He does not stand before us as

---

[11] In the essay' Appropriation' (pp.182-193) in *Hermeneutics and the Human Sciences.*
Ricoeur is here taking up and developing a theme suggested by Hans-Georg Gadamer in *Truth and Method* (Bng. Tr. London 1975) in a section in which he discusses how we appreciate a work of art.

a human individual in all the triviality of his entire biography (hence the irrelevance of psychoanalysis of an author) but in the role he chooses to adopt in writing this particular text. The author of I Peter is like any other author of an imaginative piece of literature to some extent fictitious. This would be true even if he should turn out to be the historical Peter. He assumes a voice, as surely as a narrator of a tale, or for that matter the writer of a Gospel (who may however try to burn himself out of his narrative, but nevertheless is inescapably present).

So too, those addressed are, for us as we read, fictional characters, which does not mean that they never existed. They, the baptised, the members of churches in Asia Minor at once pilgrims on their way and citizens of the Roman Empire, household servants, wives of unbelieving husbands, elders of the congregation, all have parts to play; and they are not exactly your parts or mine, although as we read a certain recognition takes place, the necessary conditions are being fulfilled for appropriation: a distance between text and reader is established, and a sense of belonging—of being drawn into the address which is the writing, takes place. The readers, that is at least potentially you and I, also go through a metamorphosis. As Aristotle knew, you do not leave the theatre or the play unchanged.

If this understanding of the process of reading a text were appreciated we should be delivered from the biblicism which demands parallels between the circumstances in which and for which the biblical author writes and our own. The whole point is that they are not parallel. The 'wife' addressed in 3:1-6 is no more my wife than is the Wife of Bath, which does not mean that there is no gain, no Christian illumination, from listening to that passage, observing that little 'playful' scene: on the contrary its very distance provides the condition of communication.

# II

If we wish to pursue further the way in which the metamorphosis of the author, actor and reader takes place in 1 Peter we should need to look afresh at the styles and forms and use of metaphor in the text. As we know, this is a long and arduous and detailed undertaking, so much so that many students never reach the end for which the whole is being undertaken. Again literary critics of non-biblical texts know our problem. As Graham Hough wrote

> It is possible to see a hierarchy in these varied critical operations ... Textual criticism is preliminary and ancillary, literary history, theory of genres, the

story of the gross structure of literature occupies the middle rank; interpretations and judgments of value are the summits of critical activity. The ultimate reason for which criticism was undertaken is that we may understand each thing rightly on its own plane, and that we may know the better from the worse.[12]

In the study of 1 Peter much excellent work has been done on the first two stages of that process. In particular a great deal of intensely scholarly attention has been given to the placing of 1 Peter within early Christianity. Selwyn[13] made himself indispensable to later students: he saw affinities of thought and phrase between I and II Thessalonians and 1 Peter and discovered hymns and other liturgical fragments (as did Bultmann[14] in his influential essay); he notes the presence of what he calls a persecution fragment; building on Carrington he discerns catechetical patterns or forms underlying this and other epistles; he records instances of *verba Christi,* and judges that they belong to the hortatory type of tradition, *halakhah.* Since Selwyn this analysis has been corrected and refined by other scholars, for instance by Elliott[15] and Best,[16] who demonstrate the improbability of Selwyn's view that 2:4-10 either as a whole or in its parts represents a primitive hymn. Best,[17] however, adds to our information about contacts between 1 Peter and the Gospel tradition by showing that the allusions 'lie in two blocks in Luke 6 and Luke 12 and also in two (Matthew 5:16; Mark 10:45) or possibly three (Matthew 5:10) isolated sayings'.

The question must be asked: what does all this kind of information do for us? Positively, it locates 1 Peter firmly in the early Christian tradition; it enriches our awareness of the manifold and varied character of that tradition; we hear voices from the early Church confessing their faith, singing hymns, catechising converts. The limitation of this approach is that it suggests that the message is to be heard in the parts or in what lies behind the document, that what is chiefly significant is that which 1 Peter has in common with other writings. The danger is that we forget to move forward and ask how exactly, that is to say for what rhetorical purposes, the author uses this material; and

---

[12] Graham Hough, *An Essay on Criticism* (London: 1966).

[13] E G. Selwyn, *The First Epistle of Peter* (London 1947).

[14] R Bultmann, 'Bekenntnis und Liedfragmente im ersten Petrusbrief' in *Exegetica* (Tübingen , 1967).

[15] J H Elliott, *The Elect and the Holy.* An Exegetical Examination of 1 Peter 2:4-10 (Nov. Test.Suppl. 12 (Leiden: 1966).

[16] E Best '1 Peter 2:4-10 - A Reconsideration'. *Novum Testamentum* 11 (1969), pp.270-292.

[17] *New Testament Studies,* 16.2 (January 1970) 95-113.

what is the message of the whole. We have put asunder what man, if not God, has joined together.

> Legends, myths, themes, rhythms and ideas, wrote Brendan Kennelly, are not like political parties and social groups. They do not thrive on identity based on a sense of separateness; they fertilise and enrich each other constantly and deliberately in order to create new legends, myths, themes, rhythms and ideas.[18]

Future work on 1 Peter will need to be concerned not only with where the images came from but how they work. A hint of how this is to be done may be found in Best's analysis of the use of Old Testament quotations in the writing. He demonstrates how in the five instances of formal quotation (1:16; 1:23; 3:10-12; 4:18; 5:5c) the citation 'confirms the argument which has preceded it and is not productive of it': they have the effect of a refrain at the end of the stanzas in a Yeats poem or a ballad. By way of contrast Old Testament phrases and clauses are worked into the argument: 'by using Old Testament words and phrases in place of his own he is obviously giving to his own arguments that authority which he allowed the Old Testament to possess'. But perhaps most interesting of all are words and phrases incorporated into sentences composed by the author,[19] in each case words necessary to advance the argument. 'They are neither prepared for by preceding midrashic comment nor are they used to confirm an argument already explicitly present in the context'. It could be shown that the tone of voice changes, the metaphor performs a subtly different function in these three instances: in the first the quotation operates, refrain like, as a signpost; in the second there is given to contemporary event what Ricoeur elsewhere calls 'a temporal density,[20] by the invocation of the Old Testament; in the third a metaphor drawn from the Old Testament carries the argument forward.

All this, of course, is only prolegomena: an attempt to approach 1 Peter with another mental set, supplementary, complementary to that which we customarily find in commentaries although dependent upon linguistic, historical critical work which is the staple diet of commentators. If these considerations

---

[18] 'Introduction', *The Penguin Book of Irish Verse* (England: Harmondsworth, 1970), 29.

[19] Best gives five instances: 2:17 = Prov 24:21; 3:6b - Prov 3:25; 4:14b = Is.11:2; 1:18 = Is. 52:3; 2:11 = Ps. 38:13.

[20] 'Why has Christian preaching chosen to be hermeneutic by binding itself to the rereading of the Old Testament? Essentially to make the event itself appear not as an irrational eruption, but as the fulfilment of an antecedent meaning which remained in suspense. The event itself receives a temporal density by being inscribed in a signifying relation to "promise" and "fulfilment"'. 'Preface to Bultmann' in *The Conflict in Interpretations,* essays in Hermeneutics (Evanston: 1974), 383.

properly raise the question of how in relation to biblical text we move from the *meaning* of a text to its *significance* (using the terms in Professor Quinn's sense[21]), then they must be followed up by a fresh reading of the parts in the light of the whole and the whole in the light of the parts; and we may consider afresh the integrity of the so-called epistle: is it one writing, or two or more bound together? That, however, would have to be a matter for another essay.

---

[21] 'Meaning, as I shall use the term, is a property of statements. Meaning is what the text says. There are limits to the meaning (in this sense), of Shakespeare's sonnet or Blake's poem, limits fixed by the text itself'. That is equally true of I Peter; and the task of traditional commentators is to fix those limits. 'Significance is what we make of what the text says'. That, we contend, cannot be achieved without help from the sensitive, disciplined process known as literary criticism. Quotations are from Kenneth Quinn, *How Literature Works* p.16 (ABC 1982).

# Shorter Papers

# Sermon preached at the
# Service of Inauguration of
# the Uniting Church
## Sydney Town Hall, 22 June 1977

*And Jesus came and said to them, 'All authority in heaven and on
earth has been given to me. Go therefore and make disciples of all
nations, baptizing them in the name of the Father and of the Son and
of the Holy Spirit, teaching them to observe all that I have commanded
you; and lo, I am with you always, to the close of the age.'*

*Matthew 28: 18-20*

## I

We cannot too often remember that these words come at
the end of a Gospel which tells of the curiously paradoxical character of this
man's authority. It is not sheer strength but is sometimes to be found in weakness. It does not win its victories by being self-evident, open to all to see, it is
exerted in conflict. It is tested in trial. The bearer of this authority is destroyed
by lesser men who know how to handle the law, manipulate the crowd and win
the political game. Yet he emerges at the end of this story, saying not 'All authority has been given to me over the hearts and consciences of few'. He does not say,
'In the hidden places, among discreet groups, I may still be remembered and
worshipped.' Rather he says, 'All authority in heaven and earth has been given to
me.' This is a claim not simply for your allegiance and mine. It is an assertion
about the nature and manner of the God who reigns in human history. We are
well to remember that, and not to be unduly preoccupied with ourselves tonight. In a phrase of Zinzendorf: 'The cross is his method and lasts until his
future.' This, to use the modem jargon, is his style: what he was, what he is, and
what he will be.

The statement may be one of triumph, but it is not triumphalist: he is the
meek King, who disclaims power and glory and moves towards the hour of his
final judgment in lowliness by way of a cross. The living crucified One still
reigns. That casts light on the period of human history in which we live—where

we are, what we can expect, how we shall be judged. It cures us of Utopian expectations, and yet it gives us hope.

Bishop Hensley Henson in one of his letters tells of receiving a seventeenth century ivory crucifix of French origin.

> I have fixed it up in the centre of the book case which confronts my study chair, and contains volumes to which I am accustomed frequently to have recourse. The top row is filled with the little volumes of the Loeb Classics Library (nearly 300 of them), the next row contains a number of volumes of history illustrating the culture of the ancient classical world. Below that is the History of the Popes and other volumes (including the works of Shakespeare), which illustrate Christian civilization. Below that again, are a whole shelf of larger volumes including the great Cambridge series of syndicated history, ancient, medieval and modern, and then all the volumes of our own National Biography. They form together a not altogether inadequate illustration of modern civilization and culture, and there in the middle, I set the crucifix, whereon one may see both the final judge of human life and the standard of his judgment. I have in mind to place there, if I can arrange it suitably, the legend from the *Te Deum*—'We believe that thou shalt come to be our judge'.[1]

Much has happened since Henson wrote those words in 1946. His picture of culture and civilization is perhaps too urbane, too Western, too literary and not sufficiently aware of the achievements and the threats which have come with advances in science and technology. All right. Replace if you will some of these books with the 20 volumes of the reports of the Commission of Enquiry into Poverty in Australia. Add the story of the relation of the white man to the Aborigine, and of the relation for better and worse of Australia with her Asian and Pacific neighbours. Put the world as you see it: our struggle with our environment, our success and failure in taming and using and abusing it; our frustrated efforts to create a society in which man serves man, the agony of our social injustices and our political ineptitude. Get as broad a picture as you can of the totality of human life; but then put the crucifix in the centre; and add the legend, 'We believe that thou shalt come to be our judge.' All authority in heaven and earth belongs to the risen Crucified One. Nothing is quite so important as to understand that.

## II

If his word is first a word about himself and the strange nature of his authority, there is also a second word addressed to his Church; a call to make disciples of all

---

[1]  *Letters of Herbert Hensley Henson*, edited by E F Braley (London: SPCK, 1950).

nations, the commission to baptize and to teach men to observe all that he had commanded.

By the time Matthew's Gospel was written, Christians had for long spoken of the Exalted Christ: of his victory over the demonic forces, of how he was Lord of things in heaven and earth and under the earth. But what is new in Matthew is the association of this with the mission of the Church. For Matthew, a consequence of Christ being the risen crucified One, is that all nations should be called to acknowledge him, men everywhere baptized into his Church, and taught the things which he has commanded. Note the repeated 'all', all authority, all nations, men everywhere, all his commandments. The universal mission of the Church is a necessary consequence of her central affirmation about Jesus Christ, who he was and who he is and who he yet will be. Because this comes from a crucified Lord, the mission of his Church is not an act of spiritual aggression, of human imperialism. It is a making of disciples, a passing on of the word, 'Follow me'. It is a baptism, an invitation to enter into a way of life which has marked upon it the consequences of his death: so that men may know themselves forgiven, no longer alienated but at home in a world over which the crucified risen One reigns. A making of disciples, a baptism, yes and a teaching, a passing on of the commandments of Jesus; and a receiving of them afresh in each generation. 'The Risen and Exalted One makes the word of the earthly Jesus obligatory upon the church on earth for all time until the end of the world'.[2]

So, if the first thing which we say to each other tonight is that we should hear the word of the risen Christ about himself, the second is that we should hear afresh the call to the Church to go out into the world on his distinctive mission.

To men everywhere, in their sorrow and in their joy, when they are broken and bowed down and when they are raised up and survive. This is a word for strong men and weak men, for women who wait and women who work, for the bound and the free. He has a word for them all.

Let me pick out a note that is struck here, and which we would neglect to our peril: *teaching them to observe all that I have commanded you.* Jesus is not just for men, beside them, with them. He has commands which he addresses to men; and he would have us pass them on: *teaching them to observe all that I have commanded you.* This is the focal point of Matthew's whole Gospel. He wrote in order that the teaching of Jesus, his commandments, might not be forgotten. The history of the Church suggests that the receiving of those commandments is at once simple and complicated. They may be received by men and women of

[2] Gunther Bornkamm, 'The Risen Lord and the Earthly Jesus: Matthew 28:16-20' in *The Future of Our Religious Past*, edited by J M Robinson (London: SCM Press, 1971).

simple faith, but they are patient of considerable sophistication in their application to a complicated world. We dare not neglect the whole story of the Church's
apprehension and interpretation of that message—the message of Christ and
the message about Christ. To say what it means for our day requires intellectual
discipline and spiritual vigour. In this Uniting Church in Australia we enter into
a tradition, catholic, reformed, evangelical, in which those who have gone before have not been afraid to confront the world with rigorous thought and spiritual commitment. Only such a doctrinal tradition, perpetuated and renewed,
will be adequate in making disciples of all nations in our day. To this end we
shall require (as our *Basis of Union* commits us) to recognize men and women as
ministers of the Word: trained in a disciplined school, educated in the story of
the Church's discipleship so that the great tradition into which we have entered
may be made vital for our day. Their commission comes from a living Lord, who
lays upon them and upon us all the obligation to teach men to observe all that
he has commanded us. To listen to him is the supreme calling of the whole
Church—of every member; and to do so we need an educated ministry—men
and women who, in a special sense, have heard the call to preach the Word.

   Anna Akhmatova, conscious of her vocation as a poet, and as a poet whose
life must be lived in Soviet Russia, was much concerned, not only not to forget
what she had lived through (the human race so easily forgets), but also with the
responsibility not to allow to be forgotten. She must put it into words:[3]

> Was it not I who stood at the Cross
> Was it not I who drowned in the sea;
> Have my lips forgotten your taste
> O pain

We have lived through a period in which the power of speech has been deni-
grated, in which confidence in communication through the spoken word has
been eroded. We live in a country in which, save for a small band of writers,
inarticulateness is exalted as a virtue. It is time for the Christian Church to
remember again that faith comes by hearing. We need preachers who share
Akmatova's sense of obligation to put the Word into words:

> If we lose the freshness of words
> The simplicity of feeling,
> Is it not like an artist losing his sight,
> An actor—his voice and movement,
> A splendid woman, her beauty?

---

[3]   The translations used here are from Amanda Haight, *Anna Akhmatova: a Poetic
   Pilgrimage* (Oxford University Press, 1976),148 & 54.

But don't try to keep for yourself
What has been the gift of Heaven:
Our lot as we ourselves know
Is to squander, not to save.

Go alone and heal the blind,
And in the difficult hour of doubt,
See your disciples jeer and gloat
And know the indifference of the crowd.

# III

And yet, you are not alone; the Church and her ministers are not alone. For if the Risen Lord's first word is about himself, so is the last: *I am with you always, to the close of the age.*

We are not alone because there is One who once was alone, who heard men jeer and gloat and knew the desertion of disciples, the antagonism of authorities, the indifference of the crowd. Because he was alone once, we need never be quite alone again. *I am with you always: to the close of the age.*

Jürgen Moltmann opens his large book on the Church, with the sentence: 'This book is intended to help the Church to find its bearing ... The fundamental questions have to be answered afresh: Where do you come from? Where are you going? Who are you?'[4]

Union means nothing, absolutely nothing, unless it drives us back to those questions. Where do you come from? From the hand of the living God who engaged with men in a new way through the death and resurrection of Jesus Christ, and the outpouring of His Spirit. Where are you going? To make disciples of all nations; to fulfil the commission with which we have been charged. Who are you? A people with whom that same Christ has promised that he will be present, to the close of the ages.

Are you and I prepared to find our bearings afresh? They are not too difficult to discern. They are not far from us; but they provide far reaching indications of the way in which we should walk. To that pilgrimage we are committed.

Now unto him who is able to do exceeding abundantly above all that we ask or think according to the power that works in us, to him be the glory in the Church and in Christ Jesus, now and forever. Amen.

---

[4]   Jürgen Moltmann, *The Church in the Power of the Spirit* (English translation (London: SCM Press, 1975).

# Address to the Second Assembly
## of the Uniting Church
### June 1979

**M**r President, my response must begin with words of gratitude. Thank you for the kind words said. Thank you for the privilege given to me to preside at the First Assembly of the Uniting Church. Thank you for the opportunities to visit each Synod, and the Church in each State: my wife, who accompanied me on most of these visits, and I have learnt much. We have also renewed old friendships and made new ones. Thank you to those who made the way easier than it would otherwise have been, not least to you, Mr President in your role as the first Secretary of the Assembly.

Perhaps a particular word of thanks to Dr John Brown and the Council for World Mission for opportunities to become more aware of the place of the Church in relation to her neighbours in the Pacific and East Asia, and especially for a memorable visit to Papua New Guinea; and also to Dr David Merritt who encouraged me to spend some of my 'presidential time' in writing Bible studies.

And thank you to my colleagues at Ormond College who made my absences and preoccupations less obvious than might otherwise have been the case.

## I

A lifelong friend of my father, and of my family, had the unusual distinction of being an Irishman who became Moderator of the Church of Scotland. After he had completed his period of office he remarked that nothing in the sphere of humanity so resembled a natural phenomenon as did an ex-Moderator of the Church of Scotland resemble an extinct volcano. I think he knew that Moderators of the Church of Scotland are frequently treated more seriously than they deserve while in office, and that it is quite good that they should be rendered innocuous as soon as possible after that term had ended. I have done my best to make sure that the Presidency of the Uniting Church will not be surrounded with exaggerated deference. I have tried, not always successfully, not to explode too often; and now, when I am about to become extinct, you give me an opportunity for a few more eruptions. I shall content myself with four.

The first concerns the primacy of the life of the congregation in the life of the Church. It is, I hope, quite unnecessary to remind you of what the *Basis of Union* says about the congregation 'the embodiment in one place of the One Holy Catholic and Apostolic Church, worshipping, witnessing and serving as a fellowship of the Spirit in Christ'.

It is salutary to observe that the *Basis* does not make any comparable claim for Presbytery or Synod or Assembly. It is of the congregation that it may be said that whether it be two or three or two or three hundred who are gathered around Word and Sacrament, there Christ is in the midst, there the Catholic Church is present in its fullness, worshipping its Lord, witnessing to him, equipping men and women to go out in his service. The rest of the activities of the Church, in Presbytery, Synod and Assembly exist to build up that life of the Catholic Church which manifests itself in the congregation of Christ's people. The Church does not come into being when all those congregations come together to constitute the Church, as we say, using secular terminology. The Church is in being where Christ is with his people.

I say this because I believe it to be important to register one clear impression: where unity matters most, it has been most effective, namely locally, in the lives of congregations. I said 'most effective', I did not say 'easiest'. It is in congregations that men and women have known the pain and the joy which go together with growing up into Christ and closer to one another. Many of you will know that, and I do not need to labour the point.

The Councils of the Church exist primarily to serve that basic unit, the congregation: to make sure that Word and Sacrament are available for Christ's people, so that they can worship, witness and serve. Presbytery, Synod and Assembly are constituted for that purpose. Of course they may have to do other things as well, but they ought to remember that the further they get away from the task of simply serving Christ's people gathered around Word and Sacrament the further they move from their own sphere of competence. That doesn't mean that they do not have to make that move from time to time; and the movement into tasks other than those determined by the primary focus will vary from time to time and from place to place. Indeed in the fulfilment of the primary task the needs of different Synods vary: the Northern Synod has a serious lack of capital, some other Synods seem to have an embarrassing surplus of capital of certain kinds. Some Synods have to take responsibilities for welfare and educational institutions while others should be shedding those responsibilities, knowing that this is neither their primary concern nor are they well constituted for the purpose.

The same thing might be said about some of the judgements on social or political questions made by Church Councils. They may have to make them from time to time, for pastoral reasons; but we, in Presbytery, Synod and Assembly, should recognize that we are not particularly well constituted for that purpose.

The *Basis of Union* makes clear that the primary function of the Councils is the building up of the life of the Church in worship, mission and service, and those who are appointed members of the Councils are presumed to know about the needs of the Church, especially as those relate to its primary manifestation in all its catholicity, the local congregation. They are not appointed because of their competence in social or political questions. This leads me to the second topic on which I should like to record a minor eruption, or earth-tremor.

## II

To put it in negative terms, we are very far from having got right or appropriate the administrative structure of the Church's life. There is not too much worry with the governmental structure, at least in principle: our commitment to conciliar government, government by inter-related councils, each with its own function to perform. Like the rest of the human race we are not good at moving from governmental structures through administrative techniques to make our purpose effective in the world. Look at the appalling amount of time spent in committees and consultations by some of our ablest members, ministers, deaconesses, elders, lay people: taking them away from the life of their congregations, from their families, from normal participation in the affairs of the world.

We no longer seem to expect our ministers to spend hours (literally hours) every week, thinking, reading, praying: so that when the hungry sheep look up they may be fed. I have sometimes thought that the eschatological hope expressed in the last book of the Bible needs to be re-written: there will be no more duplicated paper or photostats there, but only the Lamb's book of life; no more tape-recorders but a voice like the sound of many waters; no more audio-visual presentations but one from whose mouth issues a sharp two-edged sword, and his face like the sun shining in full strength. And if that is the reality, if He (one like a son of man) is the reality, then perhaps we'd perhaps better start preparing each other on earth for the day when we must meet him. And I am not wholly convinced that our Constitution, Regulations and Procedures are sufficiently and rigorously controlled by that end and purpose. I am not persuaded that they are not in danger, like some educational techniques and some mystical experiences, of becoming ends in themselves.

# III

My third impertinent eruption is this: I am afraid that we are no clearer now than we were two years ago on the answer to the question, Who speaks for the Church? Part of the reason for this is that we don't know how to be a Protestant Church in a pluralist society, nor does anybody else. We are easily pushed into becoming or trying to become another pressure group, which may (according to some views still prevailing within that Church) be an appropriate form of activity for Roman Catholicism, but the Protestant answer is not to try to emulate Rome, but to find out how Protestants should behave politically. It may be that on a series of contemporary ethical issues we have a witness to bear to the freedom of the conscience—in the case of the Christian to the freedom of the Christian man—as individuals and in groups to differ in good conscience and mutual respect from his fellow man. At the risk of causing offence, let me record that there was one verse of one hymn in the service last night which I could not sing:

> Even now we think and speak the same,
> and cordially agree;
> concentred all, through Jesus' name,
> in perfect harmony.

That may be possible for a band of like-minded men and women, a religious order within the English Churchman ship of the eighteenth century. It will not do for the Uniting Church in the Australia of the late twentieth century. There disagreement on public issues, definition of areas of agreement and disagreement, and continuing creative tension within our fellowship are more likely to be the mark of an honest Churchmanship.

There is a whole series of issues here, on which it would be inappropriate to take the time of this Assembly at this point. But both on this, and as a preliminary to a review of our administrative structures, our Regulations and so on, we need a fresh look at how authority operates (or should operate) in the life of the Church. Early this century two great theologians belonging to two of the traditions which made up our union, each in his own way drew attention to the fundamental importance for Christian faith and the life of the Church of the question of authority. I refer to John Oman (a Presbyterian) and PT Forsyth (a Congregationalist).

It is time this is taken up again before Protestantism disappears into the vacuity of sentimentality, or becomes the religious gloss on the ideologies of left wing theorists or right wing prejudice. I give it as a task to those who are younger than I to discover how authority operates or should operate in a Church and over the Christian conscience among people who belong to that brand of Christianity, of Catholic Christianity, which was purified by the Protestant reformation.

# IV

My last eruption concerns the plea for a greater sense of identity, of belonging to the Uniting Church. Simone Weil, that remarkable young Frenchwoman who lived on the edge of French Roman Catholicism in the late thirties and early forties, but always refused to be baptised, once said that what offended her was a certain 'Church patriotism'. He or she would be a brave former Presbyterian or Methodist among us who does not know what she meant: my Church right or wrong. Perhaps Congregationalists were freed somewhat from this besetting sin by the recollection of one of their forebears writing to the General Assembly of the Church of Scotland: 'I beseech you, in the bowels of Christ, think it possible you may be mistaken.'

At all events the cry for a sense of identity in the Uniting Church cannot be answered by the offer of a new kind of Church patriotism. In an important sense, we in the Uniting Church in Australia have no identity, no distinctive marks—other than belonging with the people of God brought into being by the death and resurrection of Jesus Christ on their way to the consummation of all things in him. It is a hard thing to be a reformed Catholic who believes that. We have embarked on a course in which we ask men and women to forget who they are, and chiefly to remember whose they are. The secondary things of life, denominational traditions and any new or emerging ethos of the Uniting Church, are of course valuable in their own way: they are homely, but they can also cloy. It is sometimes because of them, and it is sometimes in spite of them that we remain members of the Church. What needs to hold us (as distinct from what we hold) is what is of primary significance.

In 1966 Fr Herbert McCabe wrote an editorial in *New Blackfriars* about the recent departure from the Roman Catholic Church of Charles Davis. He was highly critical of the way in which his Church had handled the matter, his sympathies were with Davis but he concludes with these words:

> It is because we believe that the hierarchical institutions of the Roman
> Catholic Church, with all their decadence, their corruption and their sheer

silliness, do in fact link us to areas of Christian truth beyond our own particular experience and ultimately to truths beyond any experience, that we remain, and see our Christian lives in terms of remaining, members of this Church.

We have to find the equivalent. May it go something like this:

It is because we believe that the conciliar structure of the Uniting Church, with all its encouragement of good men and women to waste their time in endless committees, with all its tiresome talk and ecclesiastical chatter, still links us by Word preached and Sacrament received through the operations of a duly ordained and pastorally caring ministry, to areas of Christian truth and to a fellowship in Christ beyond our own experience, and ultimately beyond any experience, that we remain in and would call you our fellow-Australians into membership of this Church.

Then we shall have no further problem of identity.

# Mary and the
# Protestant Tradition

*A contribution to a Symposium on the Virgin Mary, made at the request of Father Anthony Clery, at the Holy Name Parish, East Preston, on August 16, 1979. Fr Clery was a founding member of the committee for the Week of Prayer for the Unity of All Christian People, in 1954: a great ecumenist.*

Ana- [MARY] gram
[ARMY]
*How well an Army doth present,*
*In whom the Lord of Hosts did pitch his tent*
George Herbert

Y ou have given me a difficult assignment tonight. It is difficult to speak of Mary and the Protestant tradition, and to do so to a Roman
Catholic audience without appearing offensive. It is difficult not to be insensitive to a devotional tradition which Protestants can really only know at second
hand. It is difficult to avoid appearing irreverent, where one would wish to tread
delicately. Yet, I must try to respond to your invitation; and must use the occasion as far as possible to say things which you will recognise as positive contributions which Protestant theologians and Churchmen would wish to make.

## I

Let me begin by quoting Karl Barth, widely acknowledged by Roman Catholics
and Protestants alike as one of the greatest theological figures of the twentieth
Century. It concerns the use of the phrase Mary, Mother of God: *Theotokos.* The
old Latin liturgy calls Mary the 'Mother of our Lord Jesus Christ'; the Council
of Ephesus (431) speaks of Mary as 'mother of God'. And in doing so, they are
drawing out the implications of the words of Elizabeth in St Luke's Gospel:
'Why is this granted me, that the Mother of my Lord should come to me' (Lk
1.43). Here is Barth on this, surely the highest title given to Mary:

As Christians and theologians we do not reject the description of Mary as the 'mother of God' but in spite of it being overloaded by the so-called Mariology of the Roman Catholic church, we affirm and approve of it as a legitimate expression of christological truth.'[1]

In other words this title, this description does two things for us:

(i) It reminds us that the birth of Jesus our Lord and Saviour was not 'a creation out of nothing, but that through his mother Jesus Christ really belongs to the unity of the human race'. No devotion will serve us well, no art or music will point us in the right direction, no dogma properly gain our assent, if it takes away from the essential womanhood of Mary. *God sent forth his Son*, says Paul, *born of woman*. We should welcome the sculptures of Epstein and Henry Moore because they represent Mary as a real woman, as a childbearing woman; for that protects the real humanity of Christ. He did not come into this world any other way than from the womb of a woman: bone of our bone, flesh of our flesh.

(ii) Secondly, the phrase 'Mother of God' reminds us that the one whom Mary bore was not some intermediate being, some demigod, some angelic creature, some second level deity, he really was God's Son: *God sent forth his Son, born of woman*.

It will be seen then that the Protestant dogmatic tradition does not reject this most fundamental affirmation about Mary, but asserts it, 'permissible and necessary', as Barth says, 'as an auxiliary christological proposition'. In other words, it is necessary to help us understand who Jesus Christ was and is. In dogma and devotion Mary is important because she points us to Christ. That is how the New Testament presents her. That is how the Church should understand her.

Because of their determination to protect the central affirmations of the Christian faith, Luther and Zwingli had no difficulty with the term *theotokos*, Mother of God. And if Calvin did not use it, neither does he contest the appropriateness of the term. So at least the first thing that I must say to you is positive. In the Protestant dogmatic tradition, the figure of Mary is treated with reverence because she points away from herself to the central figure in our faith, the Lord Jesus Christ.

---

[1]  Karl Barth, *Church Dogmatics 1.2 The Doctrine of the Word of God*, English translation, (Edinburgh: T & T Clark 1956), 138.

## II

Having said that you will perhaps permit me, in Christian charity and with a common love for the truth of the Gospel, to say quite frankly what it is that Protestants object to in the developed Mariology of Western Catholicism. We have great difficulties with the affirmation of the perpetual virginity: although ancient in origin, we believe it is not well grounded in history, and some passages of the New Testament speak against it.

We have perhaps even greater difficulties with the immaculate conception, and with the bodily assumption; and let me briefly try to explain why. They are, as we see it, attempts to put Mary alongside our Lord, albeit a pale shadow of his perfect manhood, in the work of redemption. Faith, we believe, remains response: be it unto the handmaid according to thy Word. It is not an act of reciprocity, whereby the believer becomes a part of divinity. It is a response to the divine initiative. Man/woman allows himself/herself to be reshaped according to the Divine Will; but he/she never ceases to be wholly human, perhaps still to be sinful, to be one whose salvation still and always depends on God alone.

As a Protestant I cannot but say that to me Roman Catholic dogma and devotion appear to turn Mary into something other than a genuine woman and thereby put at risk the true incarnation of Christ himself; it appears to take a view of grace which confuses God and a human being. Only once were the two combined in one person: our Lord Jesus Christ. We belong to God's family by adoption, by faith, in love, and we hope to remain there; and Mary herself, mother of our Lord though she be, still stands on this side of the great divide of the two realities which we know, God and humanity.

## III

Thirdly, I should not want to leave it there. As a Protestant I should want to ask you to go back with me to Scripture, not in any polemical spirit, but together open to its message, with the prayer that afresh we may learn from what the Gospels have to tell us. If at one time Protestants and Catholics were seriously divided in their approach to and understanding of Scripture, that time is now past. We learn from each other, and we learn together. We would hear what God the Lord would say, and he would speak 'Peace' to his children.

There is only time tonight to look at two passages; but they illustrate what I hope may be a point of common understanding: how Mary may be regarded as the type of discipleship. The first passage is from Mark 3.31-35; and its import at first sight may appear somewhat negative:

And his mother and his brothers came; standing outside they sent to him and called him. And a crowd was sitting about him; and they said to him, 'Your mother and your brothers are outside, asking for you.' And he answered, 'who are my mother and my brothers?' And looking around on those who sat about him, he said, 'Here are my mother and my brothers! Whoever does the will of God is my brother, and sister, and mother.'

With this we might compare Luke 11.27-28:

As he said this, a woman in the crowd raised her voice and said to him, 'Blessed is the womb that bore you, and the breasts that you sucked!' But he said, 'Blessed rather are those who hear the word of God and keep it!'

Here let me make just two comments.

(i) Mark's narrative is inexorable in the way in which it emphasises the isolation of Jesus. In the first period of his ministry there is a recurring pattern. Mark three times summarises Jesus' message, three times refers to the calling of disciples and sending them on the mission, three times describes Jesus' activity and teaching, culminating three times in his rejection: by the Pharisees and the Herodians, by his fellow-citizens in Nazareth, and by the lack of understanding on the part of his disciples. That last, that lack of understanding by his disciples, is so great that Mark in the second period of Jesus' ministry repeats it three more times, until in the third period (The Passion) one betrays him, another denies him, and they all forsake him. Alone he goes out into the darkness, with the cry of dereliction on his lips.

Mark's narrative is more than we can bear; for into the middle of that first period, Mark, oh so delicately, puts Mary and the brothers of Jesus 'standing outside' calling to him; and Jesus having to say 'Here are my mother and brothers! Whoever does the will of God is my brother, and sister and mother'.

And, I am afraid, that in Mark's narrative, Mary the mother of Jesus is not at the cross. There were women, and they looked from afar. He was alone.

ii) Now Mark is not the whole of the New Testament; but he is a Gospel writer to whom we must listen. He says, however, not that rejection of Jesus is the only possibility but that obedience to his word is open to all; and with that Luke agrees.

And this leads me, briefly, to allude to another passage: Luke 1:26-28.

In the sixth month the angel Gabriel was sent from God to a city of Galilee named Nazareth, to a virgin betrothed to a man whose name was Joseph, of the house of David; and the virgin's name was Mary. And he came to her and said, 'Hail, O favored one, the Lord is with you!' But she was greatly troubled at the saying, and considered in her mind what sort of greeting this might be. And the angel said to her, 'Do not be afraid, Mary, for you have found favour with God. And behold, you will conceive in your womb and bear a son, and you shall call his name Jesus. He will be great, and will be called the Son of the Most High; and the Lord God will give to him the throne of his father David, and he will reign over the house of Jacob forever; and of his kingdom there will be no end.'

And Mary said to the angel, 'How can this be, since I have no husband?' And the angel said to her,

'The Holy Spirit will come upon you, and the power of the Most High will overshadow you; and therefore the child to be born will be called holy, the Son of God. And behold, your kinswoman Elizabeth in her old age has also conceived a son; and this is the sixth month with her who was called barren. For with God nothing will be impossible. '

And Mary said, 'Behold I am the handmaid of the Lord; let it be to me according to your word.' And the angel departed from her.

On this much discussed and awesome passage, let me presume to make three comments.

(i) Verse 35: 'The Holy Spirit will come upon you'. The Old Testament has many stories of women being rescued from barrenness; but in none of these is the agent of God's miraculous power the Holy Spirit. Indeed earlier in this chapter Elizabeth and Zechariah are promised a son when Elizabeth is past childbearing; but the agent of God's miracle is not His Spirit, it is simply the promise of the angel. But here 'the Holy Spirit will come upon you, and the power of the Most High will overshadow you. ' The Spirit is now present at the new creation, the new Man (human being) will be conceived in Mary's womb. Mary stands at the end of the old creation, and at the dawn of the new day. Child of Eve, she will bring forth the new Adam.

(ii) The second thing to which I want to draw attention is Verse 28: 'Hail'! said the angel 'O favored one'. And from the Magnificant: 'he has regarded the low estate of his handmaiden.'

Let me again quote Karl Barth:

All the angels of all the heavens now look only at this place where Mary is, that young girl to whom however nothing has happened but this simple regard of God, cast on her lowliness. This short instance is full of eternity, of an ever new eternity. There is nothing greater in heaven and on earth. If ever in the history of the world, something of capital importance happened, it is indeed this 'regard'.[2]

That God should look on humanity, on the young woman, thus: that should cause us to pause and pray. For here the world began anew.

(iii) My third comment is this: the response.

Verse 38: 'Behold I am the handmaid of the Lord. Let it be to me according your word.'

Let me quote another Protestant theologian, Max Thurian:

God has not caused Christ to be born of Mary without her knowing it. He has described her acceptance, and although it is He Himself in her who said 'Yes' by the grace with which he has endowed her, He has none the less desired that she should pronounce it, and that the Incarnation should begin there.[3]

What I have been trying to say to you are three things: First, the figure of Mary always points to the Christ. The second that she is the type of all disciples, as one who could misunderstand and yet at the critical moment be is given to obey. Third: what happened in her womb was decisive for mankind. A new start was made. With God all things are possible.

I would conclude by reminding you of two works of art. A picture by Rembrandt: darkness surrounds the cross, on which alone a shaft of light shines. But as you look into it, there is another point of light, at the bottom right hand corner, on Mary the Mother of the crucified. But when you look at her, she is looking at him and your eyes must do likewise.

The second is a subject unique in Renaissance Italian painting, an image of the Madonna pregnant.[4] And where is it to be found? In the chapel of a cemetery at the little town of Monterchi in Italy. The Madonna 'waiting to give birth ... in a cemetery'. From the grave of men's hopes, comes the child who is the hope of the world. That must be the first and last word in any of our Mariologies.

---

2 *Foi et Vie*, Nos. 85-86, August - October, 1936, Paris, pp. 509-10, quoted by Max Thurian. See note 3 below.

3 Max Thurian 'Mariology (d) Reformed' in *Ways of Worship, the Report of a Theological Commission of Faith and Order*, edited by Peter Edwall, Eric Hayman, William D. Maxwell (London: SCM Press 1951), 209.

4 'La Madonna del Parto' by Piero della Francesca, See Michael Ayrton *The Listener*, 12 (November 1953).

# Mary Mackillop

*Beatified by His Holiness Pope John Paul II in Sydney in Septem-*
*ber 1994. The following address was given at a Commemorative*
*Dinner in The Great Hall, The National Gallery of Victoria*
*Tuesday 16 August 1994.*

It is a great privilege to be asked to speak on this occasion. Paul
Tillich, a distinguished Lutheran theologian was accustomed to say that Protestants were not very good at recognising sainthood. In the Protestant view—
shared today by many Catholics—every believer is a saint in so far as he (or she)
belongs to the communion of saints; and every saint is an ordinary believer, in
so far as he (or she) belongs to those who need forgiveness of sins. When Paul
says to that motley array of turbulent men and women who made up the Church
in Corinth that they were 'called to be saints' he was asserting that they all,
whatever their short-comings, belonged to the people of God. But Tillich means
more than that. He suggests that Protestants have not been good at recognising
that in a special way some places, some events, some people can be separated,
declared to be 'holy', and deserve our special attention.[1]

If Tillich is right, you give me an opportunity to make amends tonight, to
be one who is given a special opportunity to put into words something of how
we might all regard the beatification of Mother Mary MacKillop—born in Melbourne, in a house in Brunswick Street, Fitzroy on 15 January 1842. There is
more to it than raising three cheers for a 'local girl made good'. You add to the
paradoxical character of this occasion when you ask one who was born and
baptised an Irish Presbyterian to speak of one whose antecedents were Scottish
Roman Catholics. You might have expected the first Australian saint to be an
Irish Australian Catholic. Mary MacKillop would have been less than human
did she not carry some of the marks of a family of Roman Catholics brought up
in Scotland where the weight of Presbyterians must have been ponderous if not
literally oppressive. That perhaps explains why, although having many Presbyte-

---

[1]  See, for instance, P Tillich *Systematic Theology I* (Chicago, Illinois: The University of
     Chicago Press, 1951), 121-2.

rian friends and supporters she was also a little suspicious of Presbyterians, believing them to be supporters of secularist tendencies in the community.

Be all that as it may, let me take you back to Paul Tillich. In his writings he speaks of certain places, events, people as holy because they are transparent. We even speak sometimes of people being transparently honest. Saints are transparent because through their lives we see a greater reality than that of which we are customarily aware. Towards the end of his life, however, Tillich in lectures and in conversation would say that 'transparent' was not the right word; it would be better to use the word 'translucent'.

Transparent focuses attention upon us; we look through a transparent window to the light beyond. Translucent suggest that the light beyond shines through upon us. We see the world as it should be, human life as it might be because that light from the other, from what is beyond, has shone through this person or at that place upon us. 'You are not here' wrote T S Eliot[2] about the Village of Little Gidding, where a religious community had lived and prayed in the seventeenth century.

> You are not here to verify,
> Instruct yourself, or inform curiosity
> Or carry report. You are here to kneel
> Where prayer has been valid
>
> And what the dead had no speech for, when living,
> They can tell you, being dead: the communication
> Of the dead is tongued with fire beyond the language of the living.

A saint says more, not less, to posterity than she said in her life time, for the full implications of that life have to be lived out by other people, by you and me whose lives are enriched by her memory.

Tonight's celebration is a commemoration. That is to say we here tonight are asked to take Mary MacKillop into our memories. Hugh of St Victor used to speak of the memory as being like an ark (Noah's Ark) in which precious things are stored, an archive from which we draw precious information. That is what the Church does by singling her out. It says that henceforth Mary MacKillop is to be a part of our memory in such a way as to make a difference to our lives. Being the kind of person she was, she is now to haunt the imagination of Christian people of Melbourne where she was born, of Australians among whom she worked. Henceforth she will haunt our memories. She cannot be left behind in the nineteenth century. Something of the translucence, of the light of God shin-

---

[2] T S Eliot, *Little Gidding,* (London: Faber and Faber, 1942).

ing through her, will henceforth (if we are faithful) cast light on our way. But we must handle this carefully.

But how? Let me try to make two or three suggestions.

1. First, and perhaps foremost, we shall remember her preference for the poor, but without patronising them.

In the mid-70s of the last century the then Governor of Victoria, Sir George Bowen, paid a visit to England. When there he boasted that while the actual taxation per head of the population was less in Victoria than in England, of the public revenue raised nearly one-third was expended on public education.

This he claimed was without parallel elsewhere. 'In no other country is one-third of the produce of the taxes spent directly or indirectly on public instruction'. Recent statistical studies have shown that he was correct.

At the same time, in the mid-seventies Mary MacKillop wrote a letter to Rome which draws a very different picture; and she too was right. Poverty was widespread, especially in the country towns and rural areas of the Australian colonies.

So was ignorance. Children grew up illiterate, and many Catholic children were unaware of the most elementary facts of the Christian faith. Ill health was widespread, and medical care hard to come by. The lot of the Irish Catholic was particularly hard. He and more particularly she had little support from the Church. To be a deserted wife, or an unmarried mother was particularly shameful. Single parents were not known. Catholics were scattered, and were only a small proportion of the population in many areas: they were in no position to demand or receive the services of a priest. The indigenous population, the Aborigines, had been deprived of their land, and many of them like the least prosperous of the immigrant population which included many nominal Catholics, lived in squalor.

It was to these that Mary MacKillop and the Sisters whom she gathered around her were sent. The usual institutions of Church life could not reach these scattered, neglected, isolated people. Her sisters were to go and be with the poor where they were; but they must identify with them. They too must be poor.[3]

---

[3]   For details of Mary MacKillop's life and the beginnings of the order which she founded, see Paul Gardiner SJ, *An Extraordinary Australian; Mary MacKillop—the Authorised Biography* (Newtown: NSW, E. J. Dwyer in association with David Ell Press, 1993).

They must not set forth from a secure base. They were to be servants of the one who though he was rich for our sakes became poor that we through his poverty might become rich. In this way they were to be moments of translucence. Thus, the light of God's presence was to shine into the lives of the really poor.

They were to re-enact what Jesus had promised in his first sermon in Nazareth; the poor were to have the good news preached to them, but in deed as well as in word - faith and education, health and welfare belonged together, freedom for captives, recovery of sight for the blind, liberty for those who are oppressed.

If we took Mary MacKillop into our memories what would this do for us 100 years or more later? It would surely draw our attention to the hard fact that Australia still is a country where many live in isolation. The wheel has moved full circle. Many of the supports of life in rural Victoria and Australia are being withdrawn from where people are: no longer is there a local bank manager with authority to advise, schools have to be a certain size and hospitals to have a certain financial viability.

The churches alone (I sometimes think) are left to serve people where they are; and in the prophet Elijah's words, modern life seeks their life to take it away. How Mary MacKillop's vision is to be re-enacted in these circumstances is hard to know. But one thing perhaps we should say one to another: if Mary MacKillop's example means anything, a fundamental criterion for public policy as for ecclesiastical policy will be, how does this affect the poor?

At this late stage in the development of western capitalism, as has been shown all over the world, the rich will look after themselves, and are doing so very comfortably. In the Anglo-Saxon countries which we most resemble and whose economic policies we seem bent on imitating, there grow up again and again new classes of the poor. So Mary MacKillop would touch our consciences with her questions: Who and where are the poor, and who is looking after them? And can you do so without asking the comfortable to make sacrifices? Mary MacKillop is a disturbing saint. This leads to the second thing I want to say.

2. Mary MacKillop shows us how to express dissent without rancour. If she is disturbing to us, it is no surprise, for she ran up against authority, ecclesiastical authority in her own day. She suffered many misrepresen-

tations, and in what for her was a most agonising way was: she was excommunicated in the Church she loved and served. She is not however, being beatified and proposed for sainthood because she expressed dissent.

If the Pope had to canonise everyone who has disagreed with his bishops, he would have little time for other activity, and the calendar of saints would long since have been unmanageable. But Mary MacKillop shows how dissent can be expressed by a loyal member of the church, not mixing strength of conviction and will with self-importance, but humbly and strenuously holding to her vocation: let others take action against her if they must and let God decide the issue. She feared for 'the scandal that threatened the name of the bishop'; and towards priests who opposed her and whose conduct she could not explain she bore no ill-will. Faced with a plain lie, she says 'I have been able to find excuse for everything but that, but not for my own sake, but for the sake of the sacred character of him who could say what was not true'.

The morals to be drawn for our day are too numerous to mention. We in this country claim to cherish freedom, but we do not like those who deviate from the path of orthodoxy (or political correctness as we now call it). We find it easy to impute motives to our opponents. We know a lot about how to bolster ourselves, our egos, our policies, by blaming others. We not only have opponents which is an honourable role for anyone to fill, but we have those whom we regard and treat as enemies, which is dangerous. Through the freedom which Mary MacKillop claimed for her religious order, and which was acknowledged by Rome, she struck a blow for pluralism in Church life—a loyal independence which has so splendidly characterised religious orders in this and other countries.

She also set an example which might be followed in community life, for without that open, tolerant pluralism, which knows how to differ without damning, the future for Australia will be dark indeed.

3. One last note must be struck; it undergirds what we have been observing. Hers was a life of prayer without fanaticism, of strength of conviction and statement without stridency. Small wonder that she took as the model for her Sisters, Joseph the quiet provider. She quietly, persistently went on doing what must be done next: the cause of justice for the dispossessed has to be pursued, and the justice which was due to her own Sisters took her in most uncomfortable and financially insecure

circumstances to Rome. Throughout it all there is one clear mark of her personality.

She was quite simply a woman of prayer, and her prayer was centred on the sacrament for there she met and received her Lord. 'The "good tree" ', says Tillich, 'precedes the "good fruit"'. Mary MacKillop's roots went deep into the soil of Christian devotion.

In this too she challenges the Australia, the Victoria, the Melbourne which rejoices in her elevation. In our activist atmosphere, where we talk a lot about performance criteria, we need more men and women who think before they act or speak. Mother Mary rarely took a decision without consulting those who might advise her well, and certainly never without prayer. In this she was splendidly supported by members of the Society of Jesus and others.

But prayer, it is to be remembered, is not a 'cop out', an escape route to a more serene world. It may confer a deep serenity, but in the words of a great Jewish philosopher.

> Prayer is meaningless unless it is subversive, unless it seeks to overthrow and ruin the pyramids of callousness, hatred, opportunism, falsehood. The liturgical movement must become a revolutionary movement, seeking to overthrow the forces that continue to destroy the promise, the hope, the vision.

I do not suppose that Mary MacKillop was an easy woman to work with, the saints of God rarely are, largely because they challenge us. Without always knowing it they are a judgement on our easy-going ways. But they too suffer.

Mary MacKillop, born in Brunswick Street, Fitzroy, would have appreciated the cartoon which recently appeared in *The Australian*. The scene is of the crucifixion—the women grouped at the foot of the cross. One soldier says to another: 'Where are the twelve apostles?' The other replies: 'It must be ladies' day'.

She would have understood, for she made her first religious vows (or profession) as Sister Mary of the Cross. May she be a great blessing to the Church of which she was a disturbing member, and to the city in which she was born. But I am afraid it will have to be on her terms.

# What are you looking for?
## Service of Induction of Robert Gribben
### Wesley Church, Melbourne, 5 April 1995

*The next day again John was standing with two of his disciples; and he looked at Jesus as he walked, and said, 'Behold, the Lamb of God!' The two disciples heard him say this, and they followed Jesus. Jesus turned, and saw them following, and said to them, What do you seek?' And they said to him, 'Rabbi (which means Teacher), where are you staying?' He said to them, 'Come and see'.*
*John 1: 35-39*

'What are you looking for?' It comes as something of a surprise to note that the first recorded words of Jesus in the Fourth Gospel are this question addressed to two disciples of John the Baptist who are walking behind him: 'What are you seeking?' 'What are you looking for?'

The Gospel has opened with a majestic treatment of the theme, the Word of God. And the opening poem culminates in the brief paragraph studded with the words, 'And the Word became flesh and dwelt among us … and we have beheld his glory … grace came through Jesus Christ … the only Son, who is in the bosom of the Father, he has made him known'. A page or two later in his writing, the Evangelist has John the Baptist identify Jesus, 'Look, the Lamb of God'. Two of his disciples hear him and follow Jesus, who turns around and greets them not as you might expect with a word of revelation, not with one of the great declarations, I am the light of the world or the bread of life: that will come later. No word of disclosure, but a crisp question *Ti Zeteteite*; 'What are you looking for?' An unexpected, but promising, beginning for Jesus' ministry among men and women.

This may be the place to begin a sermon to a congregation on the night when we induct into the ministry of Jesus Christ in this place another preacher of the Gospel. It may be a question put to him, and to you all: 'What are you looking for?' Oh, I know that some time ago you thought about what kind of a minister, and therefore what kind of ministry you want, and you, Robert, will have thought and prayed about the kind of ministry you might be called to exercise. There will have been talk about 'profiles', as I understand is the current word; and you will have been led, and rightly so, to think that what you need in Wesley Church and what Robert Gribben has to offer match: your expectations and his gifts fit each other. The Presbytery has heard those two voices speak, and is met to induct Robert to the ministry here tonight. All necessary, all most desirable, everything done in good order. But tonight will have passed you by unless you hear another voice, the Lord of the Church addressing you both, minister and congregation with that age-old question put to would-be disciples: 'What are you looking for?'

It would be easy at this point to speak in contemporary terms of the problems facing this and other congregations, of the demands to be met by the ministers; and that too is necessary and good. But let us for a few minutes do something other. Let us stay with the text of the Gospel and ask what it says to us.

The would-be disciples were following Jesus, and it was to those who followed him that Jesus turned and addressed his question. This re-iterated 'follow' is not simply a matter of walking along the road after Jesus. The question which is addressed to anyone who comes near Jesus turns mere walking behind him into a discipleship, that is to say a learning from him. As minister and congregation we are not allowed merely to talk about or be near Jesus. We are asked to follow him. To follow him through the story which unfolds in the pages of this Gospel, and to have our expectations changed in the process. To be present with him at the marriage of Cana of Galilee and share its joy as the water of purification is turned into the wine of God's banquet with his people. To be with him when by night Nicodemus comes in the agony of his soul to find the light. To learn with the woman at the well what it means to have thirst quenched by living water. To see him take the official at Capernaum whose child was ill and transform him into the father whose son will live. To go with him to the pool of Bethesda where Jesus will ask of the man paralysed for thirty-eight years the same question, 'What do you want? Do you want to be healed?' and the man pathetically replies: 'There was no-one here to help me'. Sabbath day though it was, Jesus told him to take up his pallet and walk.

So it goes on, the feeding of the multitude with the bread of life, the growing conflict with the authorities, the granting of sight to a man born blind, the raising of Lazarus, the supper with Lazarus and Martha and the anointing of his feet against his burial by Mary, followed soon by his washing of his disciples' feet. To the celebration of a wedding, to the perplexity of the intellectual

Nicodemus, to the woman of Samaria whose life was in tatters, to the frightened official with a sick son, to the helpless man, the hungry crowd and the bereaved family the Word made flesh had gone, and his disciples had followed. Now the disciples must be prepared for what lies ahead of them. *Let not your heart be troubled. Believe in God. Believe also in me.*

His instruction to his disciples ends in prayer—the so-called high priestly prayer of chapter 17. So all our discourse about God must end in our claim upon God, our address to him. I have sometimes heard students talk about God, says Rosenstock-Huessey, in ways that made me feel ashamed. They knew everything there was to know about God but one thing, that he himself was listening. Then he added: they were theological students. The ministry of Jesus to his disciples ends in prayer. So must all our preaching. There is a point at which our talk about God must finish and end in prayer. But how is that approach made possible? Up to this point the disciples had 'followed.' Now they are at that hour of which he had spoken to Peter, 'Where I am going you cannot follow me now; but you shall follow afterwards. '

There is a decisive, determining, before and after the events which are now to occur. In them Jesus stood alone before the High Priest and before Pilate; and in the person of the Roman procurator the kingdoms of this world confront the King of kings who makes no claim to that title but asserts 'For this I was born, and for this I have come into the world, to bear witness to the truth. Everyone who is of the truth hears my voice.' From that point on, as Ernst Käsemann once remarked, Church and State is one of the great themes of human history. You in this city-Church must never forget that. But more important, in that final event was accomplished a new way between God and man, and by man to God. 'It is accomplished. '

In the scenes that lie beyond Golgotha, in the encounters with the risen Lord, there is a strange echo of the opening incident from which we started. When Peter had been reinstated with the command 'Feed my sheep', Jesus added: 'When you were young, you girded yourself and walked where you would; but when you are old, you will stretch out your hands and another will gird you and carry you where you do not wish to go'. And after this he said to him, 'Follow me.'

As at the conclusion of a short story by Chekov, an open road still lies before the disciples. A new beginning: a perpetual, never-ending command to the Church, still to be heard in our old age, and still in the maturity of the Church's life: 'Follow me.'

Let us return to the passage from which we started. When Jesus asked those who were following what they were looking for, it is as though that question loosens their tongues; and the first words ever spoken by a disciple to Jesus were a request to know where he is staying. And his response is to 'Come and see'—an invitation which Philip is to pass on to Nathaniel a little later. 'Where are you staying? dwelling? abiding?' The same Greek word variously translated with different shades of meaning. Where can they go to hear him teach, perhaps? But it goes deeper. 'It is essential to know where Jesus "lives"', says Bultmann, 'for in the place where Jesus is at home, the disciple will also receive his dwelling. '

As this Gospel is to teach us, he was at once here among us and present with the Father. So too we may be at home. To what house, what inn, what dwelling place he took those first disciples we do not know; but through everything that followed his presence with them was assured. And for us too.

> My dear, dear God! I do not know
> What lodg'd thee then, nor where, nor how;
> But I am sure, thou dost now come
> Oft to a narrow, homely room,
> Where thou too hast but the least part,
> My God, I mean *my sinful heart*.[1]

'Why do I write?' asks Isabel Allende, novelist, exiled niece of Chile's assassinated president Salvador Allende. 'Garcia Marquez once said that he writes so that his friends will love him more. I think I write so that people will love each other more.'[2]

What do we preach? And what is it we seek, what do we look for, from the preacher? Certainly it would be good if the end of preaching was that people should love each other more; but I suspect that the great end of preaching, like the great end of Jesus' ministry, is that people should love God more. And even more important than that, that men and women and little children should know that God loves them, that where Jesus dwells—with the Father—there they may be also. That too is the message of the Gospel. Commend it one to another.

[1]  'The Dwelling-Place' by Henry Vaughan (1622-95) in *Silex Scintellans* (1655).
[2]  Isabel Allende, 'Writing as an Act of Hope' in *Paths of Resistance: the Art and Craft of the Political Novel*, edited by William Zinsser (Boston: Houghton Mifflin, 1989).

# Service of Thanksgiving for the Centenary of the Association for the Blind, Wesley Church
## Melbourne, 10 December 1995

**Leviticus 19: 1-4, 9-18**

In the suburb where I now live, it has become the custom of some of the churches that on each Good Friday members of the congregation make their way in procession through the streets. Someone carries a cross, and at intervals the procession stops, at the site of factory or a school, by a busy intersection as the traffic hurries by, in a suburban street, by a block of flats. We are invited to pray for God's blessing on the activity which surrounds us, or does so on other days of the year, for the redemption of our common life, symbolized for Christians in the cross of Christ. It says, as it were, God can be with you, is with you everywhere, redeemingly—if you will but receive him. It is a simple, quiet but moving ceremony.

This year as we moved through the suburb, I noticed that many new houses have been built—some of them privately, some of them public housing, some of them on vacant blocks—infill, I think they call it—some of it where older houses had been demolished, and some of it (regrettably) where previously trees had grown. I found myself asking, Who lives in these houses? In and around this suburb where I now live, who are my new neighbours? Who is my neighbour?

The Dictionary tells me that a neighbour is 'one who lives near or close to another e.g. in an adjoining home, or in the same street or village'. It also tells me that it is used 'more widely, in echoes of biblical passages'. Indeed that is true; but the Dictionary can only define what the word signifies, describe how the word is used. It cannot disclose to me who my neighbour is, what is his or her name, what are their occupations, in what are interested. Do they like to stop for a chat? Or pass by with a nod they of the head? In the Swiss mountains people greet each other as they pass, '*Gruss Gott*'; in Melbourne suburbs, you are lucky if you get a smile. Who is my neighbour?

This is a very old question, as we may have noted as we listened to Rabbi

John Levi read from the nineteenth chapter of the third book of the Law, Leviticus as we call it. It is part of what some scholars call the Law of Holiness. It tells how the Israelites are to behave one to another, and to outsiders; but it has long been taken as a picture of a civilized society from which any community could learn. In its original setting, the section read to us ended:

'You shall love your neighbour as yourself: I am the Lord.'

This is not just a piece of good advice. This is a commandment of God, an essential condition for living: 'You shall love your neighbour as yourself'.

The passage has disclosed to us the neighbour: in a number of settings we learn who he or she is. The neighbour is the poor man or woman who has no farm of their own, no way of earning bread; so when you reap the harvest, leave gleanings after you have brought in the grain. The same with the grapes: the poor, or the traveler—the one who is just passing through to whom you might be thought to have no obligations—should find something left for their refreshment. Don't imagine that you have to get everything you can out of life, for yourself; remember that there are others, less favourably placed than you may be. Pause, and be generous. There is a great difference between the world envisaged here and the one in which efficiency is equated with employing as few people as possible, with no teacher's aids to look after the slow-learning child or the one with disabilities: the aim to get as many children as possible to complete the course with efficiency. About the gleanings of the harvest for the slow or the deprived child; little is said. The same with health, and with many of our services: we cannot afford to be generous, 'efficiency' or 'good management' as it is called will not allow it.

So we could go on through this passage, seeing afresh who is our neighbour: the hired servant who is to be paid her wages when they are due, so that she may decide what to do with them. The payment is not to remain in the hand of the employer as though the employee's entitlement was a gracious gift by the employer, to give or withhold. The employer and those who work for him are neighbours: one is to regard the interest of the other as he or she would his or her own interest. Dangerous stuff this; but the condition of civilized living. No one must want to destroy their neighbour, neither financially, nor by slander, by reducing their reputation. And it is specially important to remember that there are people with disabilities. 'You shall not curse the deaf'. It is so easy to be impatient with a deaf person. Or 'put a stumbling block before the blind': it is equally easy to forget to make access to public places easier; a society can be unthinkingly, unintentionally callous.

And within the structure of the courts, society must acknowledge that there is no distinction to be made between the rich and the poor. There must not be one law for the rich and another for the poor. The law must be impartial, and recourse to it must be open to all. Again easily said, but frequently ignored; and as we know, those with political power can deny access to the courts to omit those with little or no power between elections, and as we also know it is much easier to be well-represented in court if you have lots of money than if you have only a little.

So we could go on, and learn from this passage again and again that neighbourliness is not only a matter of how I recognise or behave towards the neighbours in my suburb, it also has to do with how we order our public life. To what do we give priority? How do we regard each other there? Any society which ignores the lessons of this ancient law of Israel does so at its peril. This is not just a historical curiosity. 'You shall love your neighbour as yourself. I am the Lord.' It is a divine command. This afternoon we meet to celebrate with thanksgiving one hundred years of service to blind Victorians, through the Association for the Blind, founded by Tilly Aston. About that, and within the context of what we have observed from the passage in the book of Leviticus, let me briefly try to say three things.

The Association is a vivid example of one of the good things that has happened to our society in the past one hundred years. It is an example of that widening of an understanding of 'neighbour' of which the Dictionary spoke. My neighbour is not only the man or woman who has recently moved into my suburb, or my street, and whose name I do not know. He, she, is everywhere around me in the community in which I live, in the global village about which publicists are so fond of telling us we all live. We must not turn back the clock. The other man or woman is not there outside us for us to exploit. He, she is there to be served. The world has become more aware of that in the last one hundred years than ever before. The cry of your Association must be: do not turn back, but go forward into a new century of service. In a day of increasing competition between people for greater material comforts, of increasing preoccupation for self-satisfaction, you rightly take a deep breath and start again on a new century of service.

Secondly, there is one important thing we learn from that last hundred years. It can be put in the words of Richard Titmuss, social administrator and thinker. The question to which we have to draw people's attention is not simply 'Who is my neighbour'? but hidden within it is another question 'Who is your stranger?' For many centuries, and in too many places still, the elderly, the blind, many others with one limitation or another have been thrust to the margins of our society. Writing about the elderly, Abraham Joshua Heschel, a distinguished Jewish philosopher of a previous generation, has said: 'What we owe the old is reverence, but all they ask for is consideration, attention, not to be discarded, forgotten'.

Blind Bartimaeus in the Gospel story cried out to the passing Jesus to have mercy on him. Many rebuked him and told him to be silent. That is typical of human societies everywhere and in every age: we want to pretend that those with disabilities, like the frail, the elderly do not exist. Fortunately for him, blind Bartimaeus cried out all the more. The blind in the community, yes and the rest of us, owe much to Tilly Aston who would not, could not be silenced; and what was said by her in organisation was supplemented by what she said in verse. So, many confronted with the question 'Who is my stranger'? found in the other man or woman 'my neighbour'.

This leads me to the third thing I want to say. Titmuss who writes much about what he calls 'the gift relationship', the attitude of service, also says that you have never completed your service until you have helped the one served to see that he or she also has something to give. Louis Braille showed us that blindness was not only a condition which he had to suffer, but was also an opportunity to open up to his fellows a way whereby the blind may read. Three hundred and eighty seven years ago yesterday, on 9 December 1608 there was born in London one of the most celebrated Englishmen to be afflicted with blindness, and that in a day when there was little to soothe physical pain. His blindness to some degree distanced him from the political preoccupations of his youth, and delivered him from polemical writings, but he gave himself so as to become one of the greatest of English poets, perhaps more than a poet, as he prays:

> So much the rather thou celestial Light
> Shine inward, and the mind through all her powers
> Irradiate, there plant yes, all mist from thence
> Purge and disperse, that I may see and tell
> Of things invisible to mortal sight.

Which of us coming away from a time spent with a friend struck with blindness has not felt that we have been the receivers of a special blessing? Our friend has listened more carefully than we are wont to do, has been grateful for the warmth of the sun, where we (accustomed to its light) have omitted to observe its other blessings.

May God bless you all, one to another, in the days and decades, as the new century opens before you.

# Each Other's Stories— Telling and Listening

## The Inaugural St Thomas Lecture
## Wyndham Chapter
## Council for Christians and Jews
## 4 July 1999

Sometimes we hear two sides to a story.

Professor John Baillie, a distinguished Scottish Presbyterian theologian, told me of how Martin Buber's book *Ich und Du* (I and Thou) came to be translated into English. Martin Buber was born in Vienna in 1878, was brought up in Germany, and was Professor of Jewish History and Religion at Frankfurt University from 1923 until deprived of the Chair by the Nazis in 1933. In 1938 he was called to the Chair of Sociology at the Hebrew University of Jerusalem. He died in Israel in 1965. Through his long and productive life he became enormously influential with both Jewish and Christian thinkers. In 1923 he published in German a relatively small book which was to become one of the classical philosophical writings of the 20th century, its title *Ich und Du*. It was from that book that Professor Baillie quoted a section to his class in Edinburgh in 1936 or 1937. In a way that Professors do, he remarked in an aside 'someone should translate this book into English. It would be a great service to us all.'

At the end of the class a young man came forward and asked if he might borrow the book. The Professor had no idea that this young man read German, but lent him the book. Imagine his surprise when a week later the student brought him some pages of English translation and asked Baillie if this would do. Professor Baillie told me 'I did not want to alter a single word.' So, in 1937, *Ich und Du* appeared in English, and was launched on its influential way.[1] Professor Baillie continued to quote Buber, to commend him to his students, and indeed reference is made to Buber's thought in Baillie's Gifford Lectures published post-

---

[1]  Martin Buber, *I and Thou*, English Translation by R.Gregor Smith (Edinburgh: T & T Clark, 1937).

humously in 1962.[2] (John Baillie died in September 1960, leaving in completed form the manuscript of these lectures.)

The young student who translated *Ich und Du* in 1936-37 was Ronald Gregor Smith, who after the War became managing director and editor of SCM Press and subsequently Professor of Divinity in Glasgow University. When we lived in London for seven years after the War Ronald Gregor Smith and his wife became close friends with my wife and me. For a short period we were colleagues; and the Gregor Smiths visited us after we came to Australia where Ronnie gave a notable course of lectures published under the title, The New Man.[3] Sadly Ronnie died in 1968. But I was able to observe the effect of that incident upon him in the Edinburgh classroom in 1936. Ronnie translated more of Buber's work, he interpreted Buber to the English-speaking world, he incorporated Buber's thought into his own theological writing. When we were working together in London, Buber visited. He, the older Jewish philosopher and Gregor Smith the young Presbyterian theologian had become friends. Ronnie wrote a most satisfying and illuminating, albeit brief study of Buber.[4]

So I had the privilege of observing three very remarkable men influencing each other.

Now, what has all this got to do with the topic which I offered for this afternoon "Each Other's Stories—telling and listening"? Well, I hope something. I would just ask you to bear that story in mind while I weave what I want to say around three other books all by a very different person from the three who appear in that opening anecdote. The figure to whom I would introduce you now—if you do not have the good fortune already to know her—is Eva Hoffman.

# 1

You will have noticed that the anecdote with which I opened this lecture hinged on a translation: how Buber's *Ich und Du* came to be translated into English. At the time of his death Buber was, along with a colleague, engaged on a fresh translation of the Hebrew Bible into German. The title of Eva Hoffman's first book to appear in English is *Lost in Translation*.[5] I shall return to that in a mo-

---

[2] John Baillie *The Sense of the Presence of God*. Gifford Lectures 1961-62 (London: Oxford University Press, 1962).

[3] Ronald Gregor Smith *The New Man: Christianity and Man's Coming of Age*, The Alexander Love Lectures 1955 (London: SCM Press, 1956).

[4] Ronald Gregor Smith, *Martin Buber* (London: The Carey Kingsgate Press, 1966).

[5] Eva Hoffman, *Lost in Translation: a Life in a New Language* (London: Heinemann, 1989).

ment, and to the pun implied. Immediately, however, let us recognize the wide-spread way in which our understanding of each other across frontiers depends upon good translation. When I was young, translations of significant literary works were always assumed to be inferior to the original. Today we are not so sure about that. It is part of the good heritage from the Reformation of Christianity in the 16th and 17th centuries that the Hebrew and Greek Scriptures were translated into German, French and English at a very fine point in the history of those languages. The editor of the recently published *Selected Poems* in English translation of Goethe has remarked:

> Translating a poem is not quite the imaginative act of writing one. All the same, the synthesis of possibilities for which a translator settles is derived from his judgment as a feature of his linguistic imagination.[6]

The imagination is at work in each case, in that of the original writer and of the translator. Attempts to produce literal translations only result in banality. By imagination is understood the power to recognize that there is more in front of us than meets the eye. If I am to express in another's language what is there before us in Hebrew or Greek 1 must meditate on what lies before me on the page.

It is not for nothing that so much in the Scriptures, Hebrew and Greek, has come to us in poetic form, sometimes indeed as poetry: the psalms of course, but also prophetic oracles, parables which are small prose poems, groups of wise sayings, fairy tales and legends. Narratives are there, to be sure, that draw the reader along 'to the end of the line', but also the intensive poetic or quasi-poetic forms which hold us up and compel us to reflect, to meditate. This is a very distinctive kind of listening, of hearing each other's story. It controls, or should control the way in which we read and hear the Torah, the Scriptures, in Synagogue or Church. The reading, and the hearing, should be meditative.

But let me return to Eva Hoffman's first book, *Lost in Translation,* which uses the word not only about moving a statement out of one language to another, but also about what happens to people when you move them from one place to another, when you translate them from one country or culture or social setting to another. *Lost in Translation* is an outstanding work of autobiography. Eva Hoffman tells the story of her own early life. Born in Cracow of Jewish-Polish parents, at the age of thirteen with her parents and her young sister she left Poland for Canada where she completed her secondary education and won a

---

[6] Johann Wolfgang von Goethe: *Selected Poems* in German and English (Goethe's Collected Works, Volume I), edited by Christopher Middleton (Princeton: Princeton University Press, 1994).

scholarship to an American university in Texas. She moved in North American intellectual circles in Texas, at Harvard and in New York and was for a period an editor of the *New York Times Book Review*. Throughout her writing she never ceases to reflect on the immigrant's problem of translation: how can she explain to her North American contemporaries what it was like to grow up in Poland in the years immediately after World War II, and what it was like to be in Eastern Europe, a Jew and not a communist. Similarly, when she returns on a visit to Poland how can she explain to her childhood friends the attitudes which characterize her contemporaries in North America? And similarly, again, how to maintain meaningful conversation with her parents and her sister who now increasingly seem to live in different worlds and use different vocabularies to describe it. Some of the most poignant as well as amusing passages describe her mother's bewilderment in this new world. Running like a subterranean stream through her narrative lies the search for a knowledge and a speech that will close the gap between her upbringing as a member of a Jewish family in Poland and her adult life in a hitherto unimagined secular society in North America. Exploring that subterranean stream she writes:

> It is possible that when we travel deep enough, we always encounter an element of sadness, for full awareness of ourselves always includes the knowledge of our own ephemerality and the passage of time. But it is only in that knowledge—not its denial—that things gain their true dimensions, and we begin to feel the simplicity of being alive. It is only that knowledge that is large enough to cradle a tenderness for everything that is always to be lost - a tenderness for each of our moments, for others and for the world.[7]

If the sad story of Jew *vis-à-vis* the secular world of the 20th century issues in that, if the story of Christian *vis-à-vis* Jew over many centuries can pass through—not pass around—that sadness to issue in a tenderness 'for others and for the world', then all will not have been utterly lost. As we all know, grief, sadness can issue in bitterness or resentment; but, as Eva Hoffman puts it, the knowledge it brings us of our ephemeral nature and the passage of time may provide a cradle large enough to contain a tenderness for everything—'for each of our moments, for others, and for the world'.

# 2

It is now long past the time to move to the second of Eva Hoffman's books, and its character too is suggested by a central thought of Martin Buber. Buber, as is

---

[7] Eva Hoffman, *Lost in Translation,* 274.

well known, broke with the tradition of philosophical thought which stressed the importance of objectifying, measuring the object to be investigated. Our dealings one with another often have the character of transactions that can be measured in, say, monetary terms; but not all, and not the most important of our dealings. Some things, some relationships are immeasurably rich or valuable, we say. Reality discloses itself in what Buber calls 'meeting' *Begegnung*. Some years ago Dr J H Oldham took up Buber's phrase 'Real life is Meeting' as the title of a series of essays that he had written. He abandoned the phrase when Christopher Dawson suggested how awful the thought if you added an 's', 'real life is meetings'! Buber himself makes clear that there are three portals (or doorways) to this life: the life with nature; the life with other people; the life with spiritual existences. Buber indeed added a Postscript to *I and Thou* in 1957:

> God's speech to men penetrates what happens in the life of each one of us, and all that happens in the world around us, biographical and historical, and makes it for you and me into instruction, message, demand.[8]

It is with that understanding that I commend to you Eva Hoffman's second book, *Exit into History*.[9] In 1990 and then again in 1991 Eva Hoffman made journeys from the Baltic to the Black Sea, listening to the stories told by people who had lived through the period of Soviet Russian dominance, and through the time of so-called liberation, of coming to terms with the ways of western Europe. She visited Poland, Czechoslovakia, Hungary, Romania, and Bulgaria. She gives us little if anything in the way of statistics, or even of historical background or social analysis—just accounts of conversations, how people found it all, what they said and what questions she asked. Here is a rich record of what Buber could have called 'meeting' in which reality is found.

It is not possible to quote without distorting: you cannot see the whole tapestry if you cut out a small section. Yet some phrases may give an impression of what the reader is likely to find if he or she applies serious attention to the whole tale. From Poland:

> Like so much of the Polish economy, the shipyard is caught between two systems—rotting Communism and raw Capitalism' (p. 61);

> 'there are no new restraints yet, either of law or etiquette, on managerial imperiousness' (p. 104).

One wonders whether Poland is the only country of which that could be said,

---

8  See R G Smith, *Martin Buber*, p. 20.
9  Eva Hoffman, *Exit into History: A Journey Through the New Eastern Europe*, Heinemann, Minerva Edition, London 1991.

the only society in which managerial imperiousness may be found.

From Pavel of Romania (not to be confused with Vaclav Pavel of Czecho-slovakia. This Pavel has participated in acts of terror and oppression in the past for which he now accepts responsibility and acknowledges guilt):

> There's no way for anyone to say to Pavel "It's all right" [comments Eva Hoffman]; the circumstances in which he was involved were too awful for that, the complicity too deep. And yet, as I listen to him, it seems to me that he has also achieved something large. Through wrestling with his angels and demons, he has converted the terrible events of his life into the stuff of consciousness and conscience—that is, a form of experience that might prove instructive in thinking about the future—into a fragment of a usable past.' (p. 289)

There is not time to quote more; but one thing we might observe about Hoffman's second book. Whereas the first book had been autobiographical, predominantly about herself and her experience of 'translation' as an immigrant, as a Jew, the second book is predominantly about the dilemmas in which the human race at least in the northern hemisphere, but predominantly in what was previously the communist world, finds itself at the end of the 20th century. The collapse of the Soviet empire has disclosed to us the fragility of other forms of so-called civilized institutions—and that situation may have become worse since Hoffman wrote that book.

## 3

Hoffman's third book, entitled *Shtetl*[10] occupies a middle ground between the individual and the total community. It tells the story of a village in Poland, the village of Bransk, east of Warsaw, not many miles from the Belarussian border. It tells the story of how for centuries that village was occupied more or less peace-fully by Polish Jew and Polish Catholic. At least there was some accommodation between the two communities. But all that was brought to an end by the occu-pation of Poland by the Nazis, and by the Holocaust, the Shoah. The Jews sim-ply (but certainly not simply but calculatedly) disappeared.

The word *Shtel*, the title of the book, is a diminutive form of a Yiddish word for town. Taking account of the long history of Jews in Poland, Eva Hoffman sets out to trace the story of the relation between Jews and other Poles, mostly Catholic, in that village. Characteristically she sought out people who had lived,

---

[10] Eva Hoffman, *Shtetl the Life and Death of a Small Town and the World of Polish Jews* (London: Secker and Warburg, 1998).

or still lived in Bransk, and from their stories and from historical records builds up her picture. The sub-title of the book aptly summarizes its contents: 'the life and death of a small town and the world of Polish Jews'.

A recurring theme is that of 'otherness'. 'The Jews', she writes in her first chapter, sketching a long historical background, 'were Europe's archetypal Other, but they were never completely absent or unfamiliar'; and then tracing the more immediate background, 'The Poles were the Jews' radical Other, just as much as the other way around. Of course, there was a crucial asymmetry ... The Jews were the minority; they knew they were in their host country as invited guests at best, on sufferance at worst'.

There is neither time, nor on my part competence, to summarize a delicate and beautifully presented verbal picture. But here is material for meditation on one of the critical questions to be faced in many parts of the world at the end of the 20th and the beginning of the 21st century—not least in Australia. In country after country groups have settled, moved in bringing with them their customs and their religion: they appear to those already there to be 'Other'. For them, but not only for them the questions are: How is identity to be maintained, and how are cultural traditions cherished? How are differences to be respected and maintained and conflicts avoided? I have great sympathy for Eva Hoffman who, towards the end of her third book writes: 'One hesitates to speak of lessons or to derive conclusions in a terrain where pieties are easier to come by than wisdom'.

Nevertheless I risk two suggestions to this Chapter of the Council for Christians and Jews.

The first is that we learn afresh, as this really rather terrible 20th century draws to its close, how in Eva Hoffman's phrase, to turn its events into the stuff of consciousness and conscience, so that the long and often unhappy story of the relations between Jew and Christian may become a fragment of a usable past. That story can come to us in many literary forms—much of it from the hands of some very great writers. I have only touched on the fringe of it this afternoon. I have scarcely touched, for instance, on that great literature that we have in common, the Hebrew Scriptures—what Christians call the Old Testament. I sometimes think that Jews and Christians and adherents of Islam should make a pact wherein we say that we will not cease to be peoples of the book. We shall not allow ourselves to be drawn into being the people of the video or of the internet.

The second suggestion, and my last point, is this: do not let us forget Buber's word about meeting (*Begegnung*). That is what you have undertaken to do in this Chapter, meet and learn from each other.

> 'I believe', wrote Buber at a rather grim moment after World War II, 'despite all, that the peoples in this hour can enter into dialogue, into a genuine dialogue with one another. In a genuine dialogue each of the partners, even when he stands in opposition to the other, heeds, affirms and confirms his opponent as an existing other.'

Recognition may then occur in most unexpected places; but we should be ready for it anywhere. Ronald Gregor Smith tells of an incident, which he had heard from Buber himself.

> Buber had just returned from a visit to the United States of America, and was full of his impressions. He told me a little story of his journey across New York City in a taxicab. The driver was talkative, and the following dialogue ensued:
>
> Driver: I have been reading an article by a strange fellow. He says that you shouldn't be angry, but should solve your differences by being patient and seeking peace with the other person.
>
> Buber: I agree
>
> Driver: He was a strange man, 700 years old.
>
> Buber: A great age.
>
> Driver: Yes. His name was Francis.
>
> Buber: I know him too. I can tell you a lot of stories about him.

So they talked of Francis, and finally Buber was deposited at the bookstore he wished to visit. The driver departed, and some time later, when the taxi was long gone, Buber noticed that he had lost his spectacle-case. Before he had time to do anything about it, the driver reappeared, spectacle-case in hand. 'Good boy,' said Buber; and before all the people the driver leant his head for a moment on Buber's shoulder, and thus they embraced.'[11]

---

[11] R G Smith, *Martin Buber*, 8.

# The Foundations:
# Prayer and Obedience

*This essay was prepared as a lecture to introduce a course on spiritual theology planned and supervised by Fr Noel J Ryan SJ in the mid-seventies for the United Faculty of Theology in Melbourne. It subsequently appeared with lectures by other contributors in a volume edited by Fr Ryan entitled Christian Spiritual Theology published in 1976 by Dove Communications, Melbourne, with whose permission it is reproduced here.*

*I cannot think of any place where I would prefer to begin a collection of theological writings than in a reflection guided by a father of the Church on prayer and obedience. These are the foundations on which other intellectual activities must be built. Nor can I think of any company in which I would prefer to be found than that of ecumenical scholars and churchmen whose names will be found in the table of contents of that volume. In one way or another I have learnt something from almost every one of them.*

It would be appropriate to begin this study of Christian spiritual theology by reading a prayer. It would be even more appropriate to pray a prayer. We offer, therefore, as the first note to be struck, three extracts from the prayers of one man. First, the preparation:

> Come now, little man,
> turn aside for a while from your daily employment,
> escape for a moment from the tumult of your thoughts.
> Put aside your weighty cares,
> let your burdensome distractions wait,
> free yourself awhile for God
> and rest awhile in him.
> Enter the inner chamber of your soul,
> shut out everything except God

and that which can help you in seeking him,
and when you have shut the door, seek him.
Now, my whole heart, say to God,
'I seek your face,
Lord, it is your face I seek.'

That, we may assume, is the heart of spiritual theology: to shut the door and say, 'I seek your face, Lord, it is your face I seek.' How does one do that? Before we can answer there is a presupposition, which is found in the second extract:

Teach me to seek you,
and as I seek you, show yourself to me,
for I cannot seek you unless you show me how,
and I will never find you
unless you show yourself to me.
Let me seek you by desiring you,
and desire you by seeking you;
let me find you by loving you,
and love you in finding you.

It may be thought that this is a shade too individualistic, perhaps even encouraging of pietism: but the third extract carries the enterprise out and shows its part in the great design of theology:

Lord, I am not trying to make my way to your height,
for my understanding is in no way equal to that,
but I do desire to understand a little of your truth
which my heart already believes and loves.
I do not seek to understand so that I may believe,
but I believe so that I may understand;
and what is more,
I believe that unless I do believe I shall not understand.

# 1

These are extracts from the first chapter of St Anselm's *Proslogion*[1] the remarkable writing in which prayer and theology are one. The extracts, and the longer treatment of the subject in which they are found, provide a useful starting point for a number of reasons, including the following:

---

[1] The translation is that of Sister Benedicta Ward, S.L.G., from *The Prayers and Meditations of St. Anselm*, Penguin Books, 1973, of which the Introduction, esp. pp. 51-82 should also be read.

(i) However unpopular it may be to say so today, theology is reflection; and that first in the sense that it demands time for reflection and a disciplined use of that time. All talk about spiritual exercises, the three ways or stages, of deepening union with the subject of theology, the Christ, are but suggestions on how that time for reflection is to be used. 'This taking oneself aside in order to have leisure for God is one of the great themes of medieval monasticism,' writes Sister Benedicta Ward; but time for thought that passes into prayer, and for prayer that passes into thought, and for prayer and thought which pass into love, is necessary for theological activity in any era or place. Spiritual theology provides a constant reminder to every other theological discipline of the need for just such leisure. The point has frequently been made that Anselm wrote his earlier works, and indeed produced all his writings, in a life whose framework was that of the monastic hours, of prayer and of meditation; and his own prayers and meditations make it clear that the disciplined monastic life was no mere formal or conventional frame; prayer was the condition of appropriate thought and speech about God.[2] The papers in this book point to many periods in which that has been the case, and raise the question of whether this condition still obtains in our day. If it does, what is the appropriate manner for us to undertake theology reflectively?

(ii) We are reminded by the second extract that theology is reflection in the sense that it is response. Unless God shows himself, there is no possibility of finding him. But that engagement has already taken place. To adapt a well-known saying: we would not be seeking unless we had already been found. Spiritual theology assumes the reality of prayer: there would not be any search for God, if he had not already quickened in us a desire for communion with him. Spiritual theology not only describes this reality, and deepens awareness of it, but also tries to interpret or explain it. Anselm elsewhere dismisses theological activity which denies or even questions the Church's affirmation of faith, as 'no better than bats and owls squabbling with eagles about the reality of the beams of the midday sun'.[3] We would perhaps want to allow a more significant

---

[2] Cf. John McIntyre: "We dare not dismiss unthinkingly ... anyone who prays as Anselm prays ... and who makes his theology a prayer." From *St Anselm, and his Critics*, (Edinburgh: Oliver and Boyd, 1954), 16, as quoted by Sister Benedicta.

[3] A remark from *the Epistle concerning the Incarnation*, quoted with approval more than once by Karl Barth in his celebrated *Anselm: Fides Quaerens Intellectum*, English translation (London: SCM Press, 1960).

place for the critical assessment of what occurs in prayer: but we do well to remember that theology proceeds from a previously given reality. That reality is the engagement of God with humanity, or at least the alleged association of the two. Spiritual theology, whatever may be the case with other theological disciplines, must begin with people praying: and Christian spiritual theology with Christian people praying, with the union of Christ with his followers.

In a notable passage in his *Church Dogmatics* Karl Barth discusses what he calls 'the goal of vocation', that perfect fellowship of Christians with Christ for which 'the terms "attachment" and "co-ordination" are inadequate in that they are not expressly understood in the sense of "union" i.e. the Christian's *unio cum Christo*.' After asserting that Jesus Christ is the unique one who unites himself with man. Barth goes on to say:

> But as this One . . . He cannot and will not remain alone, nor can He be solitary in the reconciled world on His way to His future, conclusive and universal revelation. He cannot and will not be the Master without disciples, the Leader without followers, the Head without His own, Christ without Christians . . . He does not go alone but wills to be what He is and do what He does in company with others whom He calls for the purpose, namely, with the despicable folk called Christians.[4]

Spiritual theology has to do with this union of Christ with his people, under its different aspects, with the reflection of his life in their lives, with the response of their wills to his will, with their hopes and fears, their contrition and their aspirations.

(iii) The third extract, and indeed the setting of the prayer in the *Proslogion*, reminds us that the task of spiritual theology is not merely to encourage the individual to pursue a special vocation of prayer, but rather to make its contribution to the total task of theology. The grand design is to show how men and women are to know, to speak of and to love God; how the human race is to become aware of the Eternal God, who is the very ground of our existence, the Creator and Fulfiller of our lives. It is not necessary for our present purpose to determine whether Anselm's method leads more directly to the rational argument of Aquinas or to the denial of natural theology by Barth. It is probably wise to accept Dr

---

[4] Karl Barth, *Church Dogmatics*, IV. 3. 2 (540-1).

Charlesworth's judicious treatment of that debate in his *St Anselm's Proslogion*,[5] and agree with Professor McIntyre that 'St Anselm antedates all our labels',[6] but this only makes it more important to recognize the part to be played by prayer and the discipline of the spiritual life in the whole process or 'understanding' our faith. Today that understanding needs strengthening and correction among those who are inside the faith; it also need to be commended as to its validity to those who are outside. In both cases understanding is unlikely to grow unless those who hold and argue for the faith can demonstrate that their discourse is not only among themselves, or with the world of contemporary thought, but is also an engagement with One who has already engaged their interest and attention. Theology must once more be seen to be a disciplined response to questions which theologians do not so much ask as they are asked. Theologians can only lead men and women to understanding if they themselves trying to understand what they believe, are trying to bring into articulation what is inarticulate, into present experience what has hitherto been remote. For theology to regain its relevance and cogency theologians must again and again become men and women of prayer. The study of spiritual theology may well begin by making that demand of its students, even though its task will not finish there.

## 2

If the first pillar on which a spiritual theology rests is prayer, the second is obedience. Here we may take as our norm the call of Jesus to discipleship. This theme has been very fully explored in recent years by Professor Eduard Schweizer, not only in his monograph *Lordship and Discipleship*[7] but also in his commentaries on Mark and Matthew.[8] It would now be accepted widely among New Testament scholars that the call to discipleship was reproduced by the Gospel-writers not merely out of an historical interest in the relation of Jesus to his first followers but as a call to people in every age to follow him Again and again that

---

[5] (Oxford: Clarendon Press, 1965).

[6] John MacIntyre, 'Cur deus-homo: The axis of the argument' in *Sola Ratione: Anselm - Studien für Pater Dr h.c. Franciscus Salesius Schmitt OSB*, Stuttgart-Bad Cannstatt: Kohlenberger, 1970.

[7] English translation (London: 1960).

[8] In the series Das Neue Testament Deutsch; *Das Evangelium nach Markus*, (Gottingen: Vandenhoeck & Ruprecht 1967), English translation. (London: SPCK, 1971). *Das Evangelium nach Matthaus*, (Gottingen: Vandenhoeck & Ruprecht 1973).

following is represented as costly; it involves leaving home and customary occupation (Mark 1:16-20), it may require a neglect of pious duties (Matt 8:21-22) or it may put someone back into the place of fulfilment of domestic duty (Luke 8:39). But one thing is clear; the call to follow Jesus is of supreme importance.

Perhaps no passage from the Gospels has been so influential and controversial in its contribution to the ascetic element in spiritual theology as the story of the Rich Man who came to Jesus and asked how to gain eternal life (Mark 10:17-31 and parallels). He is reminded of the Law, with special reference to its second table—duties towards neighbour; and he protests that he has kept these from his youth. 'You lack one thing', says the Jesus of Mark, or 'If you would be perfect', as Matthew puts it, 'go sell what you have and give to the poor, and you will have treasure in heaven; and come follow me'. Professor Hans von Campenhausen has taken this incident as the starting point for his study 'Early Christian Asceticism.'[9] Antony the Egyptian, the first monk, understood these words as pointing to the way of life which he must follow and literally sold everything he had and adopted an ascetic way of life. Countless others have heard the same summons in these words, and made the same response. Before Antony's day the question of the Christian's attitude to riches had been asked and answered again and again. Within the New Testament, as Dr von Campenhausen shows, Luke in particular offers us a 'theology of poverty'. Later, Clement of Alexandria was to argue that property is morally neutral. 'Jesus was concerned with setting the heart free and with a renewal of the interior disposition.' Jesus' words are not to be taken literally: they mean no more than that we are not to put our trust in riches.

It may argued that both Antony and Clement were wrong in their interpretation of the passage. The Gospels do not provide us with 'universally valid norms of Christian conduct' which can be applied either inwardly through adopting the appropriate frame of mind or outwardly through the adoption of an ascetic way of life. The Gospels transmit to us the call of Jesus to discipleship, and attach to that call a series of reminders that obedience is likely to be costly, and costly in real terms. Antony was more fully perceptive here than Clement: the Gospel, and response to it, cannot be spiritualized or applied only to the interior life. Neither can its more severe demands be understood as applying to a few who have a special vocation to holiness. It has, for instance, sometimes been suggested that Matthew's variation, 'If you would be perfect', provides the sanction for a double standard, as though there are some who are called to a perfection which is denied to the many. It is to be remembered however, that

---

[9] English translation in *Tradition and Life in the Church* (London: Collins, 1960).

behind the 'perfect' of Matthew (see, too, 5:48, the only other occurrence in the Synoptic Gospels) lies the Old Testament *tamin*, 'irreproachable before God'. What is at stake is the rich man's relation to God, not his own moral perfection. In either case the only appropriate reaction is that of the disciples, 'Who then can be saved?'; and the ground of hope is in the word of Jesus: 'All things are possible with God'.

This conclusion is not intended to rob the story of its demand upon the conscience of the reader, but to give it its true context in the Gospel of grace. The story remains a reminder of the truth asserted again and again by Dietrich Bonhoeffer: there is no such thing as cheap grace.

It is not part of this introduction to trace the story of Christian obedience. In magisterial fashion Dr von Campenhausen has traced the early history of asceticism in three areas: Christian attitudes to property, to abstinence from food and drink, and to the renunciation of the sexual life. The very different positions adopted on these by different Christian groups points not to indifferentism; on the contrary, their history indicates the seriousness with which Christians have taken the demand to 'give up' the good things of life, if that is for them a part of the cost of discipleship. A theology which fails to inform the Church of this story neglects something central to the understanding of the Christian message. The taking up of the cross and the denying of oneself are essential conditions of Christian discipleship, and therefore the understanding of what this has meant, means and may yet mean for the Christian community is a proper and necessary ingredient in spiritual theology.

# 3

On these two pillars, then, prayer and obedience, is built any spiritual theology worthy of the name. At their extremes, perhaps prayer and obedience become 'mysticism' and 'asceticism', and a fully developed spiritual theology will have to take account of both these phenomena. Spiritual theology is, however, better thought of as concerned primarily with the middle ground: it points not to special or unusual phenomena but to the terms on which every man draws near to God. Prayer and obedience are indeed ways of knowing him.

It would be tempting, and much easier, to adopt another approach. This would be to argue that prayer and obedience flow from faith, since they are not its precondition. But this will not stand investigation. Even our cursory glance at St Anselm's prayer shows the interrelatedness of prayer, and faith: they grow together.

Let me seek you by desiring you,
and desire you be seeking you,
let me find you by loving you,
and love you in finding you.

If, as is manifestly the case in some of the New Testament writings, the act of faith can be described in terms of following Jesus, of discipleship, then the cost of the enterprise must be regarded as a part of the response to the invitation to follow. Not the least of Professor Bultmann's contributions to our understanding of Paul has been his insistence on the ingredient of obedience in the act of faith.

It is timely to be reminded of the centrality of a spiritual theology which examines the place of prayer and obedience in Christian thought and practice. The danger of polarisation within the Christian community is ever-present. Today we observe a tendency to divide. We have the charismatics on the one hand for whom the experience is an end in itself; and the revolutionaries on the other for whom the giving is all. Prayer is not, however, the end; it is a part of life on the way. The end is the vision and knowledge of God, incomplete as long as life lasts; and, for the Church, as long as time and history last there is the witness to be borne. Prayer has to do with that life *in via*: we are on the way, and have not yet reached the promised end. Similarly the giving is not all, but the following until the end is reached. Christian faith and obedience can no more be subsumed into the revolutionary response or be simply equated with the giving of self to any earthly cause than they can be seen as contained in their entirety in the ecstatic experience of heaven now. Christian spiritual theology, then, speaks, out of the richness of the Christian tradition, a word of correction and hope equally to those who have their longing for God satisfied in a charismatic experience and to those whose compassion leads them to identify God's will *tout court* with the delivery of the oppressed. It will delineate something of what it means to say, in words already quoted from Barth, that Christ 'cannot and will not remain alone, nor can he be solitary in the reconciled world on his way to his future, conclusive and universal revelation'. The life of Christ with 'the despicable folk called Christians' will be its constant theme.

# 4

Nowhere are the themes of spiritual theology woven together more subtly than in Matthew's arrangement of material in the Sermon on the Mount. Here we find, as it were, the New Testament warrant for our whole enterprise. It is therefore worth recalling the structure of Matthew 5:1-6:18.

As is well known, the sermon opens with the Beatitudes (5:1-12), which declare the blessedness of those who, when the kingly rule of God breaks upon them, are aware only of their own unqualified poverty and need, and of the sorrow, turmoil and injustice of the world around them. These are the pious or righteous sufferers of the Psalms who expect nothing from themselves but wait upon God. God and the world fill their horizons: there is no place of distinction for the individual or corporate self.

In the long section 5:21-6:18 there is set forth the hidden righteousness and piety of those who thus, in grace, receive the kingdom. In the great series of antitheses in 5:21-48 we are taught that life in the kingdom cannot be measured in terms of outward observation of the law. The law's demands are radically applied: in the inner disposition and quality of the heart God is accepted or rejected as King. So radical is this that it ceases to be law. As William Manson used to say: 'The Sermon on the Mount is not the Christian law; but the Christian accepts no other law.' The way of discipleship is costly (as Bonhoeffer stresses in his monograph on the subject).[10] Here the Christian returns for refreshment and judgment. Here he is thrown back on the mercy of God. He knows that by himself he can achieve nothing.

In 6:1-18 the same radical treatment is given to the traditional acts of piety: almsgiving, prayer, fasting. They are to be performed, but hiddenly. As Bonhoeffer remarks, we like to say our prayers and hear them also. And since we have done so God will not hear them. We have had our reward. Again, God and those in need should be our whole concern. We ourselves are nothing.

Between the Beatitudes and the delineation of true obedience and true prayer, Matthew puts the saying about salt and light (5:13-16). He opens with the emphatic 'you'. This is the one moment of permissible self-consciousness. You, the unselfconscious man, aware only of God's kingly rule and the world's need, you are salt.

> To those who are persecuted for belonging to Jesus it is said: you are the light of the world! Their ethical conduct through belonging to Jesus is also grounded here: because they are the light of the world they must let their light shine.[11]

---

[10] *The Cost of Discipleship*, English translation, revised 6th edn. (London: SCM Press 1959).

[11] Gerhard Barth, 'Matthew's Understanding of the Law' in *Tradition and Interpretation in Matthew*, edited by G. Bornkamm, English translation, (London: 1963), 102.

Good works are not a cause for self-congratulation, but are to be performed for God's sake. They are to be signs of the presence of God's kingdom breaking into the texture of observable history, the bearers of 'a discipleship which should prove itself before the world to be such by its "good works."'[12]

## 5

This leads us to the last of our preliminary observations. Spiritual theology must constantly speak of the end for which all theology is undertaken, the joy of entering into the glory of God. It can never be satisfied with a secondary purpose, or not for long. Karl Barth, writing about Anselm's work, has said:

> · As *intelligere* is achieved, it issues - in joy. The dominating factor in Anselm's mind is that even the Church Fathers wrote about it in order to give the faithful joy in believing by a demonstration of the *ratio* of their faith. This reason, which the *intelligere* seeks and finds, possesses in itself not only *utilitas* (by which Anselm may have been thinking of a polemical proof) but also *pulchritude*.[13]

In our day utility of other kinds is too often the legitimating criterion for theology. Does our theology serve the immediate needs of the Church? Does it send men out with a new and liberating power into society? These and similar questions are important to ask and to try to answer: but they are secondary to the questions: Does our activity as theologians lead men further into the joy of discipleship? Does it illuminate the life of Christ among his people? Does it help men to worship the Lord in the beauty of holiness? It is worth remembering that the very argument—the so-called ontological argument for the existence of God—which is enclosed by prayer in Anselm's *Proslogion* has appealed to men down the centuries because of its beauty.

The chief end of man, we are taught, is 'to glorify God and to enjoy him for ever'. So the first answer in the *Shorter Catechism of the Westminster Assembly*. By the mouth of the reformed tradition the great catholic affirmation is reaffirmed. Here, Reformation and Counter-reformation, Eastern and Western Christianity meet, and agree. Through all the vicissitudes of the Christian's pilgrimage, in the discipline of prayer, through the costly way of the disciple, it may be given to man to share in the life of him of whom it was said that for the joy set before him endured the cross.

---

[12] G. Bornkamm op. cit. p.16.
[13] Karl Barth, *Anselm*, 15, but see the whole passage.

It would appear appropriate, then, to finish, as we began, with an extract from the prayers of St Anselm. This time, we take the closing words of the whole *Proslogion*:

> My God,
> I pray that I may so know you and love you
> that I may rejoice in you.
> And if I may not do so fully in this life.
> let me go steadily on to the day when I come to that fullness.
> Let the knowledge of you increase in me here,
> and there let it come to its fullness.
> Let your love grow in me here,
> and there let it be fulfilled,
> so that here my joy may be in a great hope,
> and there in full reality.
> Lord,
> you have commanded, or rather advised us,
> to ask by your Son,
> and you have promised that we shall receive,
> 'that our joy may be full',
> That which you counsel
> through our 'wonderful counsellor'
> is what I am asking for, Lord.
> Let me receive
> that which you promised through your truth,
> 'that my joy may be full',
> God of truth,
> I ask that I may receive,
> so that my joy may be full.
> Meanwhile, let my mind meditate on it,
> let my tongue speak of it,
> let my heart love it,
> let my mouth preach it,
> let my soul hunger for it,
> my flesh thirst for it,
> and my whole being desire it,
> until I enter into the joy of my Lord,
> who is God one and triune, blessed forever.
> Amen.

# Sermons
## Seasonal

✤

# A God Near and Far

*Am I a god only near at hand,*
*not far away?*
*Can a man hide in any secret place*
*and I not see him?*
*Do I not fill heaven and earth?*
*This is the very word of the Lord.*
*Jeremiah: 23:23*

F ashions change rapidly.

A year or two ago, to have talked about God being transcendent would have meant nothing to anyone but a few theologians. Today, at least, 'transcendental meditation' is in the news. It is not altogether clear to me whether those who practice such meditation hope to release powers from within themselves or to be brought into harmony with something (someone) beyond themselves. If it is the former—the release of hidden powers within—I am not sure that 'transcendental' is an appropriate adjective. If it is the latter, then the word may have some of its customary connotations. In meditation, the meditator hopes to come into contact with something, someone who transcends previous experience, is greater than the one who meditates.

The prophet Jeremiah would have been a little wary of people who talked about transcendental meditation in either case. He would have warned them against 'dreaming dreams': He represents God as saying *I have heard what the prophets have said who prophesy lies in my name, saying I have dreamed, I have dreamed.* Long before Freud and Jung, he knew that dreams tell you more about the dreamer than they do about the objective world around you. Yet for Jeremiah, the problem of God's distance (his transcendence, if you like) and his nearness was a real one. How do we know that we are in touch with a reality beyond ourselves? 'We' in touch with 'beyond ourselves': God at once near at hand and far off.

# I

The first criterion which Jeremiah would have used may be summed up in what in effect he said to his contemporaries: you can't hire God, and you can't fire him either. That's what it means to say that he is at once far off, and near at hand.

Many of the Jews in Jerusalem in Jeremiah's time thought they could hire God. If they stuck to the Temple, and its decorous worship, they would be safe. God was on their side, and if they only remembered this (said Jeremiah's opponents the false prophets) 'Prosperity shall be yours no disaster shall befall you'. They were quite sure that they had a god near at hand.

This isn't only a problem of two and a half thousand years ago. It has reared its ugly head in the twentieth century. In two world wars men were sorely tempted to use God in support of the big battalions, for democracy, for Hitler: a god near at hand—supporting our security, our prosperity, keeping the world safe from fascism and communism. In this context the word of Jeremiah begins to make sense: Am I a god only at hand, not far away? God is not only to be met in Jerusalem, in the worship of the Temple, or defending the city walls. He is also to be met in the triumphs of Nebuchadnezzar's Babylonian Empire, more threatening to the established order of its day than that of the Communist powers in the South East Asia of ours. There too God is at work speaking his judging word upon those who would merely think of him as on their side. 'Can a man hide in any secret place and I not see him? Do I not fill heaven and earth?' Moreover, God will be as much present with the Jews in distant Babylon in their exile as he was in Palestine—more so, for there he will be teaching them not to weep for lost glories but to accept present opportunities, to acknowledge him as in the words of the Psalm 139: *Thou hast traced my journey and my resting places, and art familiar with all my paths.*

No, you cannot hire God, says Jeremiah; but you can't fire him either. He's not simply your 'next door neighbour, at the beck and call of everyone who chooses to assume familiarity with Him' (Skinner). He is inaccessible to the impertinent intrusion of human audacity or presumption. But just as you cannot control God, neither can you escape him. If you take flight to the frontiers of the morning or dwell at the limit of the western sea, even there his hand will meet you. You can't hire God, but you cannot fire him either.

This is a lesson which has to be learnt not only by those who tend to think of God as on the side of the white races, the prosperous nations, the anti-communist forces in history and the rest. That is so obvious that it should not need saying. You cannot equate God with any human cause: you can neither hire him, nor fire him. But it is also a lesson which needs to be learnt on a fairly humdrum domestic level: I suppose we might say at the level of our education. There are a lot of people still in this community who seem to think that faith in God is all right at the extremities of life—good for children and conveniently comforting at funerals, but not much to do with the real business of living in between. They would hire God to teach their children morals, and they would hire God to comfort the women at their own funerals; but they would fire him from the real business of getting and spending, living and loving and hating. And there are young people who as a result find it difficult to grow up and become mature in the faith; for the God with which they have been surrounded is too small. He is a god near at hand, involving us in limited liabilities, not a god afar off, who comes afresh into every new day—with demands and power for our developing control over nature, our increasing awareness of the world around us.

## II

The first thing then that this question of Jeremiah brings home to us is the danger of too parochial, and self-centred a view of God. But it raises the question of how God can become real to us again today, as at once close at hand and transcending all the limits of our own petty concerns.

So, the second thing I want to say is that for the Old Testament prophet, as for Christian Faith, God is far off because He is near. *Nah ist Und schwer zu fassen der Gott.*

'Near and difficult to grasp is God', wrote Holderlin: not primarily because God is beyond our intellectual comprehension, but because his demand is greater than our capacity to fulfill it, his forgiveness greater than our need.

In human relations there are moments when those whom we know best and are closest to us also disclose to us that we do not know them, that there are hidden depths to their personalities which we have never understood, to which we have never penetrated. When a man and a woman deeply love each other, in the long intimate relation of marriage, there is frequently disclosed to them the mystery at the centre of their relationship. The most near, the most dear, is also the other one, whose distance I must recognize, whose separate existence I must respect. Woe betide the parents who think they understand their children fully–although it may be the pardonable error of children to think they understand their parents!

This experience of the other in what is most close, of the mysterious hinterland to what is near at hand, seems to have been characteristic of the relation of Jesus to those with whom he came into contact. In his teaching, his words, his deeds, men came to acknowledge that God stood beside the sick, the miserable, the outcast; and yet, when men tried to grasp him, he passing through the midst of them went his own way. When he spoke to them in homely metaphors or in stories of every day happenings—a woman baking, a man sowing, a bailiff cheating—they suddenly become aware that a lot more was at stake in the ordinary everyday things than they had previously imagined. When a criminal, handed over to Romans for death by crucifiction died in the darkness of desolation, an army officer on a period of foreign service standing at the foot of his cross was provoked to cry out 'Truly this man was the Son of God'. *Am I a God near at hand and not a God afar off?*

What used to be called transcendence, God's Otherness, is not something opposite from his presence with us, his nearness. It is as we commit ourselves intensively and intently to the present - in the relation with the neighbour, as we meet this loved or this unloved one whom God has given us as our personal, political, racial neighbour, that the claim and the grace of the God who is greater than that relation makes itself felt in our lives.

# III

This leads me to the last thing I want to say. It is not only true that God is far off because he is near, it is also true that he can be near to us meaningfully at every moment because he is also the One who is far off. He is the One who addresses us, and in doing so creates our humanity, by asking us to make decisions. The last volume of Jean-Paul Sartre's trilogy *The Roads to Freedom*[1] tells the story of a group of French conscripts, waiting in a village to be mopped up by the Germans after the fall of France. Much of the comment comes in the reflections of one of their numbers Mathieu, a peacetime school master.

> 'You said it', remarked Longin: 'the poor bloody infantry don't have no opinions'. His cold slobbering smile gave Mathieu the creeps: 'And prisoners even less', he said dryly.
>
> *Everything's* asking our opinion; *everything.* We're encircled by questions. The whole thing's a farce. Questions are asked as though we were men, as though somebody wanted to make us believe that we still are men.

---

[1] The third volume is entitled *Iron in the Soul*: published in English translation by Penguin Books in association with Hamish Hamilton in 1963. The passage printed is on page 56 of that edition. Sartre brings to our notice profound matter about the questions which we are asked, and what it does to us in being questioned, which are far beyond the scope of this sermon.

It is a farce—this shadow of a question put by the shadow of a war to a handful of make-believe men.

'What's the use of having an opinion? You're not going to be called on to make a decision'.

He stopped talking. He thought suddenly: 'Life's got to go on. Day after day we have got to gather in the rotten fruit of defeat, work out in a world that's gone to pieces, that total choice I've just refused to make. But, good God!—I didn't choose this war, I didn't choose this defeat: by what trick of fortune have I got to take responsibility for them.' He was conscious within himself of the panic fury of the trapped beast, and looking up, saw the same fury in their eyes. Let them shout together to the far heavens: 'We've nothing to do with all this'.

If there is nothing more to life than the present, with questions for ever being asked of us, if there is no meaning in it all, then we may be driven to the fury of the trapped beast. The Christian story, however, tells of the beginning of it all in the purpose of a God of grace, of how he comes meaningfully into our lives - perhaps especially into their frustrated lives; of how he shares our sufferings, even their bewilderment and despair; and of how out of the darkness there is kindled a ray of hope. Thus the One who is most near also comes from without. Our cry into the far heavens need not be of desperate defiance 'We've nothing to do with it all'; but of simple acceptance: into Thy hands I command my spirit, for (at whatever cost) Thou hast redeemed me, O Lord Thou God of truth. Because He is the most near, He is also far off; but because He is the One in whose hands are the issue of life and death, the destiny of men and of nations, He is never far from any one of us. To Him be the glory. Amen.

# The Leper

## Ecumenical Service for the Fifth Congress of the Australian Medical Association
### Melbourne, 18 August 1974*

*And a leper came to him beseeching him, and kneeling said to him: 'If you will, you can make me clean.' In indignation Jesus stretched out his hand and touched him and said to him: 'I will; be clean.' And immediately the leprosy left him, and he was made clean. And he dismissed him with this stern warning: 'See that you say nothing to anyone; but go show yourself to the priest, and offer for your cleansing, what Moses commanded, for a proof to the people.' But he went out and began to talk freely about it, and to spread the news, so that Jesus could no longer openly enter a town, but was out in the country; and people came to him from every quarter.*

*Mark 1:40-45*

This story has some peculiarities. First, the case of a leper was not like that of any other sick or diseased man. He was an outcast, no longer a member of the community, doomed to live and die outside the towns and villages, cut off from the people of God. When he saw a traveller approach, he was bound to cry out from a distance: 'Unclean! Unclean!' The introduction to the story is, therefore, surprising: a leper breaks through that centuries' old isolation, kneels before Jesus and begs him: 'If you will, you can make me clean.' This explains too, of course, the conclusion—or the near conclusion—of the story. The man is sent to the priest to receive a certificate that he has been cured; he may be restored to the community. He can have a residence permit once more.

The second peculiarity is the way in which Jesus receives him. In indignation—or perhaps more literally 'in wrath'—Jesus stretches forth his hand and touches the man. This was too much for some of the copyists; some of them left

* Previously published in the *Medical Journal of Australia*, 1:425-426, 1975.

out the word about wrath, others changed it to the word for compassion. 'Jesus in compassion stretched out his hand.' But many manuscripts have 'in wrath'; and it seems virtually certain that that is what Mark wrote. What did he mean by it? What did he mean when later on he says, literally, that Jesus dismissed the man with a snort? What but this, that he is setting forth Jesus as the one who conveys the power of God, who demonstrates in his ministry the attitude of God to the poor, the demoralized, the sick and the dispossessed. This miserable leper, who has presumed to come out of his exile to claim the power of God to heal, focuses for Jesus that disordered world which is against God's will. Confronted by the leper, Jesus sees God's good order of health being violated; and when he dismisses him with a grunt, he is doing no more and no less than saying in effect that God will not have his people get rid of their problems by turning aside from them. He has said; 'I will; be clean!' And in doing so, he has expressed the will of the eternal God himself.

The third peculiarity is this: while the story begins with the leper coming from the outside and making an approach to Jesus, it ends with the injunction to silence and with the cleansed leper disregarding it so that Jesus has to stay outside the towns, in the open country. He was driven where the leper had previously been. We shall return to that point later. But perhaps before doing so we should ask about the relevance of this story for this afternoon's service, and for the preoccupation with medical practice of most of those gathered here today.

Let me take this second peculiarity first. Whatever later apologists have made of them, as the Gospel writers present them, the healing miracles of Jesus were not performed in order to surprise or shock men into faith. They were signs of the breaking into our disordered, diseased world of God's good order of health and of peace. We waste our time if we ask about the nature of the acts performed; we do not have the information necessary to analyse the stories in medical or quasi-medical terms, speculating upon whether they are instances of psychosomatic cures. We waste our time because such considerations distract us from the fundamental presupposition of the Gospel writers, which (I take it) is also the fundamental presupposition of medical science—namely, that ill health is an evil to be rid of, if at all possible; that man's full and proper life is to be lived in a state of health before God and in community with fellow man; that that which hinders the full exercise of our powers, physical, mental, spiritual, is to be fought, and if possible, conquered; that disease is the enemy, not the friend of man. All medical practice therefore stands under the great sign: 'I will; be clean!'

This means that for the doctor there can be no slipping back into cynicism or fatalism; there can be no passive acceptance of a disordered, diseased world. It means that in a sense, the medical profession can never be content simply to be a profession: a group of men and women who know how to organize a certain section of human activity, and who can pass on the skills from generation to generation. For, in a sense, you have never arrived. You cannot sit down as though the battle was won, and all that is left to do is the rebuilding of life in more peaceful circumstances before the spoils can be divided. On the contrary, the battle is on, and is never-ending; and each victory only opens up a new section of the front. For all the great achievements of medical science in the last 50 years, the battle lines have only been redrawn.

Thus it was in the ministry of Jesus, and so it is today. Jesus did not heal all those who were sick in Palestine. To do so would, of course, have been to turn himself into a conjuror or a trickster. He was no cheap publicist. But he performed these signs, he pointed the way. Indeed he pointed in two directions. He pointed to God and his intention: 'I will; be clean!' And he pointed forward, calling men into a new determination to do battle with sickness and disease - to engage in the name of a fundamental understanding of what men and women are for, in a task which will last as long as time and history last. I take it that it is good for us from time to time to stop and see the wider context, the full dimension of that in which we are engaged; and that is why we are here this afternoon.

But the story also speaks a word of judgement on us and our society; and that comes out of the first peculiarity. We noted that the leper was an outcast, and that Jesus' act restored him to the community. In fact, Jesus took seriously the civic authority which in that case happened also to be the religious authority, the priest who had to recognize publicly that the healing had taken place, that the man was no longer 'unclean'. Many of the healing miracles of Jesus end with the man being restored to his family, to the community from which he has been cut off. The sick man is not treated only as an individual.

I see a lot of medical students in the course of their training, and talk with some of them in their early years of practice. As a class—there are always notable—they know a lot about disease, about sickness and its symptoms; they sometimes know (or come to know) a little about the individual who is the bearer of that disease, the patient—a curiously apt word for the passive sufferer, who, for the time being, is of interest because he or she has such and such symptoms of disorder in his or her body. But they know nothing, or practically nothing of the real lives of the people whom they treat and handle so kindly: the real lives made up of home and family and work and play—and all the people on whom they rely there and who rely on them to make life tolerable.

Or again, I hear frequently (although necessarily I know of this less directly) of patients leaving hospital; and that is that. Neither your profession nor our society knows how to help them back to true and full health, or how to live with limited health, in the communities from which they came and to which they must return. We are all victims of three centuries of individualizing of human problems. Those centuries brought great gains. They have also left us with much to learn about how to live socially, about social responsibility.

This is not the time or the place in which to discourse on how such matters may be resolved—nor would I have the knowledge or skill to do so. It is, however, the time and the place to remember the leper, who was essentially a social phenomenon, who was cut off from society, and whom Jesus would have returned to that society, a cleansed man.

But this leads us to the last peculiarity of the story. By the cleansed leper's folly Jesus was driven out into the uninhabited place to which the leper had previously been consigned—a strange irony. It was an irony which was to characterize the whole Gospel story. The more Jesus got to the heart of the human problem, the more isolated he became, until he was crucified outside the walls of the city. There is absolutely no guarantee—but rather a suggestion to the contrary—that those who follow in His ministry of healing will be spared from loneliness, misunderstanding or pain. In most parts of the world—not quite all—the medical profession has in these early days of modem medical science been both prosperous and prestigious. I am not sure that that is going to continue to be the case. If it is not, then the question will remain: why be a doctor? Why indeed, except for the knowledge that at whatever cost, the sick person must be healed and restored to life again, or have concluding moments before death made more bearable. We do not know whether there is more human suffering throughout the world today than at other periods of history. All we know is that we know about it, and that we know that we ought to do something about it.

From that world there comes the plea to the sophisticated, the scientifically trained, the sensitive and the socially aware: 'If you will, you can make me clean!' Happy this world will be if your profession throughout the world can hear again the voice of the eternal Lord saying: 'I will; be clean!' And having heard that voice, regard it as a call to action.

# The Godforsaken[1]

*And at the ninth hour Jesus cried out with a loud voice, 'Eloi, Eloi, lama sabachthani?' which means 'My God, my God, why hast thou forsaken me?'*

Mark 15:34

It is important and valuable to remember the many varied figures who had to do with the crucifixion of Jesus: Judas who betrayed him, Peter who denied him, the high priest who accused him, Pilate who condemned him, Barabbas who was set free in his place, the crowd who mocked him and demanded his blood, the soldier who spat upon him, and the patient women who watched him die. It is important and valuable because it reminds us that these figures represent the human race. Small wonder that Matthew has all the people cry out, 'His blood be on us, and on our children'. 'At this hour,' wrote W H Auden, 'We all might be anyone.'

Yet when that is said, when we come to this ninth hour, Jesus hangs on the cross not one among many human actors, no longer even the one man mocked by the passers-by, the chief priests and those who were crucified with him. He is alone. There is darkness over the land from the sixth hour until the ninth hour. Then Jesus, isolated, addresses not his antagonists but his Father: 'My God, my God, why hast thou forsaken me?'

## The darkness of chaos

Mark arrests our attention by his time signals: rare in Mark. From the third hour to the sixth hour (Mark 15:25-32), there is plenty of human activity: the inscription is raised on the cross and the passers-by and the chief priests and the scribes all have their say. Then is focused in one short verse (33) the three hours of darkness: from the sixth hour to the ninth hour.

---

[1] First published as an Epilogue to a series of studies on Mark's Gospel, entitled *The Gospel for Our Day* (Melbourne: The Joint Board of Christian Education, 1978).

What is the significance of that darkness? It was not merely that nature was turning aside from this horrid deed: that is altogether too romantic for this narrative. No, at this climactic moment, Mark would remind us of the darkness of chaos, of the darkness of the cosmic sea, out of which God created the heavens and the earth, brought order out of chaos, said 'Let there be light' and there was light.

What is at stake in this event is the dissolution of God's created and creative order: it is as though the God who had looked at everything that he had made, and behold it was good, now turned his face from the earth. Chaos is come again. That chaos, that state of separation from God's good purposes for men, was the condition and context of Jesus' death. Whatever it may mean, he went out into the darkness of chaos.

## Faith in the God who seemed not to be there

He died with the opening words of Psalm 22 on his lips. It is well known that in verses 1-21 of Psalm 22 we have a prayer of lamentation and supplication, by a worshipper in distress; in verses 22-31, a prayer of thanksgiving after relief has come. For our purposes we note some points in the first half—the cry of lamentation.

> My God, my God, why hast thou forsaken me?
> Why art thou so far from helping me, from the words of my groaning?
> O my God, I cry by day, but thou dost not answer;

The psalmist's cry is no reproach against God: it arises from the poet's agonising awareness of the mystery of the hidden God. Because he later uses vivid metaphors (verse 14-15), it has sometimes been suggested that the psalmist has undergone acute physical sickness and suffering; but that is to misunderstand. The acute question is that of God. The one who should be near is not there. The psalmist can only see the abyss which separates him from God. His whole existence depends upon the God who is near at hand, but he is not there.

> Yet thou are holy,
>> enthroned on the praises of Israel.
> In thee our fathers trusted;
>> they trusted, and thou didst deliver them.
> To thee they cried, and were saved;
>> in thee they trusted, and were not disappointed.

Perhaps the answer is that God's distance is what makes him so hard to reach? *Yet thou art holy, enthroned on the praises of Israel.*

It was then God, the Transcendent One who gave himself to Israel, who allowed men to approach him in worship. High and lifted up, his name holy, but also with the worshipper who is of a contrite spirit, to lift up the lowly. He is the covenant God, and the psalmist tries to remember that: our fathers trusted in thee and thou didst deliver them.

> But I am a worm, and no man;
>> scorned by men, and despised by the people.
> All who see me mock at me,
>> they make mouths at me, they wag their heads;
> 'He committed his cause to the
>> LORD; let him deliver him,
> let him rescue him, for he delights in him!'

What if all this great tradition of God's approachability by men and women does not apply to me? What if there is no contact between God and the human being for me? *What care I if good God be If he be not good to me?*

The very banality of Stevie Smith's lines expresses their modernity. It is all very well to speak of the great tradition of the covenant God; that may have meant something to others; but what if it does not apply to me?

> Yet thou art he who took me from the womb;
> thou didst keep me safe upon my mother's breasts.
> Upon thee was I cast from my birth,
>> and since my mother bore me thou
> hast been my God.

In the case of the Psalmist, however, the agonising character of this trial of faith is underlined by his consciousness that God has been his God: all his life has been in God's hands. Indirectly he has been aware of God's presence in the past. The apparently unbridgeable distance between him and God can only be covered by prayer:

> Be not far from me,
>> for trouble is near
>> and there is none to help. (11)
> But thou, O LORD, be not far off! (19)

He throws himself upon the God who seemed not to be there. He can speak to God, if only of his affliction. There is no talk of vengeance against his enemies, only of the possibility of faith.

Now we may turn again to these words on the lips of Jesus. How strange and untypical this is of stories of the deaths of heroes of the faith. Socrates drank the hemlock with calm, and as a testimony to the immortality of the soul. 'He had a cock sacrificed to Asclepius, which was done on the recovery from a severe illness'. Martyrs likewise went to their death in sure and certain hope of eternal life. Zealots and revolutionaries went in defiance of the civil authorities, certain that their deaths would contribute to the ultimate victory of their causes. But this man died with a cry of desolation on his lips. Why? And why did the Christian church preserve this particular tradition? Surely, one might think, there were nobler ways to die.

But there it was firmly in the tradition; and since it was unthinkable that his death was a mere accident, this must mean something. What it meant was not just that another pious Jew died reciting the psalms. Certainly much that we have said about the psalmist's struggle for faith in the covenant God of Israel must be said of Jesus also. But this must be added: Jesus' cry is not only to the God of his fathers, but to the God whom he called Abba, My Father. His cry is to the One, the imminence of whose kingdom he had proclaimed. The kingly rule of God is at hand, he had taught. Through his words, and his healing deeds the forgiveness of God had broken into their midst: the old had been destroyed, a new day had dawned. But now that God is afar off. He is a God who hides himself: the God and Father of our Lord Jesus Christ!

There is here a genuine abandonment; and until we have seen that, we have seen nothing or at least nothing on which we can base an adequate hope for humanity. It is out of the depths that the cry comes. This is the opposite of what men expect from God: he should be accessible. He should not abandon the heroes of faith.

> Men go to God when they are sore bestead
>> Pray to him for succour, for his peace, for bread,
>> For mercy for them sick, sinning or dead:
> All men do so, Christians and unbelieving.

> Men go to God when he is sore bestead
>> Find him poor and scorned, without shelter or bread
> Whelmed under weight of the wicked, the weak, the dead:
>> Christians stand by God in his hour of grieving.[2]

---

[2] 'Christians and Unbelievers' in *Letters and Papers from Prison*, by Dietrich Bonhoeffer, first published in English in 1953 by SCM Press, London.

Is that all there is to say: that there was a genuine abandonment? That the hero of faith collapsed? That God who was to be present with men, at the critical moment was not there?

Although the answer is 'No' it ought not to be given too easily or slickly. Jesus is not well described as a hero of faith: there is little heroic about his death. On the contrary the one who carried God's love into the midst of human life, carries it now into the midst of human death, and a despairing death at that. The paradox of Mark's Gospel—that that which is revealed is concealed in certain actions and a certain person—reaches its most acute point. What is to be disclosed of God's nearness is enclosed in the cry of this dying man. For there,

> God goeth to every man when sore bestead,
> Feedeth body and spirit with his bread,
> For Christians, heathens alike he hangeth dead;

The world into which Mark took his Gospel was unlike ours in many respects, but not least in this that it believed in too many gods, ours in too few—except that perhaps things are changing and religiosity and superstition are in vogue again. Nevertheless the most serious strain in human life and thought is atheistic. Men and women have long since learnt to think about their ordinary activities, as though there were no God; and there is justification for that: there is a proper autonomy which belongs to many of our human activities, and God has set men free to enquire according to their own understanding of the nature of economic or other relationships. Most men and women live and work (as the seventeenth century jurist claimed about law) as though their activities possessed validity, even if God did not exist. To live in this world, to work with our neighbours, is to make that assumption again and again. The danger is that it drives God from the centre to the margins of life. It forgets that this world in all its autonomy is still accountable to the Creator-Redeemer.

Into this world, in all its rejection of God, comes Jesus the crucified one, articulating the sense of abandonment. A contemporary mathematician has said of the twentieth century, 'For the first time in the history of mankind, man everywhere is faced only with himself'. But there was a place, a time, when representative Man was faced only with himself: it was the ninth hour and Jesus cried 'My God, my God, why hast thou forsaken me?' Here is one who went out into the darkness, one in whose death God and the human race of men and women seem to be completely separated; and there seems to be no future for either. When Jesus hung on the cross, God is dead and Humanity is dead.

Those who see this may hear something which speaks to that condition of despair, of ultimate meaninglessness, which is the lot of so many in our day:

what, at the beginning of our era, was called, 'Dumb unbending nothingness! Cold and eternal necessity! Senseless chance! ... How solitary everyone is in the vast tomb of the universe! I am alone with myself'. And that is not simply a proper and confident sense of the autonomy of different spheres of human activity. That expresses a sense of abandonment. To be 'alone with myself' is hell.

'In the light of his message about the impending kingdom of God', writes Moltmann, 'this abandonment on the cross is the end of Jesus' mission. But in the light of his resurrection we have to say with Paul that through his forsakenness Jesus has brought God to the Godforsaken'. It is to be remembered, however, the discretion—the discreetness—with which the resurrection is presented in the concluding versus of Mark's Gospel. The sun has indeed risen, the tomb is indeed empty, but there is no appearance of the risen Lord. There is only a word: 'He is going before you to Galilee; there you will see him'. And whatever that meant to the women and to Peter, to Mark's readers it must have conveyed that the Jesus whom they expected as Judge and Saviour would come to reign in Galilee. There they would see him, not in some geographically defined place, beside the lake, but in 'Galilee of the nations': as they went out on the Gentile mission they would go in his train. That is where he is now leading them. From the place of abandonment, out into the search for the human race, he goes. Those engaged in the mission must follow, if they are to know the risen Lord. Because he goes from the place of abandonment, there is no place where a man or a woman can go–in the first century or the twentieth–where the crucified Lord cannot find him. Because he has been there he can bring man back to the presence of God, even from the pit of hell.

> If a good man were ever housed in hell,
> Would he at last, grown faithful in his station,
> Kindle a little hope in hopeless hell,
> Sow among the damned doubts of damnation,
> Since here someone could live, and could live well?[3]

---

[3] 'The Good Man in Hell', Edwin Muir, quoted in Hugh Anderson, *The Gospel of Mark*, The New Century Bible (Oliphants: 1976), 346.

# An Obscure Pact

## A Sermon preached at College Church, Parkville
## Christmas Day 1989

*The days were fulfilled that she should be delivered, and Mary brought forth her first born son; and she wrapped him in swaddling clothes, and laid him in a manger, because there was no room for them in the inn.*

*Luke 2:6-7:*

Those who have sung Christmas carols, and for that matter those who read the glossy magazine given away by *The Australian* on Saturday, know that there are twelve days of Christmas, not just one. Christmas begins today when we celebrate the birth of Christ; it ends on January 6 when the church has customarily commemorated the manifestation or showing forth of Christ to the nations. Those two days speak of almost contradictory, certainly contrasting things: the humility of Christ and his glory. Today the birth in Bethlehem: born in a stable, no room in the inn; discreet, almost hidden. Twelve days hence, the Christ child receiving gifts, gold and frankincense and Myrrh: receiving the homage of the wise and powerful. And the other readings will speak of his baptism, the voice from heaven—This is my Son, the unique One; and of the marriage at Cana of Galilee where he turned water into wine. Today the birth; tomorrow the mission and the miracle.

So today the birth: what does it say to us?

It says quite simply what the Church has always treasured, that the one whom we worship as Lord of all was born like the rest of us: one with the rest of the human race. I don't suppose that Jesus' birth weight was different from that of the average child born in Palestine in his day. His was no hero's birth. Even when the story is embellished, as told by Luke, it has almost a folksy touch: when the angels and the shepherds have played their part they return to their proper occupations - the angels to heaven, and the shepherds to their flocks. He and his mother and Joseph are left with the cattle in the stable:

He neither shall be cloth'd
In purple nor in pall,
But in the fair white linen
That usen babies all,
He neither shall be rock'd
In silver nor in gold,
But in a wooden cradle
That rocketh on the mould.

Secondly we might observe that the lowly birth in the Christian story is not merely an eccentricity: the humility is the condition of the glory. His humble beginnings, his common humanity is not something to be put aside when he takes upon himself the garments of majesty. The humility and the humanity are the garments of his glory.

The Polish poet Czeslaw Milosz has a line: 'The night a child is conceived, an obscure pact is concluded'. When Jesus was born in Bethlehem God concluded an obscure pact with the human race: obscure because it would not have been possible to see the end from the beginning. Paul uses the mystery of birth to explain the mystery of death: That which thou sowest thou sowest not the body that shall be but a bare grain … God giveth it a body even as it pleased him.

What man or woman is there amongst us who being present at the birth of a child, or seeing one recently born, who has not asked: what is in store for this child? What joys and sorrows? What kind of a world awaits him or her? An obscure compact has been made by parents on the night a child is conceived: to watch over this girl, this boy, to protect through childhood, to guide through adolescence, to remain in trust and friendship through adulthood; but essentially it is an obscure compact. 'That which thou sowest thou sowest not the body that shall be but a bare grain … God gives it a body as it pleased him'.

Christmas Day requires us to stop and think similarly about a birth in Bethlehem. In some ways we know the story much too well any longer to savour its strangeness; and yet it comes again as a surprise that the one born in humility should through all the disciplines and sufferings of life and of death come to be worshipped as the Saviour of the world. God gave him a body, a broken body, as it pleased him.

Finally, the implications of this are quite inescapable. Humble as was his way, so our way too. Unpredictable, what is hidden in the Father's intention for the Son, so our lives as daughters and sons of God.

There is a challenge here, a perpetual Christian challenge, to the currently fashionable assumption that big is beautiful—whether it be in commerce or in education; and to our carefully calculated futures, personal or national.

From Bethlehem, little among the clans of Judah was to come forth one who is to be a ruler in Israel. He shall stand and feed his flock in the strength of the Lord.

Who is to say what may come forth from Bethlehem in the turmoil of these days. At least this year we may be a little more ready to hear of, and lay hold upon the unexpected. The implications of this for the human race are far-reaching.

They are also far-reaching for you and me, for our piety, our spiritual life.

> Lord, thou hast told us that there be
> Two dwellings, which belong to thee;
> And those two, that's the wonder,
> Are far asunder.
>
> The one the highest heaven is,
> The mansions of eternal bliss;
> The other's the contrite
> And humble sprite.
>
> Though heaven be high, the gate is low,
> And he that comes in there must bow;
> The lofty looks shall ne'er
> Have entrance there.
>
> O God! Since thou delight'st to rest
> Within the humble contrite breast,
> First make me so to be,
> Then dwell with me.[1]

Finally the implications are great for God Himself. He made a pact to dwell with men and women in the routine and ordinary things of life, as well as at a time of national census or folk festival—He comes and is present in human festivals, and transforms them: whether a Roman *saturnalia* or a Melbourne shopping spree.

> And London shops on Christmas Eve
> Are strung with silver bells and flowers

---

[1] Thomas Washbourne, 1606-1687

As hurrying clerks the City leave
  To pigeon-haunted classic towers,
And marbled clouds go scudding by
  The many-steepled London sky.

And girls in slacks remember Dad,
  And oafish louts remember Mum,
And sleepless children's hearts are glad,
  And Christmas-morning bells say "Come"!
Even to shining ones who dwell
  Safe in the Dorchester Hotel.

And is it true? And is it true,
  This most tremendous tale of all,
Seen in a stained-glass window's hue,
  A Baby in an ox's stall?
The Maker of the stars and sea
  Become a Child on earth for me?

And is it true? For if it is,
  No loving fingers tying strings
Around those tissued fripperies,
  The sweet and silly Christmas things,
Bath salts and inexpensive scent
  And hideous tie so kindly meant.

No love that in a family dwells,
  No carolling in frosty air,
Nor all the steeple-shaking bells
  Can with this single Truth compare
That God was Man in Palestine
  And lives today in Bread and Wine.[2]

God who came in his son Jesus, the child born in Bethlehem, deigns to dwell with us through word spoken and bread broken. May he thus dwell with us through the twelve days of Christmas and thereafter—within which and beyond which He will disclose to us his strange glory.

---

[2] 'Christmas' by John Betjeman, *Church Poems* (London: John Murray, 1981)

# A Tale of Two Cities

## A sermon given at Wesley Church
## Melbourne, 4 September 1994

*You have come to Mount Zion and to the city of the living God, the heavenly Jerusalem, and to innumerable angels in festal gathering, and to the assembly of the first-born who are enrolled in heaven, and to a judge who is God of all, and to spirits of the just made perfect, and to Jesus the mediator of a new covenant, and to the sprinkled blood that speaks more graciously than the blood of Abel.*
*Hebrews 12.22-24*

We are met this morning to celebrate 155 years in which the congregation of Wesley Church has worshipped in this city of Melbourne. It is an awesome thought. From 1839, the year in which Charles Joseph La Trobe came ashore to become Superintendent of the Port Phillip District, later to be Lieutenant Governor of the Colony of Victoria, a group of Methodists met to worship here where men and women had begun to gather themselves together to establish what ten years later was by Act of Parliament to be declared the city of Melbourne.

Ten years later again, between 1857 and 1861, Charles Dickens in London was publishing in serial form his shortest novel, *A Tale of Two Cities*, with its celebrated opening sentence:

> It was the best of times, it was the worst of times, it was the age of wisdom, it was the age of foolishness, it was the epoch of belief, it was the epoch of incredulity, it was the season of Light, it was the season of Darkness, it was the spring of hope, it was the winter of despair, we had everything before us, we had nothing before us, we were all going direct to heaven, we were all going directly the other way.

The words refer, of course, to the France of the Revolution; but by the time they were written gold had been discovered in Victoria, men (and some women) were entering the colony to settle in considerable numbers, and the cathedral Church of Victorian Methodism, as it was called, had been built. Some at least of Dickens words might have been applied here: the best of times for some and the worst for others, the spring of hope and the winter of despair, belief and incredulity, Darkness and Light. And the Christian Church had come to establish itself (in its various forms) in this city: this city which was destined to share with other cities a strange juxtaposition of prosperity and poverty, of civilised life and cruel barbarism.

## 1

So the first thing that we might remember this morning as we celebrate what is for this part of the world the long history of this congregation, is that the Christian Church—the great Church to which we all belong—is no stranger to the ambiguities of life lived in communities, in cities. Every era is the best of times and the worst of times, an epoch of belief and of unbelief. With this ambiguity of life in cities, the Hebrew prophets were familiar.

> ... the faithful city has become a harlot [declared Isaiah]
>     she that was full of justice!
> Righteousness lodged in her, but now murderers.
> … Everyone loves a bribe and runs after gifts.
> They do not defend the fatherless,
>     and the widow's cause does not come to them.[1]

He is speaking of Zion, a city for him with a more lofty foundation than any other. There God had established a kingdom under his servant David for the protection of his people Israel. There Solomon had built a temple, a place of worship which would attract all nations to the God of Israel. Within these walls at the end of Isaiah's life the people had remained secure against the Assyrian invader; and so there developed a doctrine of the inviolability of Zion, to be tested and proved wanting a century later when Jerusalem fell to another invader, the Babylonian, and the prophet Jeremiah laments again and again over 'this city' as he calls it: refusing as it were to name it in its shame. It was the best of cities and the worst of cities. The best of hopes and the worst of despair surround this city in the teachings of the prophets.

Jesus himself was no stranger to this ambiguity that attaches to city life. Like other Jews he and his disciples went on pilgrimage to Jerusalem, no doubt

[1] Isaiah 1.21,23

singing psalms of expectation as they ascended Mount Zion. But what hopes and fears did he harbour when he wept over the city?

> Jerusalem, Jerusalem, killing the prophets and
> stoning those who are sent to you!
> How often would I have gathered your children
> as a hen gathers her brood under her wings,
> and you would not![2]

The one crucified outside the walls of the city is the permanent reminder to his followers, and to those who look to him, of the ambiguity of civilised, that is of city life.

And here we might note that religion is no escape from such ambiguities, and that indeed as A D Hope—like the Hebrew prophets—has reminded us, religious institutions all too often have shared the deceit and corruption of the societies in which they are placed:

> The City of God is built like other cities:
> Judas negotiates the loans you float;
> You will meet Caiaphas upon committees;
> You will be glad of Pilate's casting vote[3]

The Christian Church finds herself, and citizens of earthly kingdoms will find her, immensely experienced in the ambiguities, the joys and sorrows, the devoted service and the exploitation of life together in cities. But it won't be much use, and the Christian Church will not be heard unless her members are prepared to learn from their past and face the present with humility, and with compassion.

## 2

This leads to a second suggestion for reflection this morning; and it is focused for us in some words written a few decades after the literally crucial event outside Jerusalem's walls.

> You have not come (says the writer to the Hebrews) to what you can touch, to "flames of fire", to "mist" and "gloom" and "stormy blasts"[4]

---

[2] Matthew 23.27
[3] 'Easter Hymn' in *Poems* by A D Hope (London: Hamish Hamilton, 1960).
[4] Hebrews 12.18. The translation and punctuation is that suggested by James Moffatt in the ICC Commentary (Edinburgh: T&T Clark, 1924)

You have not come to an hour in which you can demonstrate for all to see and hear, a message, which will overwhelm men and women with its awe and its majesty. It is not given to you in this generation—whatever may have been the case in the past—to enunciate a triumphal message, to subject men's minds and consciences to your understanding of your message. No physical miracles will accompany your faithfulness; but something quite different, something to be received and borne witness to, with a certain reverence and humility.

You have been given a glimpse in advance as it were of the true meaning of our lives together: not written out in any human plan for Melbourne or any ecclesiastical blueprint, but a glimpse of the city of the living God, the heavenly Jerusalem, and of a judge who is the God of all.[5] To pass on that message, to remind men and women of the one with whom we have to do; to recall for ourselves that the standards of judgement come from another, and that expediency or the making of a quick profit regardless of the means is not the true end of life, that is our task.

Alexander Solzhenitsyn has a short piece entitled *Along the Olga*.[6]

When you travel the by-roads of Central Russia you begin to understand the secret of the pacifying countryside. It is in the churches. They trip up the slopes, ascend the high hills, come down to the broad rivers, like princesses in white and red, they lift their bell-towers—graceful, shapely, all different—high over mundane timber and thatch, they nod to each other from afar, from villages that are cut off and invisible to each other they soar to the same heaven. And wherever you wander in the fields or meadows, however far from habitation, you are never alone: from over the hayricks, the walls of trees, and even the curve of the earth's surface the head of some bell-tower will beckon to you.

Then he describes the terrible desecration of these buildings: crosses flattened, graves churned, obscene inscriptions scrawled on the murals: one church locked and silent, another storing lubricating oil, and another used by groups and clubs. He adds:

People were always selfish and often unkind. But the evening chimes used to sing out, floating over villages, fields and woods. Reminding men that they must abandon the trivial concerns of this world and give time and thought to eternity. These chimes, which only one old tune keeps alive for us, raised people up and prevented them from sinking down on all fours.

---

5 Hebrews 12.22-23
6 Alexander Solzhenitsyn, 'Along the Olga', to be found in *Patriarchs and Prophets: Persecution of the Russian Orthodox Church Today*, by Michael Bourdeaux (London: Mowbrays, 1973)

>Our forefathers put all that was finest in themselves, all their under-
>standing of life into these stones, into these bell-towers.

We in Australia can rarely see such sights, although in the city of Melbourne we might fondly imagine the churches nodding to each other, saying: we stand together to recall these people to their answerability to the living God. We certainly can say 'Our forefathers put all that was finest in themselves, all their understanding of life into these stones'; and we can remember the words of Hebrews: we are come on this anniversary Sunday 'to the assembly of the firstborn enrolled in heaven and to the spirits of just men and women made perfect'. We can say to this city and its citizens: they too are part of your history, and we are in no mind to disown them. They looked for a city which has foundations and whose maker and builder is God; and just as the prophet Isaiah would conclude his vision of the renewed Mount Zion with an exhortation, so we would say to you:

>O house of Jacob
>come, let us walk
>in the light of the Lord.[7]

# 3

There is, however, one last perspective necessary for those who would live in this city as citizens of another

>'You have come' in imagination to Mount Zion; you have come by faith
>into the presence of the living God, the judge of us all, of the total life of
>our city. Finally, you have come to Jesus.[8]

Again and again, at critical points in his argument, the author of Hebrews brings his readers face to face with Jesus. Early in his writing: we do not yet see everything in the world around us made to serve human and humane ends, but we see Jesus[9] another text worthy of consideration, indeed of proclamation by a Church in a city. You are here to hold up before men and women the figure of Jesus. 'Consider Jesus' says our author again and again, touching on different aspects of his life on earth and his heavenly intercession on our behalf.

Here towards the end of his discourse he does it again. 'You are come to Jesus, the mediator of a new covenant, and to the sprinkled blood that speaks

---

[7] Isaiah 2.5
[8] Hebrews 12.22-24
[9] Hebrews 2.8-9

more graciously than the blood of Abel'.[10] To see Jesus thus is to be reminded that with God there is always the possibility of a new start. The blood of Abel cried out for vengeance. The seed of Cain was to be cut off. The mark of the murderer was to prevail. The death of Jesus speaks of new life—a new covenant re-enacted every time you celebrate the Holy Communion; and it speaks of forgiveness.

To grasp opportunities for a new start, to lay hold of forgiveness is not simply a religious experience, it is a civic virtue. New possibilities open or may in God's mercy open, surprisingly and frequently for those with eyes to see, between Jew and Arab in the Middle East, between conflicting and mutually despising groups in South Africa, between deeply antagonistic sections of the population in Ireland. Solzhenitsyn in the passage, which we looked at a moment ago, speaks of the part played by the churches in enabling the traveller in Russia 'to understand the secret of the *pacifying* countryside'.

It is at least part of your calling as a Church in this city, dominated as it is by competition, threatened in its very soul by greed, to preach peace to those who are far off and to those who are near. And,

> May the God of peace who brought again from the dead our Lord Jesus, the great shepherd of the sheep, by the blood of the eternal covenant, equip you with everything good that you may do his will, working in you that which is pleasing in his sight, through Jesus Christ, to whom be glory for ever and ever. Amen.

---

[10] Hebrews 12.24

# 'I am the resurrection
and the life'

*Jesus said to her [Martha], 'I am the resurrection and the life'.*
*John 11.25*

As far as I can make out Rembrandt represented the climax to the story of the raising of Lazarus in two ways; several times in etchings (copies of two in the National Gallery of Victoria), once in a splendid painting. The etchings bear the mark of something that Rembrandt had learnt from older artists but which he is to use in depicting biblical scenes, especially in etchings and drawings: what art critics call chiaroscuro—literally light and shade, through Italian from the Latin words *clarus* (clear) and *obscurus* (from which we get obscure). This is a style of pictorial art where only the light and the shades are represented: black and white or sepia and white. In these etchings Jesus is surrounded by light, he raises his hand and holds back the darkness. Lazarus is drawn into this realm of light, and the bystanders are illuminated: light is cast upon them. Incidentally, the face of Jesus is not particularly illuminated. It is as though his word and his gesture does it all.

The painting is quite different. To begin with it is in colour, although as in many of Rembrandt's paintings use is still made of the contrast between light and darkness. In this painting the surrounding world is in darkness. Jesus comes out of the darkness: he stands near the back of the picture, with just one disciple behind him. His arm is raised up, the hand and the forearm illumined and some (although a very little) light is cast on his face. In the foreground to the left are the faces, lit, of the Jews come from the city to comfort Lazarus's sisters, and the face of what is surely the youthful Mary her eyebrows raised in astonishment, her lips parted as though wishing to greet her brother but not knowing what to say, and her hand also raised, echoing that of Jesus on a vertical line below it, in a gesture of uncertainty—to receive Lazarus as though to say 'This is more than I can understand', or perhaps even 'This is more than I can endure'. Lazarus himself is in the foreground on the right of the picture, looking up with a weary expectation at the powerful figure of Jesus, as though to say 'Why should this happen to me?'

I may be all wrong about that; but Rembrandt is one of the greatest commentators on Scripture that we have ever had. His two ways of treating the story read to us this morning represent two ways in which we can, and I think should read the Fourth Gospel. The first way is suggested by a remark of another great commentator, Sir Edwyn Hoskyns: the author of the Fourth Gospel expected his readers to read it from the beginning to the end. I wonder how many of us ever do that: take any one of the Gospels, and read it through, if not at one sitting, then perhaps in two, from beginning to end.  None of them is longer than a long short story. If we did that with the Fourth Gospel we would find that the depiction by way of *chiaruscuro* recurs again and again: light and darkness, blindness and sight, death and life. It announces its theme at the very beginning.  In the one who was and is the Word of God, 'in him was life and the life was the light of man. The light shines in the darkness, and the darkness has not overcome it'. In the very word which the author uses for 'overcome' there is a pun which will be taken up elsewhere. It can mean 'understand' or it can mean 'hold down'. The darkness has not understood the light nor can it conquer it. Perhaps our word 'apprehend' does it: apprehend means understand with the mind. But we also speak, or writers of detective novels and journalists write about policemen apprehending criminals. The darkness does not apprehend the light. Then read on through the Gospel and you find this theme being taken up again and again in the first twelve chapters, which scholars call the Book of Two Signs. Even his mother does not understand him at the marriage in Cana of Galilee, Nicodemus comes to him out of the darkness of night, just as at the end of the Gospel when Judas receives the morsel of bread dipped in wine and goes out to betray him, the writer adds the comment 'and it was night'.

The light-darkness theme runs right through the Gospel. Try it out by reading the Gospel from beginning to end. But we also read the Gospel in sections, in quite small sections, and have it read to us Sunday by Sunday; and each piece adds to the picture of the whole, just as the pattern of a jigsaw emerges, each piece essential for the whole.

There is not time to go through this story of the raising of Lazarus this morning. There never is time. Like all great stories we can read it again and again and find more in it. But consider just two points—one at the beginning and the other at the end. At the beginning Jesus is represented as delaying going to Bethany where his friend Lazarus is sick, indeed is dying. The clue to why the author stresses this point, sets the stage in this way, is found in the somewhat enigmatic remark of Jesus, when he received the message from the sisters that Lazarus was sick:

> This sickness is not to end in death [he says]; rather it is for God's glory, that the Son of God may be glorified through it.

This story will not end with Lazarus' death. Indeed it will appear to end with his return to life; but the effect of Jesus going to Bethany, returning to Judea will be to hasten his end, the crucifixion. We are told at the end of the chapter that a consequence of the raising of Lazarus was that the authorities decided to do away with Jesus. The word 'glorify' in this part of the Gospel, from now onwards, always refers to the death of Jesus. When Judas went out to betray him, 'and it was night', Jesus immediately says 'Now is the Son of Man glorified'. His crucifixion is inevitable. So, the story of the raising of Lazarus looks forward as do all the other incidents in the Book of Signs to the Greatest Sign—the story of Jesus' crucifixion and his resurrection. There on the cross darkness and light will be brought together in a paradoxical relationship.

The story of the raising of Lazarus begins with an enigmatic saying that reminds the reader that Jesus is on the way to his own crucifixion; but what about the end of the story, what about Lazarus himself? Where does he fit in? Is he just an excuse for reminding the readers that the crucifixion of Jesus is near at hand? I think not. Extraordinarily little is said about Lazarus; but what is said is significant. Jesus, we are told, 'loved Martha and her sister and Lazarus'. He refers to him as 'our friend'. And at the end Lazarus says nothing. Jesus shouts with a loud voice, 'Lazarus, come out.' Jesus speaks this life-giving word to him.

John Donne in one of his great sermons asserts that the noise of the cannon will not wake the dead, nor will an earthquake which may shake the Church in the graveyard of which they lie disturb them. But there is a voice which they will hear: the voice of the Son of God, crying 'Arise you dead.' What the author of this Fourth Gospel is saying is that because Jesus lives we shall live also. Our resurrection depends upon him. When Cassio is dismissed from military service by Othello he cries out

> O! I have lost my reputation. I have lost the immortal part of myself, and what remains is bestial.

He is thinking of his reputation on earth, as when we might speak of Shakespeare as an immortal poet. But our immortality does not depend on ourselves. Our life beyond the grave depends on the fact that unworthy though we be, God loves us, and will call us into eternal life with himself. 'Christ is our eternal friend' writes a nineteenth century French Calvinist divine, 'and it is the law of friendship that friends support one another'.

On the tomb of the Venerable Bede in Durham Cathedral are engraved these words:

> Christ is the morning star who
> when the night of the world is past
> brings to his saints the promise
> of the light of life and opens everlasting day.

May God grant to us, and to all whom we love, and whom He loves, the fulfilment of that promise.

# Sermons
## Academic

✤

# What would you die for?

## A sermon preached on University Sunday at a service held in Winthrop Hall in the University of Western Australia, 5 May 1968

W hat are you willing to die for? What do you think a university should be willing to die for?

Perhaps these are rather melodramatic terms. After all institutions don't die, or do not wish to do so. Whether that institution be a State or a university we appoint people to protect its life, not (in a Churchillian phrase) to preside over its liquidation. The individual has a responsibility to preserve his or her own life, so what is the point of talk about what you are willing to die for? The point I take is this: you and I are unlikely to know what we should live for, if we have no idea what we would die for. Societies know this in time of war, or their leaders say they do, but in time of peace the question is less frequently asked: What are *you* prepared to die for?

The events of recent weeks have raised this question in an acute form: a new turn of events, what amounts at least to a shift in key in the war in Vietnam, the murder of Martin Luther King, and all this taking place in Passion-tide and around Easter. Even more than usual Good Friday this year brought us the question: What would *you* be prepared to die for?

Whatever else lay behind President Johnson's strange *volte face* about Vietnam and the Presidency, this much may be taken for granted: that Lyndon B Johnson, shrewd politician that he is, could no longer remain deaf to the voices of millions of people who said, 'We are no longer willing to go on suffering and inflicting suffering on our fellow-men for the sake of the Administration's theory of what this war is about. That theory is not worth dying for. '

Whatever else Martin Luther King stood for, as a realistic observer of the growth of black power in America he held to this: that any risk, life itself, is worth putting on the stake if it demonstrates to men that violence will only breed violence, that the God who made men and women one people requires justice for all and that they be reconciled to each other and walk together in the way of peace.

Whatever else the death of Jesus Christ means, it is clear that there came a point at which, if he was to be true to his own message, he must face the consequences of going to Jerusalem, of announcing there that God deals graciously with every one of His children, that there is no special privilege attached to belonging to a particular class or race, that we all stand in need of love, renewal and forgiveness; and that, if necessary, for that kind of a God to be believed in, a perfectly obedient Son must be willing to die. *For this I have come to bear witness to the truth.*

So much for the way in which the question is posed. If we stop to reflect we can scarcely escape it: What would I be willing to die for? The author of the Fourth Gospel compels us to take the question a little further. *For this I have come, to bear witness to the truth*, says Jesus; and Pilate asks *What is truth?* But the author of the Gospel has already seen that there is an essential relation between truth and freedom: *You will know the truth and the truth will set you free.* In terms used by the author of the Fourth Gospel, what Jesus was prepared to die for was the truth which sets free.

How *are* truth and freedom related? It is widely assumed, and rightly recognised in academic circles, that freedom is the condition of true learning. The university is a place of free enquiry into the truth of any matter. That can be said a little too easily, and in ways which do not touch many of us. Few of us have, as a matter of fact, had to fight for academic freedom—freedom to teach or freedom to learn, freedom to speak, freedom to enquire. Most of us have had at least the external conditions of freedom. Some have had to fight, all should be alert; but we can scarcely pretend that all our waking hours are spent in the conscious fight for freedom. But consider these cases. In the closing months of last year, men and women celebrated three events: the October revolution in Russia in 1917, the beginning of the Protestant Reformation in Germany when Luther nailed his theses to the door in Wittenberg in 1517, and the birth of Jonathan Swift in Dublin in 1667. What have these events in common? They were all, each in its way, about freedom.

It may be strange for us to talk about the Bolshevik Revolution in those terms, but it was a mighty protest against ignorance, tyranny and inefficiency by a people who were determined to live the life they believed they should live and could live, if the Tsarist regime could be overthrown. If they were to know their own true human life they must grasp freedom, be set free. However disappointing the outcome, for millions in other countries, dominated by foreign powers, that revolution became a symbol, so that in many parts of Asia national integrity or freedom and communist government are not contradictory but necessary allies. To know their own true life and culture, the nations of Africa or Asia must be free.

Or turn from the political to the personal. Although it was much else besides this, Martin Luther's protest was in the name of the freedom of the Christian man, the freedom of a man to unburden his conscience before his God and receive His forgiveness, without the necessity of winning his way into God's presence by works laid down by moralists or demands made by ecclesiastics. My guilty conscience must be set at rest by God as He comes forgivingly to me in the message of His Son, Jesus Christ. I must be free to be myself before God, to face the truth about myself, and not try hopelessly to conform to the picture of goodness given or required by another.

Or turn again to Jonathan Swift and what we might call practical freedom, freedom protected for the other by my exercise of reason, self-control and commonsense—and so the appeal, again and again, often in the form of satire, to those with power not to exercise it in tyranny but to let men be men and be women, to let us all be human. 'Last week I saw a woman flayed,' he wrote, 'and you will hardly believe how much it altered her person for the worse.' Civilisation (for Swift) meant freedom from self-delusion, the freedom to see things exactly as they are. With him it was a kind of passion.

Now, these instances—so different—have one thing in common: the passion to let men and women be what they could be and should be. Oh, I know that they each provide instances of the corruption of the good. There is no need to illustrate that from the horrors of post Revolution and Stalinist Russia, from the savagery of Luther in his attitudes to the peasants, from the crimes committed in the name of the freedom of the individual conscience, from the strident partisanship of a Swift, cruel and ungenerous to his enemies. But they at least suggest that freedom is not a negative neutrality: it calls for a passionate commitment. That is perhaps what Jesus meant when he said to the Jews, *If you continue in my word, you are my disciples and you will know the truth and the truth will make your free.* Obeying the truth, committed to discipleship, that is the way into freedom. So much of the freedom which is demanded and claimed is freedom to do differently or to think differently from our predecessors, and of course that is important. But it is a shallow thing—it may be no more than a mere reaction against a previous generation who are scarcely worth reacting against in any case. Is the present fashion for non-conformity on the part of the young only a reaction against us older people, as some psychiatrists and psychologists and elderly moralists are busy telling us it is—and so patronisingly insult the young—or is it a genuine demand for freedom, to be free and open for a new future, with all the risks implied?

Is some of our academic demand for freedom to enquire, to ask new questions, anything more than a search for novelty, a novelty which twenty years from now will seem utterly banal? Or is it marked by that intellectual passion, that discipline, that discipleship which is concerned only with the truth, and cannot rest until it is uncovered? What we want—in the sphere of intellect and of morals—is a passionate commitment to let people be what they were made for, and what they may become—and that includes a life before God, lived in dependence on His power and forgiveness, in His capacity to raise the dead, to release the fetters which tie men and women to their own and other people's pasts—a passionate and compassionate commitment to what may really be.

One last word: the man or woman who is committed to freedom must themselves be free, truly free. Return to the story of Jesus before Pilate. Pilate is feeling around for categories in which to understand Jesus: 'So you are a King.' Jesus, as it were, slips through his fingers. *Those are your terms ... I came to bear witness to the truth.* Just as on an earlier occasion when they came to take him by force and make him a king, he withdrew to the hills by himself, or as when (as Luke put it) they would stone him, passing through the midst of them he went his own way, so now, to the court of Herod and the court of Pilate he remains an enigma, he is free of them and their estimates of him. He goes his own way.

There are, says Bonhoeffer, four stations on the road to freedom: *Discipline*, and we might remember the association of that word with discipleship. It begins there, hearing the word and following. *Action*, 'to do and be—not what you would but what is right'. What I called the passionate commitment: *Suffering*, for a passionate commitment means one that hurts and no one should live and work in a university unless he is prepared to think until he has a pain in the mind. And the fourth station on the road to freedom, *Death*. This has, for some, been the supreme test. I pray that it may not be so for any of you, or for me, for I do not know how we should face it. When Martin Luther King died, a young man wrote to me from America that this was the first contemporary Christian martyr. He was too young and too protected to know at the time of the death of Dietrich Bonhoeffer. The twentieth century has had a number of martyrs. They are like saints of whom Paul Tillich said that they were moments of translucency—places where the light shines through. That's what men ought to be like. When a saint dies, he is a martyr, a witness. So death can be a station on the road to freedom. For Jesus Christ it was the supreme test of whether he was prepared to go his own way, which was God's way, to the bitter end; and some in every country have to follow.

Ought there to be just a little bit of the quality of sanctity about a university? Ought the light to be shining through such a place, so that men see in our endeavours a little more clearly, the ends for which they were made—to rejoice in the truth and in freedom to pursue it? I imagine that we would wish our answers to those questions to be 'Yes': the university should be a place of moral and intellectual passion for the truth, and for man's freedom. If we know that, we know what we would be willing to die for.

# Things New and Old

## Centenary of St Andrew's College
## University of Sydney, 1970

*'Have you understood all this?' They answered him 'Yes'. And he
said to them, 'A scribe who has become a disciple in the kingdom of
heaven is like a householder who can produce from his store things
new and old.'*

*St Matthew 1: 51-52*

The author of Matthew's Gospel is what, in today's parlance,
we would call a Christian educator—if not a Christian intellectual. Of all the
Gospel writers he stresses particularly the element of understanding in discipleship. Mark had said that the disciples had not understood the parables of Jesus.
Matthew takes these parables, adds others to them, reorganizes, adapts them,
and presents them to his readers afresh; and then at the end of the group of
parables he has Jesus say 'Have you understood all this?' Have you exercised
your intelligence upon it? Have you really thought what it means to be a 'scribe',
a man with a trained mind, who is at the same time a disciple in the kingdom of
heaven, a learner in the Kingdom of God? Do you *know* what it means to accept
your human gifts and divine gifts, your human calling as a divine calling? 'Have
you understood all this?' They answered him 'Yes'.

In a sense, Matthew is justifying himself and his own procedures. He himself, a Christian scribe, an educator committed to the kingdom of heaven, a
disciple, had brought new meanings to light. He had been, or hoped that he
may have been, a householder who had produced from his store things new and
old. With that astonishing freedom and daring which the Gospel writers show,
he had not merely repeated the teaching of Jesus, he had adapted it. For him
Jesus was not simply a Rabbi who had lived and taught and died in Palestine 50
years before. He was the Risen Lord of His Church in Syria as the century drew

to its close. Here and now, the One to whom has been given all authority in heaven and earth, addresses his Church. 'Have you understood what I am saying to you now?' he asks through the words of Matthew. The answer can only be 'Yes', if like a householder the Evangelist can produce from his store things new.

# I

The first thing to say this afternoon to a university college which is a Christian foundation, at the end of the first century of its life, is that if it is to be true to the nature of Christian faith and to the genius of the University, it must continue to give priority to things new. That is the way this saying of Jesus puts it: things new before things old. That is what Matthew had been doing, and he is justifying innovation in his interpretation of the teaching of Jesus himself.

Let us pause upon this for a moment. Here Christian faith and modern scientific culture come together and belong together—if each is properly understood. For each demands of its disciples that they should be open towards the future. Faith demands that I should be willing to receive new claims into my life, that I should look for new powers to meet those claims in each new day. Forgetting those things which are behind (as the apostle Paul puts it), I am to press forward, not as though I had already attained.

And learning—at any rate the kind of learning pursued in a university— requires of me that I should always be seeking the answer to the new question, that I should never be satisfied, that what addresses me in my subjects of study, requires of me that I should give my whole mind and person—if need be, health itself—to trying to find the answer.

This openness to the future which should characterize both faith and learning is supported by an unquenchable hope. It was not always so, and it is not always so. It has been accurately said that in the world into which the Christian Church was born, that of the Roman Empire, hope was hope that it wouldn't happen. The Christians struck a new note: they lived as men who hoped that it would. Pagan hope was a kind of despair, marked deeply in the lines of the faces which have come to us in contemporary sculpture. The world was in its decline. The golden age was in the past. A sensitive man could at best look forward hoping that the worst would not happen in his time. The Christian had here no continuing city but looked for one to come. Or, as Cyprian put it: we are not as those who grovel having no hope, but we stand upright among the ruins.

Modern scientific culture has had this hope, not that it is going to manipulate the world (this is a travesty of its aim), but that it will be given to us to understand more, that the question which comes from what is not known is a question worth hearing and trying to answer, even though we know that our answers will be imperfect and that a generation coming after us will have to take up the quest again.

This afternoon is not the occasion to develop this further; but it is perhaps the occasion to say this. Unless St Andrew's College begins its second hundred years with a greater sense of excitement about what the future holds, with a greater faith in its future than was possible one hundred years ago, a greater sense that there are new things to be brought forth from the store of faith and learning than was then possible, it will not be worthy of its past. More important, it will not be true to the essential character of the Christian faith which from the first demanded that men should look forward to the coming glory; and it will not be true to the genius of the university, which, when it understands its own life fully, is committed not only to the preservation of what is past, or to the passing on of what is already known, but also—and with priority—to what is new.

# II

Having said that, and not wishing to take away from it, let us note in the second place (but only in the second place) that the intellectual who is a disciple of the kingdom will produce things new *and old.*

It is almost certainly unnecessary to stress here that the new frequently has its roots deeply in the old. Matthew was fighting on two fronts in his day: on the one the hand the traditionalist Jewish Christian wanted to keep the new faith within the confines of the old Judaism (and to them the radical newness of faith, with its openness to the future, had to be stressed); on the other hand the enthusiast who wished to live only by the new inspiration had to be reminded of the long road along which God had led men, disciplining their minds and spirits.

So too in our day. There, of course, has been a danger that, in a new country and in a new age like that of the twentieth century when change takes place with a rapidity previously unimaginable, we should begin to think that wisdom was born yesterday. I suppose that to many in the past one hundred years a college like this has stood—or seemed to stand—for the older virtues, the ancient wisdom; and that is very impressive, none of us should scorn it. Yet, today something different is happening. The rejection of yesterday is not simply a Philistine rejection of culture. That we have always had, that we shall always have, and that we shall always have to fight. Wisdom was not born yesterday any more than it died with our fathers. The rejection of the past to which we have now to pay attention is of a quite different order. It is sketched in Theodore Roszak's *The Making of a Counter Culture*. It is a rejection of the way in which we have domesticated the past, made it a good and gentle place to live in, to escape to from the cruelties and disharmonies of the present. Before it is too late and the destructive forces of nihilism which we have provoked are unleashed in their full power, we had better learn to reinterpret the past, under the pressure of this criticism. Roszak has called the protest of the young today 'The Great Refusal'. But what is being refused? It must not be the past properly understood: a past which has as its articulate moments the death of a Socrates, the cry of an Antigone, the judgments on successful and affluent societies of an eighth century prophet, the denigration by an apostle of the wisdom of the wise and his exaltation of the folly of a Crucified Lord.

The old things which are to be brought out of our store for use in a new day will be less urbane, less comfortable to live with than we have sometimes suggested or supposed. The past will be less the story of successful solutions and more that of agonizing reappraisals. It will be one through which there comes the word of a risen Lord who tells men repeatedly that he was the Crucified One.

# III

This leads me to the third, and last thing I want to say. Behind Matthew's Gospel lies Mark. Matthew, like all good educators, was most anxious that his readers should understand. Mark, like all great artists, asked men to stand before the mystery. Over all our yesterdays and tomorrows, and within all the pressures of today, are the things new and old which we do *not* understand. Even for Matthew, within the question 'Have you understood all this?' resides the doubt about whether the answer can ever be other than in the negative. Beside and behind the Jesus of Matthew who is our teacher stands the Jesus of Mark who questions us; and whose final question is not addressed to us at all, but to a greater court of appeal 'My God, why has thou forsaken me?'

There is not time, nor would it be appropriate to speak more of this afternoon, except to say this. A Church college affiliated to a university must never be ashamed to point to the dark hinterland of the things we do not know, to the mystery with which we are surrounded. It must have the courage to suggest that a part of the educated man's awareness of his world resides in the acknowledgment of that mystery. Without that acknowledgment there will be no humility, without which (in turn) neither faith nor learning can flourish. Without that humility true gentleness and courtesy will fail. It will be in these profounder depths of the human spirit that St Andrew's College in its second century will succeed or fail.

At the end of Lampedusa's novel *The Leopard*, the proud and noble Prince from Sicily refuses to become a member of the Senate of the recently united Italy. He had supported the revolution, but will not take part in the administration of the new State, because, he says, 'Now you need young men, bright young men, with minds asking 'how' rather than 'why', and who are good at masking, at blending, I should say, their personal interests with vague public ideals'.

May God deliver St Andrew's College from producing simply bright young men who so easily grow into calculating old men who, masking or blending private interest with vague public ideals, only ask the question 'how'. May God grant St Andrew's College to put it into the minds of future generations to ask the question 'why'; and though he may never give them to answer that question to their satisfaction in this life, may he hold them in his presence and that of his Son, till we all come to behold the Crucified One as the King in his Glory, in whom all things old and new are one.

# The Commemoration of Benefactors

## A Sermon preached in Ormond College and Trinity College in the University of Melbourne April and October 1979

*And he taught and said to them, 'Is it not written,*
*"My house shall be called a house of prayer for all the nations?"*
*But you have made it a den of robbers.*

*Mark 11: 17*

At first sight the lessons read—Jeremiah's attack on the invio-lability of the Temple, and Jesus driving the money changers and traders out of the court of the Gentiles—do not seem to speak to our condition this afternoon; but on reflection there may be some things to be learnt from them.

The story of Jeremiah is well known, how he stood at the entrance to the Temple and warned the worshippers as they went in not to put their trust in the institution. Don't go on saying 'the Temple of the Lord' 'the Temple of the Lord' as though that automatically provided you with security. It can be destroyed as certainly as other holy places have in the past been razed to the ground. It is what the Temple points to which is important. You are using it as an escape from life, from social justice, concern for the poor, and human compassion. There is no escape for you into religious security away from your obligations to your neighbour. The Temple was founded for the worship of God, the God of justice and mercy; but you (says Jeremiah) have filched it away from its true purpose: you have made it a den of robbers.

Immediately there is focused for us one of those insights to which many of the writers of the Old Testament return again and again, until it is stated in all its starkness in the New Testament story of the crucifixion of Jesus: no institu-tion gains its validity simply by existing. It has to justify its existence by what it stands for and what it does. To put it in the religious terms of the Old Testa-ment: God does not confer inviolable holiness on any institution, even those which he himself has brought into being—written law and temple. He does not say 'This place is holy, come to this sanctuary and you will live. Touch these stones and you will be safe.' He says rather: if men cease to use this institution for the purpose for which it was brought into being, it will be discarded and others will be put in its place. Or if you like to put it in other terms again: there is a law of history whereby that which ceases to serve the purposes for which it was created will atrophy and die. Oh! the shell may remain, an object of archaeological interest; but the institution will no longer live.

This is true of the great institutions of history—the Temple in Jerusalem, the republic of Rome, the Church in North Africa, the *pax britanica*; the institution of monarchy in Western Europe, Imperial Russia, yes (and in the long run) the Soviets also—that if they cease to fulfil in whatever changing forms the function for which they were created they will perish. It is also true of small institutions: of schools, of universities, of colleges. A Service of commemoration of Founders and Benefactors provides us with an occasion for asking each other: why were we founded? What was the purpose for which this college was created?

The actions of our benefactors remind us of a point which can first be made negatively: the college was not brought into being simply to provide convenient residence for students attending the University of Melbourne. Had it been that alone there might have been, and there might still be cheaper, more comfortable, more convenient ways of housing students. No, living together was to be part of the educational process. We were to be a cross-section of the life of the university, in which students from various disciplines could learn from each other, where teachers and taught could gain illumination from each other in their common interest in the subject of study, where minds could be sharpened, imaginations kindled and consciences quickened.

It is sometimes asked, and rightly asked (I think), why the State and the community should provide funds for the housing of students especially in periods when it so signally fails to provide adequate housing for many other sections of the community. Why provide for this group of young people? As I say, the question is a good one: to which of course there is a general answer 'This do but leave not the other undone.' But a more particular answer to the question, why a corporate collegiate life for university teachers and students? still needs to be given. It is to be found, I think, in the nature of university education.

It has been pointed out (by the philosopher Karl Jaspers) that the university today is the inheritor of three great traditions of human teaching and learning. It will neglect anyone of them to its peril. The *first* it learnt from the Jews: the Rabbinic tradition whereby what was learnt by the human race is passed on, with amplification, comment, correction, no doubt. But the process is essentially one of transmitting a tradition of learning. The *second* we learnt from the medieval guilds, whereby young people become apprentices in a trade, the trade of learning in this case. By seeing the master craftsman at work they learn what it is to be a scholar. It has often been pointed out how many Nobel Prizemen in Physics were pupils or pupils of pupils of Nils Bohr, the great Danish Physicist. And the curious fact that perhaps most of the psychoanalysts of the twentieth century were either psychoanalysed themselves by Sigmund Freud or psychoanalysed by someone whom he had psychoanalysed to the third and fourth generation. A strange kind of apostolic succession: essentially the passing on of the skills of a master craftsman. But there is a *third* place to which the Universities return again and again, a third person, that is the figure of Socrates. Whereas in the first two instances the teacher stands before the class, or the master craftsman is an example to the apprentice, in this third model teacher and taught sit before the same questions. Indeed they are themselves questioned, confronted by the mystery of what we do not know, compelled to acknowledge that man's life and thought are problematic, that his knowledge is fragmentary, his achievement fragile, and that we must walk humbly together in the search for truth.

This College, like the University to which it belongs, must try to keep before its members these three ways of learning. By the provision of libraries, by the establishment of fellowships, by the appointment of tutors, by keeping the door of the college open to students regardless of their capacity to pay for being here, benefactors from the past enable us at least to have this threefold ambition. First, that we should be able to learn from each other what is known. And this can even apply across disciplinary boundaries: something of what the other man or woman is studying, its integrity, its discipline, its scientific validity, may rub off on me, so that while I cannot myself go out and talk sense about economics or architecture or physics, I can at least suspect that sometimes other people are talking nonsense. More important, I know that there are people who know more about matters that are only of casual interest to journalists or of short-term interest to politicians; and that it is to them that I should listen.

At least that first tradition of learning should give students a nose for nonsense: I hope that you who are graduating have acquired that sense of smell. Our whole tutorial programme should be helping to achieve that end. There is an authority which rightly belongs to the truth of the matter. Second, we should be a society in which the trade of learning is, if not taught, then (to use a cliché) caught. That is why in a college like this you have senior members in residence; that is why you make room for visiting scholars amongst you. As we go about the business of learning, from the greatest scholar to the youngest student, we provide each other with (as it were) a guild within which this peculiar trade may be learnt. Thirdly, in a community like this we learn to question and in questioning to be questioned. That is uncomfortable. It is uncomfortable to be asked to think for yourself. It is uncomfortable for society to have sent into it graduates who would critically appraise what is going on. university students and university graduates will never be altogether popular members of society if they are doing their job, being Socratic, asking questions, allowing themselves to be asked questions of which they do not know the answer. (What is the use of a university education–it is asked–if it doesn't give you the answers?) Yet on such, if they would but demonstrate an appropriate clarity, restraint and humility, the health of society might come to depend.

About thirty years after this college was founded, away in Berlin, Adolf von Harnack was giving an important series of lectures, later to be published under the title *What is Christianity?* He opened them thus:

> John Stuart Mill has somewhere observed that mankind cannot too often by reminded that there once was a man of the name of Socrates. That is true; but still more important is it to remind man again and again that a man of the name of Jesus Christ once stood in their midst.

Something of that insight was present in its own way in the minds of those who founded this college, and in that of many of its benefactors. The impact here of mind upon mind, of imagination upon imagination, should raise (although not necessarily resolve) the question of faith. That too is part of our heritage to be entered into in the same threefold manner as the rest of learning.

Of that I do not want to say more now, but to recall your minds to the words of Jesus spoken (like Jeremiah) in the Temple. This house was to be called a house of prayer for all the nations. He stood in the Court of the Gentiles. The old dispensation had envisaged that the representatives of nations other than the Jews could come this far. Here, even though it be in the 'outer', the Gentiles could stand. But their ground had been occupied by those who would change the Roman coins into what was legal tender in the Temple, who would sell the doves for the sacrifice. What was a sign of universal access to God had been taken away and used for purely religious purposes. The Court of the Gentiles was now a den of robbers. The intention that God should be worshipped by everyman was now hidden behind the buying and selling which was a necessary part of the legal requirement of worship. What was to be open was now closed.

The Christian Church and the university come together in this conviction: that what is capable of being offered by way of the search for truth, the passing on of knowledge, the pursuit of learning, ought to be available to all who can take advantage of it. The day that my College was opened the then Moderator of the Church said:

> Ormond College like all our Church schools will be open to students of whatever creed or country coming up to the required standard of scholarship and bearing a stainless moral character and they will be untrammelled in their choice of a profession by any ecclesiastical authority or influence.

When I read that to a friend she asked whether they had closed it the next day for lack of suitably qualified candidates. But that was the 19th century way of saying 'those who had enough brains and would behave themselves.'

It is not often enough remembered that the word university refers not to the whole universe of knowledge, but to the fact that it aims to be an open society, open to those who would enter it from any place—any, that is, who are capable of taking advantage of what it has to offer. A house of prayer for all the nations. And indeed its commitment to learning is like a prayer. It is difficult to demonstrate that learning will necessarily benefit a nation, certainly impossible to show by cost benefit analysis the advantages of teaching many things we teach in the university. You have to believe in them. They are an aspiration: men and women opening their spirits to that which is beyond them, allowing themselves to be questioned; not seeking here a security which the world does not afford, but exposing ourselves to the mystery of that which we do not know, to the suffering we do not understand. Here is no continuing city, we seek one to come.

Perhaps by the mercy of God some who pass through this college, and who have worshipped (however infrequently) in this chapel may come to remember that at the centre of our perplexities, holding us in life was one whose sign was a cross. For he replaced the Temple with his own crucified body, that all men might have available to them an awareness of God in and not outside human suffering and perplexity. To whom be the glory for ever.

# Commemorations

✦

It has been my privilege and responsibility to speak either at the funeral or at a service of thanksgiving for a friend who has recently died. Such addresses are commonly referred to as eulogies. I do not like the word. It suggests, in the Latin phrase *de mortuis nil nisi bonum*, that one speaks only well of the dead. The occasion, however, calls for something different: not for a moral assessment, but for a way of saying 'Thank you' before God for the particular gifts and graces seen in this man or this woman, in the employment of which they had enriched the lives of others, their families, their colleagues, the congregation gathered at that particular time and the community in which they had lived and worked. If such a description is to avoid being only a catalogue of virtues something more is required: an attempt has to be made to put this particular life and death into a wider setting. Readily at hand for the Christian are the Scriptures, in which we obtain a glimpse of God's ways with the human race. This particular man or woman whom we commemorate—that is, bring in to our memory—has been and is a part of a wider purpose working itself out in our midst.

The setting of the addresses was that of worship in which the Christian faith and hope are expressed in readings and in our prayers. Customarily the address was followed by a short litany of praise in which those present are invited to make a response.

Eight addresses to commemorate Church leaders and theological colleagues follow:

> Hector Maclean (1885 – 1968)
> James Marshall Young (1912 – 1977)
> Murray Edwin Norman (1954 – 1981)
> Marjorie Smart (1911 – 1982)
> Rolland Arthur Busch (1920 – 1985)
> Marius Willem Jan Geursen (1914 – 1988)
> Frank Woods (1907 – 1992)

# Hector Maclean

## 1885 – 1968

*Born in Lismore, NSW, educated at Otago Boys High School and the University of Otago, Glasgow University and the United Free Church College, Glasgow. Ordained to the ministry of the Presbyterian Church of New Zealand in 1915, Minister of Invercargill 1915-20, St. Andrew's Church, Dunedin 1920-28. Professor of Old Testament Studies, Ormond College, The University of Melbourne 1928-57, Principal of the Theological Hall, Ormond College 1942-57. Moderator of the Presbyterian Church of Victoria 1943-44.*

> *Thy steadfast love, O Lord, extends to the heavens,*
> *and thy truth to the clouds*
> *Thy righteousness is like the mountain of God,*
> *thy judgments are like the great deep;*
> *thou comest to the help of man and beast.*
> *How precious is thy steadfast love, O God:*
> *The children of men take refuge in the shadow of thy wings.*
> *For with thee is the fountain of life,*
> *in thy light do we see light.*
>
> *Psalm 3: 65-7,9*

Early in my time in Australia I came away from a Service such as this with Principal Hector Maclean. He was (I gathered) of the opinion that more had been said than should properly be said on such an occasion; and then in two unforgettable phrases (which however he would not have wished to be repeated from a pulpit) he indicated what he hoped might be said about him when his time came. The words were to be few, they were to be honest, and he hoped the judgment might be generous: it ought not to be difficult in his case to follow those injunctions, except perhaps in brevity for his personality was complex.

Those of us who were received into his friendship when he was already old, soon realised how much every experience of life had become a part of him. His early struggles for education gave him a lasting sympathy with the many students who had to battle along with inadequate support as they trained for the work of the ministry. His early training as a scientist gave to a mind that was unusually sharp, a precision which could be devastating equally in the courts of the Church or in the classroom, at detecting the superfluous and the non-sensical. His skill at Rugby football gave him a permanent interest in sport: for years he trained the Melbourne University Rugby Football team, and made many friends thereby; and University sport of all sorts had no more interested follower in the years when he lived in Ormond.

If New Zealand at High School and University discovered in him the brilliant student, it was Glasgow that made him into a scholar. It was the Glasgow of Denny and McFadyean. There, he became a Hebraist, and laid the foundations of his remarkable knowledge of the Old Testament. Not the least of the influences which bore upon him was that of Adam Welch, the distinguished Old Testament scholar, to whom he was assistant, and whom he (in some ways) so closely resembled, as preacher, pastor, teacher and scholar. It was appropriate that many years later, long after Welch's death, Welch's old University of Edinburgh should confer on Hector Maclean its doctorate in divinity, honoris causa.

The future Dr Hector Maclean, as a young man, was undertaking further studies in Glasgow when the 1st World War came, and instead of further study it was fighting. The frustration and the waste and the suffering left a permanent mark on his spirit, as surely as the physical hazards left him with weakness in his lungs against which his otherwise powerful constitution had to battle for the rest of his life. Human injustice, unnecessary pain, whether caused by callousness, cruelty or stupidity, called forth his sympathy for the sufferer and his wrath upon those who inflicted suffering.

He returned to New Zealand, and there, while in a parish, began that ministry to students which continued until (and indeed after) he left Ormond. There also began that home given to hospitality from which many of us have received a rare quality of friendship, and in which we were received with a distinctive courtesy. In 1928 he was called to the Chair of Hebrew and Old Testament Studies in the Theological Hall at Ormond College, and from 1942 until his retirement in 1957 he was Principal. It was here that most of us in this Church this morning came to know him, as teacher, as scholar, as colleague, as Churchman: as teacher perhaps most frequently remembered for his exposition of the Hebrew prophets, as scholar possessing one of the most theologically distinguished minds in this Church (or perhaps in any Church in Australia), as colleague encouraging especially those of us who were younger than he while often surprising and humbling us by an awareness of recent developments in fields other than his own; as Churchman serving the Church in many capacities some of them normally regarded as remote from his scholarly interests, for instance in his membership of the Board of Investment and Finance, and (more expectedly) in other capacities on school Councils and as Moderator of the Assembly during a difficult year of the war. An exacting teacher (I understand) he was yet one who could take a generous view of the frailties of students, particularly in relation to what they regarded as the intricacies but he the simplicities of Hebrew grammar and syntax. He was not a comfortable colleague, but a challenging one, and a corrective influence; for while his mind was open to new approaches to old topics, he was deeply suspicious of intellectual fashions.

And so one could go on bringing to mind the many facets of his personality: how, although older people frequently regarded him with some awe, and recalcitrant students perhaps sometimes with terror, children approached him easily for he treated them with great gentleness. But to continue would be inappropriate, except to ask one question: what lay at the depths of his complex personality? Some say that he was like one of the Old Testament prophets whom he expounded with such loving care; and there is something in that. His eyes could flash; but Archie Colquhoun's splendid portrait of him now hanging in Ormond College, catches a quieter more reflective moment. I sometimes think that he is best understood as one whose spirit, like that of his Lord, Jesus Christ, was nourished upon the Psalms: the psalms which mirror a wide range of human experience, where mood succeeds mood with great variety. There evil is called evil, and mean-ness mean. There men wrestle with the problem of how to distinguish between one's own enemies and the enemies of God. There men are invited to put their trust in Yahweh's steadfast love which extends to the heavens. There Hector Maclean had his conviction strengthened that the righteousness of God stands like the strong mountains, that his judgments are like the great deep.

I sometimes think too that no one really ever understood Hector Maclean who had not heard him read the Scriptures or who had not by him been led in prayer. For in the Scriptures he believed that men could find what might be supremely precious to man, the *hesed*, the steadfast love of God; and in prayer the children of men could take refuge under the shadow of his wings.

His long life on earth is ended, more than fourscore years, surrounded by that mercy and grace of which he taught that, prefigured in the Old Testament, it was supremely found in Christ. Because of that same Christ we now look to the resurrection of the dead and the life of the world to come; and so in words still taken from the psalms we pray with hope:

> With thee, Lord, is the fountain of life, and in thy
> light we shall see light.

May the God of hope fill you with all joy and peace in believing, so that by the power of the Holy Spirit you may abound in hope.

# James Marshall Young
## 1912 – 1977

*Parish Minister, Balwyn Presbyterian Church 1940-1954. Dean of the Theological Hall of the Presbyterian Church, Ormond College, 1954-76. Assistant Registrar of the Melbourne College of Divinity from 1966, Associate Dean 1976-77. Foundation Dean of the United Faculty of Theology.*

*Who then is the faithful and wise servant, whom his master has set over his household, to give them their food at the proper time? Blessed is that servant whom his master when he comes will find so doing.*

*Matthew 24: 45*

There is a great deal in the previous paragraph of Matthew's Gospel about watchfulness, about being ready. Two men will be in the field; one is taken and one is left. Two women will be grinding at mill; one is taken and one is left. Watch therefore, for you do not know on what day your Lord is coming. But Matthew seems to have had a certain distrust of general exhortation, unsupported by illustrations of what they mean. In concrete terms, in what consists this vigilance? What is the man or woman like who watches and is ready? It is a vivid enough military picture, a man on duty at the lookout; the sentry on the walls; but what does it mean in civilian, in everyday terms? What does a man do who is ready?

So Matthew attaches three stories to suggest what he does *not* do. He tells of the majordomo, the steward in charge of the household who says 'My master is delayed', and proceeds to beat up his fellow-servants, and eats and drinks with the drunken. He follows this with the story of the ten maidens, five so foolish that they only took enough oil for the immediate needs, but not sufficient to be ready when the bridegroom came. And then the parable of the talents, and in particular the condemnation of the servant who buried his and is condemned as wicked and slothful.

Matthew does what a good many educationalists tell us we should not do: he gives us negative illustrations, he shows us what we should not do. But maybe Matthew, and behind him Jesus, knew better. Maybe the stories are there to make us pause and think; to make us go back to the question with which he introduced the sequence: *Who then is the faithful and wise servant?* What are the positive attributes of the watchful man? The question is thrown at us. We must think for ourselves. We must be roused out of mere receptivity. We must find the answers. They are not to be handed to us on a plate. No, they are discovered in life, and sometimes in the lives of those around us.

So it has been for some of us as we have reflected, been shocked into reflecting, on the particular characteristics and gifts of James Marshall Young, colleague and friend, for whom we give thanks to God this morning.

Jim Young shared with the author of Matthew's Gospel, and with his Lord, a certain distrust for general statements and exhortations which did not result in actions of a concrete kind. Which of us who worked with him has not been reproved at some point in a committee or a discussion by some such intervention as: "That is all very well, but what have you decided?" Once the decision was taken and was minuted, then action must follow; and he saw to that. And thus those stories told by Matthew draw our attention to positive possibilities.

# 1

The majordomo, our household steward, violated his office, and also expressed disbelief in the reality of the Lord's return, by creating chaos. He was disorderly in a sphere intended by his master to be an example of decency and order. The faithful and wise servant creates order. What this parable says to us is that this is not to be taken for granted. We human beings, in small things and large, run so quickly to disorder; and that is a denial of God's good intention for our lives. Disorderly administration shows a lack of compassion. To be kind to those with whom we have to do, to be loving, they must know where they stand. Only then will they be delivered from the feeling of being pushed around.

It was my privilege to be working here in the Theological Hall in Ormond when Jim came to take up the duties of Dean in 1954, an office he held until the end of 1976. Before that, since 1940 and while busy building up a congregation in Balwyn and getting them their Church building, Jim had been secretary of the Theological Education Committee. It has been suggested that he had a longer period of continuous service to theological education than anyone else in the history of the Presbyterian Church of Victoria. I suppose that it would be possible to count the number of students he had to deal with, their courses to be arranged and approved, their accreditation received, their bursaries to be made available to them; but if possible, very difficult, difficult to assess what his orderly mind and purpose did to make sure that the Church which he served would have available to it a constant supply of suitably trained men and women for the ministry. And each a person, for whom the basic requirement was that he or she should have the call to the ministry received from God, heard, tested and understood in the life of the Church. Literally, God only knows how many lives Jim's work touched in this way. Many of them themselves did not know what they owed to him; for he could be discreet to the point of reticence.

## 2

The second story also provokes a reflection assisted by our memories of Jim. The foolish maidens were imprudent. They couldn't look forward. Their lamps went out. We could exactly translate our text: Who is the faithful and prudent servant? The prudent servant is one who looks forward; and that requires foresight, preparation. When we look back on Jim's life and work, there were things for which he prepared himself and, even more importantly, there were ways in which God prepared him.

He came from Scotland in his early 'teens, and went to school at Geelong College where he developed that love for games which never left him, that skill in playing them in which he rejoiced for much of his life and brought him friends and acquaintances with men in many walks of life. This was an aspect of his sheer humanity which was to be important for him when he went to Scotland as a postgraduate student on the Archibald Main scholarship; and that very experience of friendship with Professor Main and of working with him was to give him a wide sympathy with men of varied interests. On his return he became minister of the congregation in the then rapidly growing suburb of Balwyn; and the experiences there prepared him again for what lay ahead. His time here in Ormond constantly required foresight, prudence, preparing for the future.

When he first came he was able to spend much of his time in teaching, and in particular, tutoring other subjects and teaching English Literature to students, mostly older students, who were thus enabled to undertake a course other than university studies before proceeding to theology. For him, and for them, this was one of the most rewarding experiences of his life; helping men to read carefully, to penetrate below the surface of some of the most significant writings, mostly contemporary or near contemporary novels, in our literature. He was ready to see what had to be done, and prudent in his preparation for it.

Similarly he served the Melbourne College of Divinity. Beyond the call of duty he assisted first Calvert Barber, and later Alfred Bird in preparation for the changes which would need to take place if the College of Divinity were to play a still larger role in theological education in this State and beyond. Related to this, if still distinct from it, was the emergence of the United Faculty of Theology; and as in other instances, some here know better than I the extent of his contribution to its creation and administration, so that at the time of his death he was still its apparently indispensable Dean.

For all these, and many other developments, he knew that you'd better have oil for your lamps: a little prudent planning wouldn't go astray.

## 3

This leads to the third story. What is condemned in the man who buried his talent is that he was slothful. Everything to which Jim Young put his hand and mind required hard work, some of it behind the scenes, discreet and patient, but necessary if the Master were to have a faithful and wise servant who would give his children their food at the proper time.

Dr Samuel Johnson said to Sir Joshua Reynolds: 'If a man does not make new acquaintances as he advances through life, he will soon find himself left alone. A man, then, should keep his friendship *in constant repair*'. The presence here today of men and women representing so many areas and periods of Jim's life would suggest that for all that he was a somewhat private man, he was ever making new acquaintances as he advanced through life. Here we are colleagues and friends from his days in Balwyn, from St. Andrews Hospital, on whose Board he sat, from the Ormond College Council of which he was a member for over 30 years, from the staff of this College of which he was such a proud and loyal son, from Presbytery and Synod, from former days in the Theological Education Committee of the Presbyterian Church of Victoria and the College Committee of the General Assembly of Australia, not to mention his closest colleagues in the United Faculty of Theology and the Melbourne College of Divinity and what is now the Hall of the Uniting Church. Here we are met together with his family and intimate friends to thank God for friendships kept in constant repair, for work done and relationships kept good, without haste and without sloth. Some of us know that there have been times when we have acted more sensibly, have looked at our neighbours and colleagues more charitably because Jim Young was there to prompt us. I certainly know that this College (and its Master) have been delivered from mistakes which we would otherwise have committed, had it not been for the discretion of Jim Young.

All this takes work and courage. Those who in the parable of the talents took the more venturesome line, invested their talent and looked to the future, eventually heard a voice address them: 'Well done, good and faithful servant, you have been faithful ... Enter into the joy of your Master'.

It is not too difficult for us here this morning to hear that verdict spoken over the life and worth of James Marshall Young.

# Murray Edwin Norman
## 1955 – 81

*This address was given in memory of Murray at a Service held in the Chapel of Ormond College, of which he had been a member, on 22nd January 1981: a loving man and a dissenter.*

We are met here this morning, the family and friends of Murray Norman, who died on Sunday morning at the early age of twenty-six. We meet to strengthen each other in our loss, to remember Murray together– each with his or her own precious recollection–and to thank God for what he meant to us.

A long time ago Bishop Butler said: 'Each thing is what it is and not another thing.' Each man, each woman is who he or she is, and not another person. Each life is what it is and not another thing. We may be inclined to mourn what Murray could have been, would have been had he lived for longer. But that is a fruitless occupation: 'each life is what it is and not another thing.' So we recall Murray's life as it was, or those parts of it which were known to us; and we are grateful that he was given to us, and perhaps we would learn something in the recollection.

It was even more than for most of us a life of light and shade: he could be supremely happy and he knew despair. A shadow was cast early by his father's death when Murray was four years of age: an event which he and others came to see as having a lasting effect upon his life. And yet he was a happy member of a happy family: years later he came to have a specially close relationship with his step-father, whose loss he was also to mourn, and shewed a particularly gentle side of his character towards his step-sister, Emma. He loved to talk with his grandparents.

He was destined to belong to a generation, many of the most sensitive members of which, throughout the world, rose up in protest against the world they had inherited. He took part in demonstrations against the Australian commitment in Vietnam: he had a loathing for violence. His stand was one which in some circles was likely to cost him reputation and opportunities. He could see through the pretence which encases so many of our institutions, impenetrably as it seemed; and our failure in the last ten years to learn the lesson of that protest will be a lasting shame until we face those questions again. Do the institutions of our society protect the weak or the strong? Among the papers in which in prose and poetry he tried to express his deepest feelings, Murray wrote: 'The most important aspect of Australian society is the right to dissent, and the material base from which to justly enjoy such freedom.' There speaks an old tradition of Anglo-Saxon dissent, going back through the seventeenth century to the Middle Ages—the right to dissent, and sufficient material security for all so that freedom might be enjoyed without let or hindrance.

Despite all the things that so frightened and disturbed us about the Counter-Culture of ten years ago, we should have heard this voice from our past articulating itself anew in Murray's generation. It was a generation in which, as it were, humanity's nerve ends were exposed.

Yet their very desire for new experiences, new perspectives, left them open to exploitation by evil men, who offered (at a price) a new perception by way of drugs. Murray, and many another, was vulnerable where the rest of us were secure. So he suffered; but he was fighting his way back to health, to mental and physical health, when unexpectedly his heart gave up and he was asked to fight no more. In an autobiographical fragment among his papers he tells how–a year or two after he himself was established in school–he overheard a father delivering a somewhat frightened small boy at the school and say to another boy: 'You'll look after him. Won't you?' 'This', wrote Murray, 'was probably my first contact with the consciousness of the need to help the oppressed peoples of the world. I don't know why I remember this saying but I do remember repeating it often and saying to myself "I must remember that".' And elsewhere he wrote: 'What is my path when I ask only to serve the universe? I have written it myself that to serve is my task.'

Yet he was also seeking for peace, for rest. According to his poems he did not yet know where or how: where to live, from whom to learn—the Buddha or another?

Are not psychic phenomena sometimes true?
What the hell happened to the mystic self of my youth?

*Now we see in a glass darkly but then face to face.*

Kathleen Raine has a poem entitled *Amo ergo sum*—I love therefore I am[1]. It is, of course, based upon, perhaps a correction of, Descartes' philosophical dictum: *Cogito ergo sum*—I think therefore I am. Murray Norman is to be understood, not through his thoughts but through his love. *Amo ergo sum*—I love therefore I am. His true existence is revealed in his love of family, of friends, of fun: his humour, it has been said, was not destructive, it may have been teasing (as indeed in the last days of his life he used it to provoke his nurses) but like all he would be and do it was essentially creative—creating a new relationship of confidence, of trust with those at whom it was directed.

What lives in our memory is his love, and his loveability.

A longstanding friend put this into words in *The Age* on the day after he died:

> For the countless marvellous moments, gentle spirit and lovely friend, thank you.

To give love, and to evoke love: to love and be loved. That is near to the heart of things. That is what Jesus called being 'not far from the Kingdom of God'.

Kathleen Raine has a series of three *Poems of Incarnation*. In the third she addresses the Christ child who is about to enter the world:

> Who stands at my door in the storm and rain
> On the threshold of being?
> …………
> Go back, my child, to the rain and the storm,
> For in this house there is sorrow and pain
> In the lonely night.
> …………
> I will not go back for sorrow or pain,
> For my true love weeps within
> And waits for my coming.
>
> Go back, my babe, to the vacant night
>
> I will not go back for hate or sin,
> I will not go back for sorrow or pain,
> For my true love mourns within
> On the threshold of night.

---

[1] *llected Poems of Kathleen Raine*, (London: Hamish Hamilton, 1956). The poem 'Amo ergo sum' is to be found on page 135; and the third section of 'Three Poems of Incarnation' at page 156.

Murray would have been slow to identify himself with Jesus Christ; but the Christ is the precursor and type of us all: he identifies himself with us, especially with those who are poor and suffer, and he would have us do likewise.

If we ask why Murray was sent into the world of sorrow and pain which at times looked as though it would break his sensitive spirit, then the answer is that we needed him. 'You'll look after him. Won't you?' 'My true love weeps within.' Now for him sickness and sorrow are ended, death itself is past, and he has entered into the rest that remains for the children of God. Thanks be to God who gives the victory through the Lord Jesus Christ. Amen.

# Marjorie Smart
## 1911 – 1982

### The following address was given at a
### Memorial Service in Melbourne
### 3 June 1982

*Born in Winnipeg, and educated in Canada, began her professional life as Secretary to the Rt Hon. Malcolm Macdonald, UK High Commissioner in Ottawa (1942-46); was Personal assistant to Sir Gordon Munro, UK Treasury Delegation, Washington (1947); an officer of the Canadian Department of External Affairs (1948-53); the Canadian Vice Consul, New York and Press Officer, Canadian Delegation to UN (1949-5). In April 1953 she married Lt Gen. E K Smart who died in 1961. Principal of St Hilda's College, The University of Melbourne (1964-1975).*

M arjorie Smart once told me that when a member of her family was about to leave home her father would gather them on the previous evening and read the 121st Psalm.

We cannot be quite sure, but it seems likely that this Psalm was composed as a dialogue between one starting on a journey and those who speed him on his way.

'I lift up my eyes to the hills', says the departing one. I am about to go out, to leave the old securities. 'From whence does my help come'? And the answer of those who are speeding him on his ways is:

> Help comes from the Lord
> Who made heaven and earth

And one of them speaking on behalf of all, no doubt, offers the blessing—at once a promise and at intercession:

> May he not suffer your foot to slip,
> may he who keeps you not slumber!
> Behold he who keeps Israel
> will neither slumber nor sleep

The God of your father will be your God:

> He will keep your soul (life itself)
> He will keep your going out
> and your coming in
> from this time forth and for evermore.

There is nowhere you can go from his presence. There is a great deal of Marjorie Smart's story in that little Psalm.

Not once but many times did she say 'I lift up my eyes to the hills'. I leave behind the old securities. I seek out the new. Born and brought up in Winnipeg, where she died less than two weeks ago, she graduated from the University of Manitoba, and almost immediately left Canada first for London and then for Washington, working with and for two distinguished diplomats, Malcolm McDonald when he was Secretary for Dominion Affairs and Sir Gordon Munro when he was head of the UK Treasury Delegation. In 1947 the Canadian Foreign service was opened to women. She returned to Canada, took the necessary examinations and became one of the first women to enter the Canadian Department of External Affairs. She was for a period Vice-Consul for the Canadian government in New York in charge of information, and a member of the Canadian delegation to the United Nations. During this time she met and married Lieutenant General E K Smart, Australian Consul-General in New York. When he retired she return with him to Australia where she soon became known in University affairs, particularly during the University Building Fund Appeal.

When her husband died in 1961 she once more found herself having to make a new start. I know that she found this perplexing. After the happiness of those years a great loneliness. Despite the affection of members of her husband's family, and many friends she was once more alone. With characteristic decisiveness, however, she chose to remain in Australia, took an appointment with the Immigration Department, travelled to England and back advising migrants, and preparing them to settlement in a new country. She knew what it meant to get up and go out, to face the challenge of the new.

It was at this time that St Hilda's College was being founded, and the Interim-Council was looking for a Principal; and she was invited to accept the position. She was very uncertain that she should accept. Indeed she had virtually refused, believing that she was not suitably qualified for the post. I think she would not object to me repeating what she said to me years later: 'You and others told me I should accept. Raynor Johnston pursued me with letters and telegrams at every port at which the ship called, which implied that if I refused I would be violating some principle that undergirt the universe'. I think that St Hilda's should know that they owe their first Principal at least in large part to the persistence of the then Master of Queen's College.

For eleven years Marjorie Smart was Principal, the first Principal of the College; and it was here and in that role that most of you came to know her best. If she was diffident about accepting the appointment there was nothing tentative about the way she fulfilled her responsibilities or exercised her authority. Her charm of manner, the warmth of her friendship and her gaiety of spirit did not conceal and were not intended to hide her decisiveness. She was determined that St. Hilda's should take its place with independence and dignity among the Colleges of the University, should have something distinctive to offer to its members, and should make its own contribution to the University of which it was a part. She had a will of steel in pursuing her objectives. Yet she would not have been the great Principal that she was, had she not had an unusual sympathy for students.

When asked by someone who did not know her why I thought that St Hilda's should appoint Marjorie Smart as Principal I remember saying: 'Few young women will go in and out of a College over which Marjorie Smart presides without having their horizons widened'. And if that is not what Colleges and Universities are for, I don't know what they are about. Many here today will confirm that this happened, partly because her contacts with men and women in touch with wider affairs in this community visited St Hilda's because they were friends of Marjorie, partly because of what she was in herself.

She served for a period on the Council of the University of Melbourne, and advised La Trobe University about the setting up of its Colleges. Her period on the Council of this University was somewhat turbulent. With great skill she chaired a committee containing some of the most senior outside members of the Council, senior academic staff and some troubled students. I think she gained the respect and affection of them all, and she served the University well in providing insight into some of its problems and their solution.

In all this she brought to fruition here three elements which were strong characteristics of her distinguished Canadian family: a commitment to the Church, an understanding of the University, and an awareness of a call to public service. Faith, intellectual integrity and duty: she shared them all. The God of her father was her God.

But we are not here this morning to tell the story of the Gordon family to which she was so attached and which has supported her through her last trying years. Nor are we here to tell the full story of its distinguished daughter Marjorie. We are here to thank God; and some of us cannot do that without remembering her last great struggle against a crippling disability.

It is well known that Marjorie Smart had planned for herself an active retirement, in which she would learn a new language and make herself useful in new ways. Once more she would lift up her eyes to the hills, make a new way not depending completely on the old securities. She was not to know, nor were we that the new language which she had to learn was of weakness and of suffering. Crippled by a stroke on the eve of her departure for overseas she was to spend many months in hospital, and for the last six years of her life was physically dependent on other people in a way she had never before experienced. It was a hard way for her to go: a woman who was accustomed to making her own decisions, who not only had learnt to control her own career and accept sorrow in her own life and that of others with sympathy and love but who had also bought into being a College, every detail of the life of which she seemed to have influenced. There might well have been applied to her the words, 'When you were young you girded yourself and walked where you would; now you are old, you stretch out your hand, and another girds you and carries you where you do not wish to go'. At first, indeed for months (as some of us know), she seemed to be afflicted and crushed, perplexed to the point of despair. So in sadness we asked: where is that Marjorie we knew?

Then, with the passing of time and that extraordinary courage and resilience of character which was hers—and thanks in no small measure to the devotion of her sister, Ruth—her vision turned outwards, her old interest in her family, her friends, her College, the world around her, reasserted themselves: 'afflicted but not crushed, perplexed but not unto despair'. Some of us in recent months have received from her letters in which there is no self-pity, but an acceptance of the limitations of her life and a joyful appreciation of those around her. Well might she be thought to have heard again the promise read to her by her father as she first set out from Winnipeg:

> The Lord will keep your soul
> He will keep your going out
> and your coming in from this time forth and for evermore.

Thanks be to God for his gift to us of Marjorie Smart, now entered into the joy of her Lord.

# Rolland Arthur Busch
## 1920 – 1985

*Professor of New Testament Studies, Emmanuel College, 1961-78, Trinity College 1978-85, Brisbane. Moderator of the Synod of Queensland in the Uniting Church in Australia 1977-79; President of the Assembly of the Uniting Church in Australia 1982-85. Staff Captain (Air) HQ NG Force 1943; CMF Chaplain 1954; Senior Chaplain HQ Northern Command 1962-68; Chaplain General 1968-81.*

*Therefore take the whole armour of God, that you may be able to withstand in the evil day, and having done all to stand.*
*Ephesians 6: 13*

### And having done all to stand

Whoever wrote the Epistle to the Ephesians, or whenever it was written, whatever the circumstances which called it forth, its import is clear. It aims to give security and stability to the life of the Church. Mature Christians will not be subject to trends, carried about with every wind of doctrine. Jew and Gentile are secure before God, because he has reconciled them both in one body through the cross. Indeed all things in heaven and earth have been put under Christ's feet. So what the Christian has to do, surrounded as he or she may be with cunning wickedness and spiritual evil, is to stand firm, wearing the armour of God, servants of Christ doing the will of God from the heart. So the Christian has a confidence which is not his own. Thus he is enabled to stand.

These words, and this epistle come vividly to mind when we think of Rolland Arthur Busch, Rollie Busch to so many, whom we are met together to remember with affection and gratitude, for whose death we cannot but grieve, but for whose life and work we give praise to God who called him to his service in this life, and now has called him into the communion of saints and to the life everlasting.

It is neither possible nor appropriate on an occasion like this to give a biographical sketch of Rollie Busch or to list his many services to the Church and the community. It is right, however, that we should pause a while, remember and give thanks, and that we should seek strength anew to complete the responsibilities laid upon us.

The words from the epistle to the Ephesians read to us bring to mind much of Rollie's witness for which we give thanks.

We are told to stand *having girded your loins with truth*. It is well-known that it was after periods in the public service before and after the Second World War, and distinguished service in the Army during the war, that Rollie began studies at the University of Queensland and Emmanuel College with a view to entering the Ministry of the Presbyterian Church. It would be an understatement to say that he was a good student. He was literally a first class student both in Arts and in Divinity. He followed this with postgraduate studies in New York, chiefly in Christian Education. In a day of increasing specialisation he had competence in many fields and had a well-stocked mind. We can think of characteristic remarks like: 'We can be very grateful to So-and-So (quoting some important author whom he may have read some years previously) for making the distinction Such-and-Such which we apply to this problem'.

It is perhaps not so well known that if his teachers in the University had had their way he would have spent much of his life teaching Philosophy, but he had heard the call to the Ministry and after a period in a parish was appointed Professor of New Testament Studies at Emmanuel College of which he was also for 16 years Principal—a role in which he commended himself and his interests both in the University and among his colleagues, the Heads of University Colleges throughout Australia.

We remember these things because they were all a part of having loins girt with truth. The mind was to be used for the clarification of issues; and at its centre the Christian faith made a claim for, and a demand upon its adherents for concern for the truth.

But for the author of Ephesians truth is closely related to righteousness and holiness. 'Be clothed with the new man, the one who is according to God, created in righteousness and holiness which derive from the truth', he says elsewhere; or here, more briefly, 'having put on the breastplate of righteousness'. Righteousness, that true and renewed relationship between God and man which should be reflected in relationships between members of the human race, among God's children: the righteousness for which if we hunger and thirst we are indeed blessed. Blessed are those who earnestly desire the vindication of the right.

Some of us have good reason to know how much the Uniting Church owes to Rollie Busch for the wisdom and firmness with which it was able to stand in difficult days. I think by way of outstanding example of the part which he played in representing the Church, facing government and community leaders in the interests of the people of Aurukun and Mornington Island in 1978. It was not surprising although gratifying to learn that the Uniting Aboriginal and Islander Christians Congress this year at the Assembly a few weeks before his death conferred upon him the title of 'honorary member of the Uniting Aboriginal and Islander Christian Congress'—the only person so to be named.

'And having shod your feet with the equipment of the Gospel of peace—a sublime paradox, as Harnack called it, the Christian warfare to be about peace. Rollie knew that. If a degree of independence is necessary for a people or a race, interdependence is a necessary expression of their reconciliation. In war and peace he knew the paradox worked out in the secular affairs of men of having to bear arms in the interest of peace. After the experience of his own military service he could not desert his companions in arms, but to the end served them as chaplain and guarded their religious interests. Indeed he was helping chaplains to understand their faith and their task when he was stricken by the heart attack which proved fatal. 'Having your feet shod with the equipment of the Gospel of peace' had a realistic component in it for Rollie.

And so we could go on: 'above all taking the shield of faith ... the helmet of salvation, the sword of the Spirit which is the Word of God'. Which of us could ever doubt for a moment those fundamental orientations of Rollie's life? Through that warm humanity, that almost but never quite irreverent sense of humour, that delight in family and friends, in travel and in the world around him shone the firm conviction of faith, the assurance of salvation, and the vocation to the exposition of the Word of God.

Solzhenitsyn has a short piece entitled *Along the Oka*. In it he says:

> When you travel the by-roads of Central Russia you begin to understand the secret of the pacifying countryside. It is in the churches. They trip up the slopes, ascend the high hills, come down to the broad rivers, like princesses in white and red, they lift their bell-towers—graceful, shapely, all different—high over mundane timber and thatch, they nod to each other from afar, from villages that are cut off and invisible to each other they soar to the same heaven. And wherever you wander in the fields or meadows, however far from habitation, you are never alone: from over the hayricks,

the walls of trees, and even the curve of the earth's surface the head of some bell-tower will beckon to you.

Then he describes the terrible desecration of these buildings: crosses flattened, graves churned, obscene inscriptions scrawled on the murals: one church locked and silent, another storing lubricating oil, and another used by groups and clubs. Then he adds:

> People were always selfish and often unkind. But the evening chimes used to sing out, floating over villages, fields and woods. Reminding men that they must abandon the trivial concerns of this world and give time and thought to eternity. These chimes, which only one old tune keeps alive for us, raised people up and prevented them from sinking down on all fours.
>
> Our forefathers put all that was finest in themselves, all their under-standing of life into these stones, into these bell-towers.

We of the Reformed Churches can rarely boast such splendid reminders cover-ing the countryside; and in Australia we rarely hear church bells or see their towers. But God does raise up among us men, men and women; and there are some of whom we can say 'Our forefathers put all that was finest in themselves, all their understanding of life into that man, that woman'.

And so like Rilke standing in front of the commemoration tablet in the Church of Santa Maria Formosa we find ourselves asking the question: 'What do they require of me?' You and I would be doing less than we should if we did not ask that question this afternoon: 'What does this hour, these memories, require of you and me?'

## Stand fast, and having done all to stand

On the morning after he was admitted to hospital Rollie Busch, lately President of the Assembly of the Church, said to David Gill its secretary: 'David, for the first time in my life, I am staring death in the face. And you know, I am not afraid.'

> Then there came forth a summons for Mr Standfast ... the post brought it him open in his hands; the contents whereof were, that he must prepare for a change of life, for his Master was not willing that he should be so far from Him any longer ...
>
> ... When Mr Standfast had set things in order, and the time being come to haste him away, he also went down into the river. Now there was a great calm at that time in the river; wherefore Mr Standfast, when he was

about half way in, stood awhile, and talked to his companions ... And he said, "This river has been a terror to many; yea, the thoughts of it also have often frighted me; but now methinks I stand easy ... I see myself now at the end of my journey; my toilsome days are ended. I am going now to see that head that was crowned with thorns, and that face which was spit upon for me ... I have loved to hear my Lord spoken of; and wherever I have seen the print of his shoe in the earth, there I have wanted to set my foot too ... His voice to me has been the most sweet; and his countenance I have more desired than they that have most desired the light of the sun ... He has held me, and hath kept me from mine iniquities; yea, my steps hath he strengthened in his way.

Now while he was thus in discourse his countenance changed; his strong man bowed under him: and after he had said, 'Take me, for I come unto Thee', he ceased to be seen of them.

But glorious it was to see how the upper region was filled with horses and chariots, with trumpeters and pipers, with singers and players on stringed instruments, to welcome pilgrims as they went up, and followed one another in at the beautiful gate of the city.'

God grant us grace to join that procession, to follow after, and to enter the gate of that city. And to Him be the glory.

# Marius Willem Jan Geursen
## 1914 − 1988

The following sermon was preached at the memorial service in the Uniting Church, Camberwell, on 22 February 1988.

*Pastor of congregations of the Dutch Reformed Church in Holland: Rumpt (Betuwe) 1942-1946; Leiden 1946-52, with an interval in Indonesia 1948-1950 at request of Dutch Synod. Minister of the Presbyterian Church of Australia, with the special task of ministering to migrants 1952-1958, as parish minister of Thornbury 1958-1961 and Hartwell 1961-1977. Minister of the Uniting Church in Australia, in the Canterbury parish in Victoria 1977-1980.*

> *For the love of Christ constrains us, for we are convinced that one has died for all; therefore all have died. And he died for all, that those who live might live no longer for themselves but for him who for their sake died and was raised.*
> Therefore, *from now on we regard no one from a human point of view alone;*
> Therefore, *if anyone is in Christ, there is a new creation.*
> *II Corinthians 5: 14-17*

We have the privilege this afternoon of pausing for a few minutes to reflect together on the life and faith of Marius Geursen, and to thank God that it was given to us to know him.

We are told that in music counterpoint consists in the combination of two or more melodic lines. We hear those two or more melodies sounding together.

We cannot hear the line which was Marius' life without also hearing something of the story of the human race in the central decades of the twentieth century. The two melodies are interwoven.

Marius Willem Jan Geursen was born in 1914, on 4 June exactly two months before the outbreak of the World War which was to shatter so many of the illusions of men and women about the progress and perfectibility of the human race. He completed his studies at the University of Utrecht in the early years of the World War II, and in 1942 was called to a country parish. In that year he married Yoke and began a family life in which he was to have great joy. In that country manse, Jan and Gabriel were born; and there too several fugitives from the German occupation of Holland were to find refuge. When later he came to Australia it was noteworthy that no one better than he knew that the Nazi occupation of Europe, the struggle in which the German Church had been involved, the resistance to the occupying authority to which the Dutch Church had been committed, had all disclosed to us the shallowness of so much of our religious life, the need to find rock on which to build, for when the storm came it blew down the house built on sand. Already the melody of his life, joyous though it was, was to be heard along with some of the more sombre themes of our days.

In 1946 he was called to the university town of Leiden, with a special charge to minister to non-Church people. There, after that war, there was no facile hope of a world fit for heroes to live in, but a great alienation: men and women separated from the Gospel, outside the fellowship of the Church. But Marius, in Paul's phrase, could not know any one from a human point of view alone: they had to be brought the Gospel where they were. That was now the story of his life, his task. During his first two years in Leiden, Rieteke was born and a daughter added to his joy in life.

In 1948 the call came to go out again: to go to Indonesia to take up the work of Dutch ministers who there had suffered in the prison camps during the Japanese occupation. To do this he had to leave his family in Holland, and undertake the work on his own. The fractured life of the twentieth century in the East as in the West called for the word of reconciliation which he was commissioned to preach. Its story and his story were intertwined.

He returned to Leiden in 1950 and continued his ministry there; but after two years he once more heard a call through the Presbyterian Church in Victoria to minister to Dutch migrants to this country, and to help those who belonged to the Reformed Church to find a spiritual home here in the Presbyterian Church. Mankind was on the move, and once more Marius had to move with men and women of his nation and faith as they put down roots in a strange land. He and Yoke and their children became, as it were, migrants among migrants, so that they might all make this country their new home. The birth of Julie here was, as it were, a pledge that here they were to stay—for the enrichment of many. I think too that Marius' decision to study Philosophy at the University of Melbourne, where he obtained his MA degree, expressed a determination to understand better the, to him, strange ways of thought to which the Anglo-Saxon mind was subject. Culture was meeting culture in a new way in the new Australia, and he had to be at the meeting place. The Dutch Government recognised his services to the Dutch community by making him a Knight in the Order of Orange Naussau.

After seven or eight years in this work Marius became in succession the Minister of Thornbury Presbyterian Church and of Hartwell where over a period of 16 years he came to mean much to many, helped to guide that congregation into the Uniting Church, and make his own considerable contribution to the theological thought which was to provide a foundation for the Uniting Church. Of the last seven years he spent three very happily as a minister at Canterbury, and despite failing physical strength continued until his death, to read and think, write letters to his friends, and articles for Church newspapers and journals, enjoy his family—his children and grandchildren—his books and music. The melodies had come together and found a peaceful conclusion.

We have thought so far of the ways in which two melodic lines—his personal life and the public scene–sounded together in the life of Marius Geursen. But of course there was a third line, which held the whole together. We heard it resoundingly in the passage from Paul's second letter to the Corinthians read to us this afternoon.

*Knowing the fear of the Lord, we persuade men.* At the centre of his life Marius knew himself to be called by God, and to be called to preach. This was an awesome thing. For Paul the fear of the Lord did not mean anxiety or terror but a certain profound seriousness. *Do not become proud but stand in awe,* says Paul elsewhere. There was nothing unduly solemn about Marius: indeed the reverse - his sense of the absurd would bubble forth, and he would laugh at himself. But to take up the Word of God and to try to persuade men of its cogency, this was a serious undertaking, requiring patience and careful preparation. No preaching or writing was ever undertaken lightly by Marius Geursen; few preachers have been more faithful to the claims of their study. It was a serious but not unduly solemn duty, rather a joy for, as Paul also puts it, *the love of Christ constrains us.* Marius knew that by that phrase Paul meant primarily the love which Christ has towards us, a love made effective in Christ's death - so that we might live no longer for ourselves but for him who for our sake died and was raised. Christ had touched the life of his servant Marius Geursen, and he could no longer live for himself, but could only seek to pass that love on to others, 'the brethren whom he loved and longed for, his joy and his crown'.

Then come the two great 'therefores'.

*Therefore*, from now on we regard no one from a human point of view alone.

Like the great apostle, like the true pastor that he was, Marius looked out and saw every man and woman as belonging to Christ, as responsible to Christ, as loved by Christ—and therefore as someone who would be immeasurably impoverished if he or she did not know this. It was Marius' calling to bring to them this good news.

And the second great 'therefore':

*Therefore*, if any one is in Christ—a new creation.

The world is opened up in a new way: the whole created order is now seen as belonging to Christ, and will be shewn to be his at the end.

Something of this vision of the world, in all its sorrows and yet placed under the hope of its re-creation in Christ, informed Marius' life. That is why, like his mentor Karl Barth, he was a great Christian humanist. Like the Lord Christ himself, nothing human was or should be alien to such a man. We think of Marius' love of music: his desire to understand the new which was strange to him and to enter more deeply into the old which he already loved. I do not think that he would have regarded it as frivolous of me to suggest in this setting that it is easy for us to imagine Marius in the new life which awaited him,· settling a few points of doctrine with Karl Barth, and then one or other of them breaking off the discussion by saying 'Let's listen to some Mozart'! Because of his intense commitment to the Christian Faith, because his life was deeply rooted in that of Christ, he lived in this world with an unusually wide range of human sympathies: in music and all the arts, as well as awareness of political and cultural change. At one stage it was difficult to name a really interesting and worthwhile film or play showing in the city which he had not seen; and he was a great attender of concerts and lectures, still making time to read widely. Not the least of his achievements in recent years was a fine paper on Erasmus. It took a Barthian and a Dutchman to appreciate that great humanist.

Through his death we in this Church have lost a dear husband, a loved father, a brother, a friend, a Churchman of such individual character that he cannot be replaced. For us the loss, for him the triumph, the resurrection life in which the praise of God is sung.

George Herbert addressed himself in his *Easter* poem; but we can think

today of a voice greater than that of Herbert addressing his servant Marius
Geursen:

> Rise heart; thy Lord is risen. Sing his praise.
> Without delayes,
> Who takes thee by the hand, that thou likewise
> With him mayest rise.

With thanksgiving we hold him and ourselves in Christ's presence, looking for
the resurrection of the dead and the life of the world to come. *Praise the Lord, O
my soul; and all that is within me, praise his holy name.*

# Frank Woods
## 1907 – 1992

*Archbishop of Melbourne 1957-77; Primate of the Anglican Church in Australia 1971-77. The following is one of several addresses given in St Paul's Cathedral, Melbourne at the funeral of The Most Reverend Sir Frank Woods on December 4, 1992.*

## Standing on the Christ-ward side of our lives

It is my privilege to speak for a few minutes of Frank Woods as I knew him, while we all continue to think of him each with his or her own memories, and give thanks to God.

I first became aware of Frank Woods almost 60 years ago when he was chaplain of Trinity College, Cambridge; his youngest brother was a close friend and Frank was one of the college chaplains who gave unfailing support to the Student Christian Movement, where Christians from a variety of Church background learnt to recognise each other, and learnt much about the message and mission of Christ and his Church in the world. The Student Christian Movement was, I was going to say 'the cradle', but better 'the kindergarten' of the Ecumenical Movement.

It was therefore no surprise when years later in Melbourne and Australia we knew Frank Woods as a leader in the ecumenical movement in this state and in the Australian and World Council of Churches. He taught us all that you must recognise in the other man or woman, one whom God has recognised, that you must rejoice that Christ has called into his service men and women of diverse races and traditions, that in the gift of the Holy Spirit we all belong to the one family of God. In Australia he inaugurated a new era of better relations between the Anglican Church and the Church of Rome, beginning with his call on Archbishop Mannix soon after his arrival; and I often thought that he understood better than some of us did what we were trying to do in bringing three churches together in the Uniting Church. Like many of us he regretted that the Anglican Church was not a party in those discussions, although thanks to his initiative we had Anglican observers throughout.

My second picture is of Frank as senior chaplain to the British Army in Northern Ireland at the end of World War II. Our closer friendship dates from then, now almost 50 years ago. We saw much of him in our home. He even came from time to time to hear me preach, a singular act of friendship. He persuaded me to join with him in conducting some Bible studies for the chaplains of all denominations stationed in that area. We were required to work from the text of the Bible alone, for the chaplain on active service might only have two books with him, a New Testament, preferably but not necessarily in Greek, and his prayer book.

It was therefore no surprise to me when we met again in Melbourne to find in Frank Woods a strong supporter for better theological education for the clergy and for better-instructed people. Nor was it a surprise to see him present at schools of theology, humbly learning afresh truths in which his life was deeply embedded.

My third picture is of Frank Woods, companion, friend and pastor: entertaining companion whose company was enjoyed by so many and who was so readily accepted by young people: loyal friend and pastor. The instances are too many and, in some ways, too intimate to recount. Wherever you went, whatever you were asked to do, you knew that Frank was encouraging you and supporting you with his prayers. He once gave me a book which he had read with some satisfaction, entitled *The Shadow of the Galilean*. He lived his life in the shadow cast on our ways by that Galilean, Jesus of Nazareth; or it might be better to say, in the light cast on our ways by that same Jesus, and he in turn shed light on our ways. He stood on the Christ-ward side of our lives.

I last saw him not much more than twenty-four hours before he died. As I came away I reflected that the next day would be Advent Sunday; and I remembered the opening words of a great sermon I had heard on Advent Sunday twenty-six years ago in a church in Heidelberg in Germany: 'God would make a new beginning with you; and would have you make a new beginning with him. That is the message of Advent'.

Thank God, that message was fulfilled in the life of Frank Woods last Sunday.